Public Goods and Private Wants

Public Goods and Private Wants

A Psychological Approach to Government Spending

Simon Kemp

*Associate Professor of Psychology,
University of Canterbury, New Zealand*

Edward Elgar
Cheltenham, UK • Northampton, MA, USA

Published by
Edward Elgar Publishing Limited
Glensanda House
Montpellier Parade
Cheltenham
Glos GL50 1UA
UK

Edward Elgar Publishing, Inc.
136 West Street
Suite 202
Northampton
Massachusetts 01060
USA

A catalogue record for this book
is available from the British Library

Library of Congress Cataloguing in Publication Data
Kemp, Simon
   Public goods and private wants : a psychological approach to government spending / by Simon Kemp.
      p. cm.
   Includes index.
   1. Government spending policy—Public opinion. 2. Taxation—Public opinion. 3. Expenditures, Public—Public opinion. 4. Public welfare—Public opinion. I. Title.

HJ7461 .K46 2003
336.3'9—dc21   2002072185

ISBN 1 84064 973 9

Printed and bound in Great Britain by Biddles Ltd
www.biddles.co.uk

Contents

List of Figures

List of Tables

Preface

How do people value what the government does? This topic interests all of us personally, and it is a professional concern for many. Obviously it is important to politicians and public servants, particularly those concerned with government finance. Answers, or at least partial answers, to the question might also be expected from many academic quarters: from those interested in finance and accounting or government administration, from economics, sociology, political science, and even psychology.

My own training is in psychology and an important theme of the book is the contribution that I believe psychology, and particularly psychophysics, can make to the valuation of government-provided goods. I hope those trained in other disciplines are able to see some value in this contribution. I also hope for a little understanding when such a reader comes to places in the book where he or she perceives that I have distorted, oversimplified, or misrepresented the contributions from other disciplines. Obviously, I have done my best to represent these contributions accurately and fairly; equally obviously, I will not always have been successful.

I received financial support from a number of organizations for the empirical work that is referred to in this book. I should like to record particular gratitude to the New Zealand Foundation for Research Science and Technology, who funded some of the earlier studies done in New Zealand, and to the Alexander Humboldt Foundation. The Humboldt Foundation supported me during stays in Kiel and Frankfurt an der Oder, and during these stays I was not only able to do empirical work but also had the time to think through some of the theoretical issues involved.

A number of people have, over a period of years, made contributions to this book, sometimes by collaborating on the empirical research, sometimes by reading what I have written, sometimes by listening to me describe some aspect of the work, and then, seconds later, pointing out some way in which I could have thought about it more clearly. A partial list of such contributors includes Jonathan Baron, Friedel Bolle, Chris Burt, Jo Crawford, Peter Earl, Brian Easton, Garth Fletcher, Alexander Fisher, Geoff Fougere, Sharon Fussell, Peter Gorringe, Werner Güth, Dieter Heyer, Seamus Hogan, Stephen Lea, Anthony MacLean, Mandi Miller, Folke Ølander, Ray Stanton, Dirk Wendt, and Karyn Willetts. I should particularly thank my wife, Cora, and daughter, Alice, who have had to put up with more monologues from me on this subject than anyone else.

I would like to record my special thanks to four busy people – Tom Keenan, Michelle Mahoney, Shlomo Maital, and an anonymous reviewer – who took the time to read through complete drafts of the book and offer constructive criticism and helpful suggestions for improving it. I should add that the team at Edward Elgar Publishing have been invariably helpful, skilled, supportive and sympathetic.

A theme of this book is the use of psychophysical scaling techniques to measure value. My interest in these techniques owes a good deal to two admirable mentors. I first became aware of psychophysics during a very lucid series of lectures given by John Irwin when I was an undergraduate at Auckland University. I first came to use a psychophysical scaling method seriously when I was investigating a quality of sound known as its roughness doing postdoctoral research in Eberhard Zwicker's institute at the Technical University of Munich. I owe a great debt to both these men.

1. Introduction

How valuable to us are the activities of government? This book explores psychological approaches to answering this question.

A moment's reflection will convince the reader that the question is not trivial. Governments take in money, largely through various forms of taxation, and then allocate it to services, many of which are provided to its citizens free of charge. The sums of money involved are huge. Even in those countries that are regarded as free-market economies, government taxation and expenditure make up substantial fractions of the total income and spending for the country. There are a number of different ways of calculating this kind of figure, not all of which produce exactly the same answer, but one reasonable way is to examine the proportion of the Gross Domestic Product (GDP) taken up by tax receipts. In 1997, the tax receipts in my own country, New Zealand, made up slightly over 36 per cent of GDP. In Germany, the figure was 37 per cent, in Sweden just under 52 per cent. Even in the United States of America, generally regarded as a country with a rather low level of government involvement in the economy, the tax take was only just under 30 per cent of GDP. (All figures are taken from the Organization for Economic Cooperation and Development, 2000, September.)

Governments – local, state, national – spend all of this money on a range of different services. Some of the more common services they provide are pensions and other social welfare payments, health, education, defence, police and roadways. Governments may also undertake the subsidy or financing of artistic and cultural events, subsidizing farmers to produce (or not produce) food, providing food for children at school, providing facilities to imprison or even to execute criminals, and a host of other facilities and services. While the range of government-provided services is vast, it is also somewhat variable between countries. Indeed, within a country the services provided often change over time. For example, thirty years ago the New Zealand government used to provide free milk for school children, but it no longer does so. One might ask whether differences in the provision of services, whether between countries or over time, reflect differences in the values of the citizenry.

Leaving aside for the moment the macroeconomic effects of taxation and government spending, if a government taxes its citizens to provide services, the services are provided at the cost of goods or services the taxpayers might have bought themselves on the open market. Obviously a number of related questions might arise here. Do we really want the services the government provides? Does the government provide the particular services we want? Do we get enough value from government services to compensate for the money we pay in tax, that is, to compensate for the goods and services we might otherwise have bought from some other source.

Of course, the question of whether one is getting value for money is not limited to goods and services provided by the government. It is also an important question for the goods and services you buy in the market. However, the problem is more difficult to assess for government activities than for market-supplied goods and services because the individual has fewer choices with respect to government activities. To illustrate this point, imagine a conversation between Janet and Sarah at their local café.

'What do you think about the way the government is going to spend fifty million dollars on new fighter aircraft?' Janet says, as she toys idly with the small chocolate that has come with the coffee.

'God, it makes me mad, especially when there are waiting lists for hospitals', Sarah replies. 'Do you know that my mother has now been waiting six months for a hip replacement, and there is still no word on when it's going to be? Six months! If they have the money to spend on toys for the air force, why don't they spend it on things that people really need?'

'It beats me. But they didn't ask us, did they?... By the way, I don't think much of this coffee, do you?'

'No, I think this place has gone downhill since it was taken over.'

'Mmm. What do you say to going somewhere else next time?'

'How about that place that has just opened up on Wellington Road?'

'Good idea, Sarah. I have been meaning to try it anyway.'

There is something relatively immediate and effective that Janet and Sarah can do in response to the poor quality of the café's coffee. It is very much more difficult for them to do anything about the way the government spends money. Moreover, it is not at all clear that they necessarily *should* be able to do anything about it. Perhaps there is a real external threat to the country. Perhaps the majority of people agree with the government's decision. Perhaps Sarah's mother is a hypochondriac and really does not need a new hip. In short, there is a real problem in assessing what the government should be doing, and individual people do not exercise choice about it as they do about coffee or other goods and services that are available in the market.

The 20th century saw a large number of attempts to solve this kind of problem on theoretical or ideological grounds. For example, under communism the majority of goods were produced by the state, and where prices were charged for the goods these tended to be set by ideological rather than market considerations. The governments of Eastern Europe set artificially low prices for urban transport and certain kinds of foodstuffs, which were considered to be necessities. 'Luxury' goods – bananas were a well-known East German example – were often sold at artificially high prices or were rationed.

At the other extreme, a number of influential thinkers have suggested that government should restrict itself largely to the provision of a particular class of goods, those that are termed 'public goods' by many economists. The term as used by economists is much more restrictive than when it is used by ordinary folk, and the economic theory of public goods is discussed in more detail in Chapter 2. For the moment, we note that economists usually think of public goods as those that, once provided, are necessarily provided for all the citizens. Moreover, as a rule the cost of provision is not dependent, or at any rate is not heavily dependent, on how many users there are. Defence is an often cited example of a more or less pure public good in this sense. The argument is not that other types of good that governments provide, such as education, elective surgery, or superannuation for the elderly, are worthless things to have, but rather that they can be more efficiently and effectively provided by the free market than by governments.

At an everyday level, almost everyone has ideas for what the government should do. But even at an academic level, the debate has often featured protagonists who are not economists. Economics is mainly a theoretical discipline and it often proceeds by setting up more or less plausible assumptions about the state of the world and the way people think and behave in it and then proceeding to derive conclusions from them. People trained in other disciplines have often taken other perspectives. For example, sociologists and political scientists have had important contributions to make. In particular, political scientists have been interested in how people's desires are translated into political decisions, including political decisions about government spending.

PSYCHOLOGY AND GOVERNMENT SPENDING

If one took the view that government spending can be valued independently of what people value or what makes them happy, there would probably be little room for much psychological contribution to the topic. In fact, however, most economists concerned with the issue (see, for example, Musgrave and Musgrave, 1984) have felt that government spending should be matched to individual preferences and the value that individuals receive from government services rather than to an absolute value that is determined by transcendent ethical considerations. Value – a frequently used economic term for this is 'utility' – is essentially conceptualized in economics as a subjective quantity, and economists have often been sceptical about attempts to measure it precisely because it is a subjective quantity. However, the measurement of subjective qualities has long been the subject of psychological endeavour.

A potentially important contribution of psychology to the study of government spending is thus the suggestion and validation of measures of value that can be applied to government services. The measures reviewed later in this book have in common that they are subjective and often derived from psychological measurement techniques that have been developed for other uses.

In general, subjective scales of measurement of sensations, attributes or concepts in psychology have often been used to study how the sensations, attributes or concepts are represented in our minds. Similarly, measures of value can be used in this way, and some of the research discussed in this book is an attempt to explore the way that people represent the value of government services. So, for example, the question of whether the economic theory of utility appears to form part of this representation, and the way in which people's perceptions of value might be linked to their perception of the cost of a service are investigated.

So far I have argued that psychology can help in studying government spending, and much of the rest of this book focuses on this psychological approach. However, I should make it clear that I do not believe the study of government spending would be advanced by discarding the work of economists and political scientists and substituting that of psychologists. Instead, a psychological approach should complement these other perspectives rather than attempt to supplant them.

ORGANIZATION OF THE BOOK

The two chapters that immediately follow discuss some of the contributions of economics and political science to the study of government spending. I am neither an economist nor a political scientist and in consequence these chapters provide less sophisticated – and probably in places oversimplified – accounts than are available in the writings of those trained in these disciplines. However, these chapters are important for some of the agenda of studying government spending. Moreover, the concepts that are introduced are interesting ones and, in my view and in that of other people, provide real insights into the issues of government spending.

Chapter 2 focuses on the contributions of economists. The notion of utility is introduced and ways in which economists have measured it (or not measured it) are considered. The chapter considers reasons put forward by economists as to why it might be better to have government supply some services than leaving it to the market to supply them. In particular, the notion of a 'public good' as defined in economics and some research on the concept by experimental economists are discussed.

Chapter 3 considers contributions by political scientists and those economists who have worked in the public choice area. The main theme is the median voter model, and the chapter outlines the theory, objections to the theory and empirical research on it. The chapter concludes with a discussion of how public choice might be different if people voted directly for the levels of spending they wanted rather than for representatives to decide on the levels on behalf of the electorate.

Chapters 4 and 5 focus on some of the subjective measures, largely derived from psychology, that could be used to evaluate government spending. Chapter 4 mainly considers measures related to quality of life, in particular general measures of well-being and the measures of quality of life that have increasingly been used in medical decision-making. Chapter 5 covers attempts to value, or to assess the utility of, various goods and services supplied by governments. These attempts include contingent valuation, the 'more, the same, less' method, budget games and psychophysical scaling.

Chapter 6 focuses on the results of studies where people have been asked to value different government services using methods based on psychophysical scaling. A feature of the chapter is the demonstration that the way people value government services differs in important respects from the way they value market-supplied goods. The question of whether people value government services for their own benefit or for that of society at large is also considered.

Most people like the government to spend money on them, but are not so enthusiastic about being taxed. Chapter 7 reviews a little of the research on the psychology of taxation and then goes on to consider research on people's perception of the relationship between taxation and spending, and whether they know how much they pay in tax. This research leads naturally to the questions of how much people know about what the government spends on particular services, and how this knowledge might affect their valuations. Some answers to these questions are provided in Chapter 8.

Chapter 9 presents a little, rather scattered, research on what people appear to want the government to do. The chapter introduces lay theories of economics, and then moves on to consider people's preferences about how goods should be supplied and who should supply them. Two brief studies that have looked at the way people perceive the way government allocates resources among different services conclude the chapter.

Finally, Chapter 10 draws conclusions regarding methods for valuing government services, results obtained from the psychological approach to government spending, and political implications.

APPENDIX: GOVERNMENT IN NEW ZEALAND

Many of the studies that I and my co-workers have carried out have entailed questioning New Zealanders about services supplied by the New Zealand government. Obviously, this raises the question of how much one can generalize from these studies to those that might be carried out in other countries. Thus, it might be helpful to readers from other countries to know a little about New Zealand and in particular about the way that its government services are provided and funded.

New Zealand is a self-governing representational democracy with a population of around 3.8 million in 2000. Broadly speaking, it has a mixed economy with a tradition of government involvement, although since the fourth Labour government (1984–1990) the level of this involvement has been reduced.

Perhaps because of the country's relatively small population, New Zealand government structures are somewhat simpler than those in many larger industrialized democracies. Effectively, there are only two levels of government – central and local – and many services which in other countries are often carried out and funded at local or state level (for example, education, police and the administration of social welfare) are carried out by the central government. Thus, asking people to value the merits of different central government services against each other covers a wider range of services in New Zealand than in many other countries.

The funding structure that supports these services is also relatively simple. Almost all central government tax revenue is paid into a single Consolidated Fund, and (with the minor exception of Accident Compensation levies) the average worker pays all of his or her income tax into this account in a single transaction. (So, for example, there are no separate deductions for unemployment or health insurance or for the government-funded old-age pension.) Taxes on company profits, a tax on goods and services, and various other minor taxes are also paid into this fund. Local government is funded largely by a tax on property (known as rates).

There is a British-type health system and at present all social welfare payments are paid out of the Consolidated Fund on a pay-as-you-go basis.

Finally, while it would be a gross exaggeration to say that it is easy to find out exactly what the New Zealand government spends its money on, the official government accounts of New Zealand are perhaps a little more straightforward to follow than in many other countries. In part this is because of the rather simpler overall structure of government, in part the consequence of the policy of recent past governments to try to make the process of government accountable and transparent (for example, Campos and Pradhan, 1997).

2. Economics and Public Goods

Unsurprisingly, the role of governments in taxing the public and using this tax to fund an array of goods and services has long been an important area within economics, and one that has been extensively researched. This chapter introduces and briefly reviews some of the issues that economists have looked at.

We begin by considering the idea of utility and how this applies to government services. Then we move on to consider briefly some of the reasons that economists have advanced for why government should involve itself in the economy. Third, the economic theory of 'public goods' is outlined, and some of the experimental research on public goods that has been conducted by economists is reviewed. Next, we consider an economic concept that is related to public goods, that of externalities. This is followed by a section on the relevance of some of the economist's concepts for the provision of government services. Finally, the use of behavioural measures to infer the utility of government-supplied goods and services is discussed.

UTILITY

Utility is a central concept in economics, although it is somewhat variably defined in the various dictionaries of economics. For example, Black (1997, p. 489) describes it as 'a synonym for individual welfare', Rutherford (1992, p. 480) as (more typically) 'the satisfaction derived from an activity, particularly consumption'. Knopf (1991, p. 305) states that utility is 'the satisfaction derived from the consumption of a good or service', and goes on to remark that the concept 'is subjective and cannot be quantified objectively'. There is, in fact, general agreement that the concept is essentially subjective and it is often thought by economists to be unmeasurable.

In particular, present-day economists have usually taken the view, firstly, that asking people about their personal well-being, values and utilities is fraught with difficulty, and, secondly, that there is no obviously valid way to compare or to sum up different people's well-being, values and utilities. So, for example, if I am out with a stranger for dinner it is not easy to tell whether my preference for a bottle of red wine is stronger than her preference for a bottle of white wine. On a societal level it is similarly not easy to tell whether a certain level of unemployment, and ensuing unhappiness for those who are unemployed, is compensated for by possible benefits to other, employed members of the community from an efficient economy. Thus, when considering the role of government in the economy, two valuation questions need addressing: how can we tell whether one outcome is better than another for a single individual? and how can we compare values across individuals?

These problems seem at first glance to be more obviously psychological or philosophical ones than economic ones – we shall return to considering them in Chapters 4 and 5 – and so it is not very surprising to find that economists have often adopted the reasonable strategy of trying to sidestep them. One useful sidestepping device is to infer people's values and preferences from their behaviour, particularly from their purchasing and consumption behaviour, rather than asking them to introspect about them. This indirect inferential measure only yields us information that one (purchased) product has more utility than another (unpurchased) product, not how much more utility it might have. Hence, the preference measure so obtained is often described as one of ordinal rather than cardinal utility (for example, Eatwell *et al.*, 1987, vol. 4, p. 778), another measurement issue we shall return to in Chapter 4. Regardless of the scale of measurement, however, a key difficulty in allocating resources to government-provided services is that it is not easy to estimate the utility that an individual receives from such services because behavioural choices are not much involved (for example, Endres, 1999; Quiggin, 1999).

In a market economy where people are free to choose, the behavioural method of inferring utility within an individual works fairly well. If I regularly buy Kentucky Fried Chicken rather than McDonald's hamburgers, it is reasonable to suppose I get more pleasure or value or utility from the chicken. Of course, even for the market system there are still difficulties with this kind of inference. For example, if you are purchasing a new type of product you cannot rely very heavily on past experience to estimate the utility that the good is likely to provide. One might also question whether the widespread consumption of substances like tobacco is really adding to the consumer's utility. Nevertheless, despite these kinds of difficulty, choice in the market system does often provide at least a reasonable guide to utility.

When one comes to consider goods and services that are provided free of charge or at reduced cost by the government, this kind of behavioural inference is not always possible. Indeed it is not often possible. If a good is provided free and someone makes use of it, clearly that person must assign some value to it, but there is no guarantee that this value is sufficient to make it worthwhile to provide the good. Nonetheless, as we shall see, sometimes some kind of estimate can be made if a certain amount of ingenuity is applied to thinking up possible behavioural measures, and in the final section of this chapter we look at some of the attempts that have been made to infer the utility of government-provided services from people's behaviour.

There is a vast variety of ways of attempting to deal with the interpersonal comparison problem and economists of different schools have experimented with many of them. A frequent starting point adopted by present-day economists is to make use of the principle of Pareto optimality for making social decisions (for example, Eatwell *et al.*, 1987). The basic idea is that a given distribution of goods is Pareto optimal when no kind of alteration to it is possible without someone being made worse off. So, for example, suppose I have two desks and Margery has two chairs. If I exchange one of my desks for one of Margery's chairs we might both become better off (or at least, neither of us may be worse off). But there it is likely that the redistribution will stop. For example if my second desk was taken from me and given to Margery to use as firewood, I am likely to be made worse off. If we assume that Margery and I are capable of making rational decisions about our furniture, then Pareto optimality is obtained when we exchange until neither of us wants to make any more trades (or to be spontaneously altruistic and give our furniture away to each other). A subtle point to note here is that if we make this trade it is reasonable to assume we both gain utility from it, but it is hard to make any judgement about how much utility we gain from it. It could be, for example, that Margery gains only a little extra benefit from having a desk instead of a second chair because she has a very small office, while I gain a great deal of extra benefit because I really disliked sitting on the second desk. Thus, the use of this principle is compatible with the economist's frequent focus on ordinal rather than cardinal utility.

It is fairly easy to see from my simple example that one might expect there to be a tie-up between the use of the principle of Pareto optimality and the use of the market system to exchange goods freely, and, indeed, subject to a few assumptions, it turns out that Pareto optimality is assured by having perfect competition. An obvious corollary of this conclusion is that economists who make use of the principle of Pareto optimality are likely to focus on the distribution of goods and services by the market system. *The New Palgrave Dictionary of Economics* states that 'Pareto-efficiency and the neoclassical paradigm go hand in hand' (Eatwell *et al.*, 1987, vol. 3, p. 813). If the government intervenes in the economy and, for example, takes over the distribution of tables and chairs, clearly this would stop the free market operating, and generally one will end up with outcomes that are not Pareto optimal. In particular, it is likely that someone will be made worse off if any redistribution takes place.

For some theorists (for example, Harris and Seldon, 1979), the inability to infer utility from behaviour because of the lack of relationship between purchase or use of a product and its cost of production and because of the difficulties of validating interpersonal comparisons of utility are good reasons to make the public sector of the economy as small as possible. However, the matter is not quite as simple as that.

Firstly, there is a clear and acknowledged weakness of the principle of Pareto optimality as a criterion in the face of pre-existing inequities of distribution. Is Pareto optimality really optimal? If I am the only member of a community with any money or other resources then, leaving altruism aside for the moment, I have nothing to gain by any exchange at all and the condition for Pareto optimality is already reached. It would be hard to argue, however, that human well-being is well served by such a state of affairs, and economists have rarely made any attempt to do so. But one might still question whether we should hold onto the free market and attempt to ensure a more equitable distribution of resources at the outset.

A second problem comes about when it is thought desirable to limit the free market for some reason. For example, we may wish to limit the free market in pharmaceutical drugs in order to ensure that antibiotics do not lose their potency through uninformed people not taking the full course of medication, or in order to ensure that addictive or damaging drugs such as heroin or barbiturates are not freely available. If we decide that a completely free market is unacceptable in such situations, a number of further choices emerge. One such choice is between retaining a market in drugs that is regulated in some way or having the state control and supply them. The problem in economic theory is that there is no general way of knowing which of these procedures is actually more efficient. Although a completely free market ensures the conditions of Pareto optimality, it is not necessarily true that a little bit of market is more efficient than no market (Boadway, 1997; Lipsey and Lancaster, 1956). This problem, sometimes known as the theory of the second best, turns out not to have a general solution. Thus it is quite possible that a state-provided service funded by taxation and for which no charges are made may actually be more efficient than a service that is provided by the market but heavily regulated by the government. This is not simply a theoretical issue. It is both questionable and important whether, for example, a heavily regulated insurance-based health system (as, for example, exists in the USA or Germany) is actually less or more efficient than the kind of state-run system that exists in the UK or New Zealand. (For some recent work on this issue, see Gerdtham and Jönsson, 2000; Hurley, 2000.)

Finally, there are a number of situations where it is either known or at least heavily suspected that the market system fails to deliver the best solution, either in the sense of Pareto optimality or when other definitions of optimality are admitted. In the following section we review some of these situations. Before moving on, however, another issue needs addressing.

If the average person is confronted with an apparent failure of the free market to produce a desired outcome, he or she will often think that the government should step in and correct the situation. So, if the continued existence of an important privately owned firm (an airline or a large bank, for example) is threatened, people will sometimes advocate government intervention to stop the firm collapsing. If there is a shortage of a health care service, people will often advocate that the government regulate the service (for example, Kemp, 1996).

Economists are more cautious. It has often been pointed out that there is no guarantee that government involvement in the economy will necessarily improve matters, because there are a number of reasons to expect government decisions to be flawed and government activity to be inefficient. For example, the bureaucratic apparatus of government is costly in time and money; government decisions may be unduly influenced by special interest groups (for example, Olson, 1982); much government activity involves coercion rather than voluntary cooperation or exchange. Hayek (1945) in an influential paper on 'The use of knowledge in society', argued that central planning was intrinsically inefficient because 'the "data" from which the economic calculus starts are never for the whole society "given" to a single mind which could work out the implications and can never be so given' (p. 519). Particularly where the economic problem entails adaptation, decentralized decision-making, he claimed, is generally superior and this is greatly aided by the price system.

In the next chapter, we investigate in more detail how decisions about government spending are made by democratically elected governments. For the present, however, it is worth simply bearing in mind that there are good reasons to expect that government intervention will not always be a panacea for real or perceived defects of the free market. As a corollary, given that there may be a defect of the market system, it is often possible to suggest a number of rather different ways of remedying it.

ECONOMIC REASONS FOR GOVERNMENT INTERVENTION

A number of reasons are commonly given by economists for why the government should play an important role in the economy (see, for example, Samuelson, 1955; Stiglitz, 1988, ch. 3). In the first place, there is an obvious need for a system of regulation and justice to allow a free market to operate at all.

Secondly, as pointed out above, the Pareto efficient outcome may simply be unacceptable, because the distribution of resources was very unequal at the outset. The perception that the free market system left to itself might produce inequitable income or wealth distribution thus provides a reason for government intervention. Attempts to secure more even income distributions, and in particular to alleviate the lot of the least fortunate members of society, may be relatively direct. For example, governments often attempt to force wealthy people not only to pay more tax but also to pay a higher proportion of their income as tax. The process is known as progressive taxation. Poorer citizens may be given direct payments of money as social welfare benefits or via negative income tax. However, redistribution need not be direct. It is often argued that the provision of free education or health services by the government has the advantage of enabling poorer members of society to have access to these services.

Thirdly, a number of goods may be most efficiently produced by a single firm. According to microeconomic theory, however, monopolists make higher profits when they restrict output to attain higher prices. Thus, it is often thought to be in the public interest to regulate efficient monopolies to ensure that the output is not restricted. Similarly, Stiglitz suggests that under some circumstances the private sector may fail to provide goods even though there are individuals willing to pay the cost of the goods. The market is thus incomplete. There is some evidence that this occasionally occurs in certain forms of insurance, for example.

Economics often assumes that people are in possession of all the information they need to make rational decisions. This is not always a reasonable expectation with consumer products. There is no real way, for example, that I can tell that a particular can of food might have been contaminated or whether a new marque of car has some safety defect that will only become apparent after I have driven 20 000 kilometres in it. In these kinds of situation we have information failure and there may be a case for government intervention to ensure, for example, that people do not end up being inadvertently poisoned by food they thought was safe to eat, or buy cars that are especially dangerous in crashes.

Obviously, there is a great variety of possible adverse consequences of information failure and a great variety of ways in which the information failure can come about. Hence it is unsurprising to find that consumer protection takes a number of different forms. Some products and services, such as heroin and pyramid selling schemes, are banned outright in many countries. Other products and services are subject to detailed regulation. For example, restaurants and other places where food is processed are usually subject to registration and health checks. Governments often specify that detailed information should be made available about many products, for example, pharmaceutical drugs or processed food. The question of which means of regulation are most suitable for which products and services has been the subject of intense debate and some research (for example, Mayer, 1999). But there is not much debate that some kind of action is required (although it need not necessarily be a government that undertakes it).

Even if individuals are in possession of all the relevant information, it is debatable whether they will always make the best decisions. Yet another justification that is sometimes advanced for government regulation or the provision of government goods is to try to compel or persuade people to consume more of the goods that are 'good for them' but that are otherwise under-consumed. These goods are sometimes known as 'merit goods'. Examples of goods that are provided by the government because they are thought to be merit goods include primary education (which one presumes children would be reluctant to attend if left to choose for themselves) and old-age pensions, because it is often believed that people will not save sufficient money for their retirement themselves. Again the government need not supply such goods itself. For example, central governments in New Zealand and elsewhere have sometimes run advertising campaigns to encourage people to take up some kind of physical exercise, because physical fitness is regarded as a merit good, but many of the sports facilities are privately owned.

There is also a class of 'demerit goods' where the government might wish to stop people from over-consuming or from consuming at all. Many western countries at present are involved to some degree in trying to prevent people from smoking, eating fatty food, and excessive alcohol consumption, particularly before they drive. Similarly, the action taken by government ranges from outright prohibition (for example, in many countries it is illegal to drive with more than a certain level of alcohol in one's blood) to warnings against the product or activity (consider, for example, the health warnings often printed on cigarette packets).

Although paternalistic government actions of these kinds are quite common, many economists are uncomfortable with them. In part this is because economics normally stresses the rationality of the individual and the assumption that he or she is capable of making the decisions that are in his or her best interest. Thus, there have been some interesting attempts by economists to explain how the consumption of heroin, which is commonly thought to be a demerit good, might actually be rational for the addict (for example, Becker and Murphy, 1988). Moreover, while it is very likely that individuals do not always act in their own best interests, it is questionable whether government intervention will always improve matters. If the individual is not competent to decide, who is? (Musgrave, 1986, ch. 3).

Two important and related justifications for government intervention in the economy are to ensure the adequate provision of public goods and to correct for externalities. These justifications are dealt with in more detail in the following sections, but for the moment we note that public goods, as defined by economists, are those which once provided are freely available to all, while externalities may be thought of as side-effects, which may be either positive or negative, of the production or consumption of goods. Defence is often thought to be a good example of a public good. Probably the best-known example of an externality is industrial pollution.

In principle, as Stiglitz (1988, p. 81) points out, the argument for government intervention because of externalities and the argument for intervention on the grounds that some goods are merit or demerit goods are quite separate. Externalities usually affect other people; merit goods are where the individual cannot properly recognize the benefit for him or herself. In practice, however, the two arguments are often entwined. For example, someone might support government advertisements to try to reduce alcohol consumption by arguing that alcohol is an addictive demerit good, but one can also argue against it on the grounds of negative externalities. For example, one could point to the devastating effect on the many people who have close contact with alcoholics or the expenses borne by state-run health systems in trying to cure them or to alleviate the health problems brought on by alcohol.

Finally, there is a general belief that the government should act as a macroeconomic manager so as to alleviate temporary dysfunctions (sometimes called coordination failures) of the market place. Thus, for example, the well-known Keynesian prescription of increasing social spending without raising taxation so as to attempt to stimulate the economy and reduce unemployment when the economy is in recession or appears to be heading towards it. In this case, the government acts as a manager of the economy as a whole in the attempt to obtain such macroeconomic benefits as low unemployment, low inflation, and high economic growth.

Musgrave (1986, ch. 2; see also, Musgrave and Musgrave, 1984) suggested that it would be valuable to split a government's budget into three parts: a service branch, a distribution branch and a stabilization branch. He envisaged the service branch as being concerned with the provision of the appropriate level of public goods (in the economist's sense of the term) or goods that have at least some of the features of public goods; the distribution branch as the transfer of resources from richer to poorer members of society; and the stabilization branch as being concerned with macroeconomic management.

THE ECONOMIC IDEA OF PUBLIC GOODS

To the lay person, the term 'public good' may suggest any type of good or service provided by a central or state government or a local body. In economics, however, the term is often used in a technical way that tends to cut across the question of who actually provides the particular good. In brief, a public good in economics is one that once made available is automatically made available to all. Examples of such goods that are frequently mentioned by economists include the provision of lighthouses, which can be seen by any ship in the area, mosquito control, as anyone who lives in the area benefits if the insects are exterminated, and defence spending, whose effects are felt by anyone living in the country.

The seminal work on the theory is generally credited to Samuelson (1954). In this early paper, Samuelson defined 'collective consumption goods' as those which 'all enjoy in common in the sense that each individual's consumption of such a good leads to no subtraction from any other individual's consumption of that good' (p. 387). Samuelson went on to demonstrate mathematically that leaving the provision of such goods entirely to the market would lead to their undersupply. Thus, for example, the market would tend to produce less mosquito control or fewer lighthouses than would really be beneficial when their cost was taken into account. Furthermore, Samuelson could not identify a voting procedure that would lead to the optimal outcome if people voted on how many lighthouses or how much mosquito control to provide. Samuelson's conclusions followed from 'the inherent difficulty of ever getting men to reveal their true tastes so as to attain the definable outcome' (Samuelson, 1955, p. 355). The basic point is this: why, for example, should I contribute towards the cost of a lighthouse, if I think you might be persuaded to carry the full cost of it, and if I can convince you that I do not value it even if I really do?

The economic theory of public goods has been worked on and developed a good deal since Samuelson's work, and it is accessible in a number of standard treatments. There are also occasionally slight changes in perspective. For example, pure public goods, according to Stiglitz (1988, ch. 5), have two critical properties: it is not practicable to ration their use and it is not desirable to ration their use.

In his presentation of the theory of public goods, Buchanan (1968, ch. 2) considers a simple world in which there are two people, Tizio and Caio, living on an island. There are two goods, coconuts and mosquito control. Coconuts are a private good and mosquito control a public good. Thus, both coconut harvesting and mosquito control can be undertaken by either individual and it is assumed that there is no gain in efficiency from any collective action. The essential difference between the goods is that if Tizio gathers coconuts there is no automatic gain to Caio (although of course Tizio may choose to give him some coconuts out of some benevolent motive), but any action taken against the mosquitoes automatically benefits both people equally. The point here is that when night falls the mosquitoes are just as likely to attack Tizio who has spent the day trying to drain the freshwater ponds they breed in as they are to attack Caio who has spent his day lying in a hammock watching the work.

In this case, it is possible to derive an interesting mathematical result in microeconomic theory. For purely private goods, the marginal rates of substitution for all the private goods an individual consumes equal the marginal rates of transformation. A simple way of thinking about this is to consider an individual who consumes a range of goods and spends her or his budget on them. Then the marginal utility to be derived from consuming an extra dollar's worth of each of these goods should be the same. For example, suppose that I generally prefer red to white wine, and consequently buy and drink more red than white wine. Nevertheless, according to the microeconomic theory, provided I purchase and drink some white wine, the marginal utility for me of receiving, say, an extra small amount of white wine will be the same as receiving an extra small amount of similarly priced red wine. (If this were not so, then presumably I would cut down my purchases of white wine even further and buy more red.)

Now for public goods, it turns out that the result is a little different. Where there is a purely public good (for example, mosquito control) and a purely private good (for example, coconuts), the sum of the marginal rates of substitution (taken over individuals again) between the public and the private good equals the marginal rate of transformation. Thus, the marginal utilities to the individuals of the public good should be added up to achieve Pareto efficiency.

Although the terminology here may be a little off-putting to the non-economist, the meaning is both straightforward and important. So, for example, in the community of two people, if both Tizio and Caio obtain one unit of extra utility from an extra coconut which one of them consumes individually and which takes one unit of labour (or other cost) to produce, then it is more efficient for them collectively to devote one unit of labour to producing extra mosquito control if the *total* extra utility to them is greater than one. So, for instance, let us suppose the value to each of them of the mosquito control is 0.6 units of utility per hour spent on this control. This is less than the value of a coconut to each, so, as Samuelson points out, it is quite possible that neither Tizio or Caio will undertake mosquito control. For each of them their labour or time produces more benefit for themselves if they use it to obtain coconuts (1 versus 0.6). However, the total utility to the two of them would be greater if one of them spent an hour controlling mosquitoes (utility of 1.2 added up over the two of them) than an hour spent by one of them harvesting coconuts (utility of 1.0 to one of them). The naïve outsider might ask why they do not each spend an hour controlling mosquitoes (total utility of 2.4 or 1.2 each) rather than each spending an hour gathering coconuts (total utility of 2.0 or 1.0 each).

In practice, there are a number of difficulties with the theory of public goods. Buchanan (1968) identifies and investigates a number of these, and suggests theoretical solutions to some of them. For example, given that we can see that there is an optimal efficient solution, how is this actually to be arrived at? This is important practically because it is all too easy to imagine situations in which Tizio and Caio are unable to resolve their labour or distributional disputes and spend their time sulking at opposite ends of the island rather than controlling mosquitoes, which is what any moderately intelligent outsider would think they should be doing.

Incidentally, readers who know something of recent thinking on evolutionary theory might see parallels here between the economic theory which makes it hard to see how Tizio and Caio are going to get their heads together to cooperate sensibly and the modern theory of the 'selfish gene' which emphasizes the evolutionary fitness of the individual rather than that of the species. Theorists in this tradition (for example, Dawkins, 1989) have made the point that genetic improvements must be to the benefit of the individual and his or her descendants, and not to the species as a whole. The parallel here is to ask why Tizio, for example, should voluntarily begin the work of mosquito control.

As a further aside it is worth noting that attempts to explain why it is that in fact humans often cooperate rather than ruthlessly compete all the time have led to the suggestion that evolution might have furnished us with altruistic or cooperative genes (for example, Ridley, 1997). After all, and the experiments we consider in the next section are a good demonstration of this, human beings frequently do cooperate to provide public goods.

EXPERIMENTS ON PUBLIC GOODS

A recent movement within the discipline of economics has been the growth of experimental economics. Researchers in this area have been concerned with carrying out experimental research, usually within a laboratory setting, to provide empirical evidence for or against different propositions of economic theory. A characteristic of much of the research has been a focus on the actual financial transactions between the experimental participants or between the participants and the experimenter that result under different experimental conditions.

A number of these economic laboratory experiments have investigated the provision of public goods. The details of these experiments have often been rather complex (see, for example, Ledyard, 1995, for a discussion of public goods experiments), but essentially they often look like this. A largish number of subjects is divided into groups of 4 people each, and each person is issued with, say, 100 tokens. Each person is given a choice. She can invest all her tokens in a private good, which might return, say, 1c/token in an experimental session. Alternatively, she can invest them in a public good, which will return, say, 2c/token to the group or 0.5c/token to each member of the group, regardless of how much the particular member has contributed or, indeed, whether he or she has contributed anything to the public pool. As a rule, subjects are free to choose how much of their token fortune they invest in the public good.

In this simple example, clearly the payoff to the group as a whole is maximized when all the group members contribute all their wealth to the public good. If everyone invests all their tokens in the group, then the group receives 800c (200c per member). On the other hand, if no one invests in the group, the group collectively receives 400c (100c per member). However, the individual does best if she puts all her tokens into the private good, while all of her companions contribute to the public good. In this case, she would obtain 250c (100c of her own plus a quarter of 600c).

Obviously there are a vast number of features of such an experiment that can be varied and, in fact, quite a number have been varied and the effects of the variation investigated. For example, thresholds may be set for the public good so that it is only provided if the total contributions exceed a certain amount. If not, the contributors get their tokens back (Bagnoli and Lipman, 1989). Alternatively, the amount of the public good might not vary continuously, but might jump up when a certain threshold is reached (for example, Marwell and Ames, 1979). For example, the public good might be set at 500c for the group if between 100 and 199 tokens are invested, but then leap up to 1000c once the group investment reaches 200 tokens. The size of the payoffs, and particularly the amount of extra benefit that might be gained from group investment as opposed to the individual investment, is obviously a key variable. The subjects may be able to interact freely with one another or they may be completely unaware of each other's identity. The experiment may be set up for a single (one-shot) trial, or it may be repeated. If the experiment is repeated, group memberships may or may not change. Non-contributors may be excluded (for example, Smith, 1980). The research has normally involved real cash payments to the subjects, but deception as to group size and what other members are doing has sometimes been employed. Sometimes, indeed, only one of the members of the group really exists, and the behaviour of the others is simply simulated by the experimenter.

Curiously, there is currently a controversy over the use of this kind of deception by experimental economists, with some claiming that a reputation for honesty is a public good possessed by economists – but not by psychologists! – that is undermined by the use of deception (for example Bonetti, 1998; Hey, 1998; McDaniel and Starmer, 1998).

In most of this experimental work, the public good has been financed from voluntary contributions, and an important practical focus is whether or not it is possible to finance public goods in the long term by voluntary contributions. This relates to a fundamental issue of whether humans are to be viewed as basically selfish or as basically cooperative (for example, Ledyard, 1995). While an elaboration of all the findings from this research is not really relevant to the present book, a few of the basic results are worth noting.

First, public goods do get provided in these experiments. The amount of investment in the public goods is, as one might expect, dependent on the actual features of the study, but it is not uncommon to find subjects investing about half of their issued wealth in the public good. Second, allowing subjects to interact with each other tends to improve the rate of contribution to the public good. Third, particularly where face to face contact does not take place, the rate of contribution tends to decline over time.

EXTERNALITIES

As Samuelson (1955) points out, there are a number of goods that are neither pure public goods (in the economic sense) nor pure private goods. For example, if I choose to have an influenza injection this autumn, then clearly I benefit from this because I am less likely to become ill. But other people in my community will also benefit from my decision, because I would then be unable to catch the illness and pass it on to them. (They might also be better off if I turn up to work instead of lying in bed at home.) As with pure public goods, I have no control over this benefit, which extends to anyone who comes into contact with me. Thus, we might consider my injection to be an impure public good.

There are a number of approaches in economics to dealing with goods that have a mixture of the properties of public and private goods. Perhaps the best known of these is the theory of externalities. Externalities occur where the production or consumption of a private good affects other people in some way. The externality may have negative effects on other people – the best known and most studied of these effects seem to be environmental pollution and resource depletion – or positive effects. The latter have been rather less studied but are not uncommon. The classic textbook example is that of beekeepers and orchardists. Orchard production is enhanced if there are sufficient bees around at the time of fruit blossom; honey production is enhanced by having large numbers of flowering trees in the neighbourhood. My influenza injection also has positive externalities.

Both positive and negative externalities can be generated by either producers or consumers. Pollution, for example, is sometimes caused by industrial concerns and sometimes by the activities of private households. Beekeepers and orchardists are producers; on the other hand, it is my consumption of the influenza injection rather than its production which creates the positive externalities mentioned above. Characteristically, individual action in a market system should in theory – and sometimes in practice does – lead to the overproduction and consequent over-consumption of goods with negative externalities and the underproduction of goods with positive externalities. This is because, for example, a polluting firm does not bear most of the social costs that arise from the pollution it produces. Obviously here the reluctance of the firm to fund a reduction in the pollution it produces but does not much suffer from is similar to the reluctance Tizio might feel to undertaking mosquito control when his own time would more profitably be spent gathering coconuts.

A reasonably well-known formulation of this problem is known as the 'tragedy of the commons' (Hardin, 1968). The example alludes to the medieval European practice of having an area of grazing ground that was common to all the villagers. Hardin points out that if, say, the optimal carrying capacity of the common is 10 cows, this should not deter me as an individual from grazing an extra one there, since the costs of the overgrazing in terms of thinner animals and eventual pasture deterioration are borne by all, while I personally gain from being able to raise an extra cow, even if that cow (like everyone else's cows) does not quite get the optimal amount to eat. The most obvious modern application of this reasoning is to fishing. Each individual fisherman gains virtually nothing from his own efforts to conserve fish stocks if his fellow fishers do not cooperate. Indeed, the over-exploitation and subsequent depletion of fishing resources in seas all around the world in the last part of the twentieth century provides a reminder that the issues here are not just theoretical ones.

The existence of externalities is often thought to constitute a reason for government or at least cooperative intervention in the economy, and indeed collective interventions of different kinds are often undertaken. However, as Coase (1960) points out, the existence of well-defined property rights and the ability to buy and sell those rights without extensive transaction costs, are sufficient to deal with externalities. Coase considers the case where a cattle farm borders on a crop farm and shows that production value (summed over the farms) should be optimized under these conditions regardless of whether or not the cattle farmer is liable for his cattle eating his neighbour's crops.

If the government does intervene, what form should the intervention take? Different countries have tried to deal with the problems of industrial pollution by regulation, for instance by an outright ban on producing some products (fluorocarbons are a recent example) or by stipulating maximum pollutant levels that an industrial plant may produce. Alternatively, they may subsidize firms to install plant that produces less pollution, as was done in West Germany when the problem of acid rain was perceived. Yet another approach is to have a restricted number of licences to pollute. In the USA, in particular, such licences have often been sold. (See, for example, Stiglitz, 1988, ch. 8, for a discussion of the relative merits of these measures.) Incidentally, as an historical aside, it is sometimes thought that Hardin was describing a gradual historical process by which common land actually did come to be overgrazed in the Middle Ages. This is not true. In fact, medieval villagers were generally well aware of the potential danger of overgrazing common land and the rights to use it were strictly regulated and codified in many medieval communities.

With respect to pollution, it is worth remarking that government intervention may not necessarily improve matters. For example, Binswanger (1991) has produced cogent reasons for believing that the deforestation of the Amazonian rain forest has actually been encouraged by measures – for example, exemption from taxation of much agricultural income – taken by the Brazilian government. Subsidizing coal production leads to increases in the concentration of carbon dioxide in the atmosphere that are currently thought to be leading to global warming.

Governments may try to increase the supply of goods that are thought to have positive externalities. For example, it is often held that there are widespread benefits to a community from having an educated workforce and electorate. It might lead to more civilized standards of behaviour, and certainly there are communication advantages if one can assume that one's fellow citizens can read. It is possible that leaving education entirely to individuals to choose in the market place would lead to undesirably low levels of education for society as a whole as well as for individuals. Again, there is a range of options, by no means mutually exclusive. Many countries have regulations that prescribe when children should attend school. Governments may subsidize schools or universities. Often these institutions receive a large part of their funding from governments. The New Zealand government recently had an explicit assumption that 25 per cent of the gains from tertiary education accrue to the individual, 75 per cent to the community. Thus it was thought reasonable that tuition fees paid by students should cover 25 per cent of the costs of running universities and other tertiary institutions.

The provision of goods with positive externalities does not always come about through government intervention. It has been remarked that in many ways the Internet functions like a highway, which in most countries is normally a government-funded public good. This makes reasonable economic sense because often the effective marginal cost of an extra user on either a highway or the Internet is close to zero. But many of the costs of providing the Internet have not been met by governments, nor have they been funded via the market. Hallgren and McAdams (1997) claim that in this case, as in some others, universities have played crucial roles in providing the good.

RELEVANCE OF THESE CONCEPTS FOR GOVERNMENT SPENDING

In this section I briefly review the relevance of the concepts discussed above for the issue of which services are thought valuable for governments to provide. A little reflection will convince the reader that the economic concept of public goods is not at all the same as that of a government-provided good. Certainly, some public goods are provided by national or local governments. Defence is probably the most cited example, but the maintenance of a police force, sewage disposal and the treatment of infectious diseases are also common and at least in peacetime more prominent examples.

On the other hand, a number of public goods are not provided by the government at all. As Coase (1974) points out, one of the most frequently mentioned examples of a public good, that of the lighthouse, was actually sometimes built and maintained by private enterprise in Great Britain. Little difficulty was in practice encountered in charging ship owners for their use: light dues, usually a small fee that varied with the tonnage of the vessel, were routinely extracted when ships berthed at the ports whose approaches were marked by the lighthouses. Moreover, this user-pays system was still in use at the time Coase wrote, although the authority that set the fees was then governmental rather than private. Similarly, although roads are usually available as a public good they can be charged for by tolls and turnpikes, although questioning the efficiency of this way of providing and charging for them goes back at least as far as Adam Smith's *An Inquiry into the Nature and Causes of the Wealth of Nations* (Smith, 1776/n.d., Bk 5, Ch. 1, Pt 3, Art. 1).

There are a number of everyday examples of the private provision of public goods. Street performers are one of the more visible. As a little aside, my own city holds a busker's festival in the summer. Performers come at their own expense from various parts of the world, and their reimbursement is from completely voluntary donations made at the various (mainly outdoor) venues they perform at during the festival. The festival has run annually for the last eight years and is extremely popular, and there are sufficient entertainers who wish to perform at it that the city council limits well before the festival which performers may perform at which venues. The continued existence of this festival and of street performers generally serve as a demonstration that public goods can exist without government financing over quite long periods of time.

Similarly, as economists with an interest in the public sector have repeatedly noted, many of the services that the government provides are not public goods in the economic sense. Indeed, many of the most important government provided services – at least in terms of how much is typically spent on them in many western countries – are not pure public goods: for example education, most health services, subsidies to selected industries, old-age pensions and unemployment insurance. Each of these services is really a private good, even though equal opportunity of access might be provided by the government. For example, a single primary school teacher can only teach a limited number of children effectively. It is simply not true that all can benefit if a primary school service is established in a particular locality. Nor does your obtaining an old-age pension mean that I can obtain one too at no extra cost to the taxpayer. Although control of infectious diseases is a reasonable example of a public good, much of the work carried out by hospitals, for example mending broken bones or treating cancer, clearly involves supplying private goods.

Ever since Samuelson's formulation of the concept of public goods, there have been arguments, particularly from those on the political right, that government spending should be largely limited to the provision of such goods. Possibly the way that modern economists have used the term 'public good' to refer to a theoretical class of goods rather than to all the goods that governments normally supply may inadvertently reinforce this thinking. In this context, it is worth noting that Samuelson's original 1954 paper used the term 'collective consumption goods' rather than 'public goods' (although the latter term appeared in another paper of his published in the following year). Similarly Musgrave (for example 1986, ch. 4) generally uses the phrase 'social goods'.

Samuelson himself was well aware that most government spending was not on pure public goods, that many goods were neither pure private nor purely public goods, and that there were a variety of other justifications for government spending (including many that we reviewed earlier in this chapter). Although he did tend to the view that whether a good is naturally public or private should be an important consideration in whether the state should provide it, his summary statement on the point contains little that even a confirmed Marxist could object to: 'One might even venture the tentative suspicion that any function of government not possessing any trace of the defined public good ... ought to be carefully scrutinized to see whether it is truly a legitimate function of government' (Samuelson, 1955, p. 356).

One might also remark that a number of economists have produced theories suggesting that there may be situations in which it is efficient for a government to supply private as well as public goods (for example, Forte, 1967; Blomquist and Christiansen, 1999). There has been at least one attempt to show that it might be efficient to have a mixed health-care system in which services are supplied both by the government and the private sector (Gouveia, 1997). Thus, overall, it would be quite wrong to suppose that all economists believe the government should limit itself to the supply of public goods as defined by economists.

Even when these caveats are taken into account, the theory of public goods is still important for our thinking about government goods for a number of reasons. One important contribution is that it provides a rigorous theoretical account of a particular breakdown of the market system, and thus justification for at least occasional intervention in that system.

The relevance of the economic experiments on public goods for the question of what goods the government should provide and how they should be allocated is also difficult to ascertain. The key point here is that these experiments have largely focused on people's individual willingness to provide public goods voluntarily. In reality, while there are goods that are provided in this way, very few of them are provided by the government. Typically, people are not given a choice as to whether they wish to pay taxes to support government in general, and still less are individual taxpayers given any choice about which government goods they would like to see their contributions go to support.

Again this does not mean that these experiments are irrelevant to the real world. Some public goods are often voluntarily provided. Street performers are one example as we have just considered. It is quite common for cultural organizations to receive a proportion of their income from subscriptions from interested companies or individuals. A number of American radio and television stations receive funding in this way. All over the world a large number of charities are funded mainly by private contributions, although it should be noted that the welfare they provide is not really a public good in the sense of either the theory or the experiments, since those who contribute most to these organizations are not often those who benefit from them materially. (Of course, the donors may derive considerable utility from acting altruistically or from perceiving social inequities to be alleviated, but that is a different issue.) Also, most of the work done by charities is not a public good in the economist's sense of the term. For example, a soup kitchen can only provide a reasonable quantity of food for a more or less fixed number of people.

There is another important issue here. In principle one can define a very clear difference between being compelled to pay for the goods that the government provides through a legal obligation to pay taxes and voluntarily contributing to a fund that provides such goods. In practice, the matter is a little more murky. There is a good deal of research suggesting that people do not pay taxes simply because they are compelled to by the government. In every country, there is a fair amount of tax evasion, and the probability of being caught for it is usually quite small. Moreover, in many countries the penalties for tax evasion are often not excessive, partly because it is widely acknowledged that there is enormous scope for genuine error in tax declarations.

Such considerations have led researchers in the area (for example, Cullis and Lewis, 1997) to ask the question: why actually do people so often pay the taxes they are legally supposed to? While fear of the consequences of not doing so is undoubtedly an important motivator, it does not appear to be the only one. Hence, there have emerged a number of theories of tax evasion which stress the importance of social norms, altruism, perceptions of fairness and personal support for what the government is doing in the decision to pay taxes. The psychology of taxation is revisited in Chapter 7, but for the present we should note that the influence of social norms, fairness and other variables of this kind is precisely what has been examined in many of the public goods experiments. In short, the public goods experiments are not quite so irrelevant to the way government works as one might think at first glance. There is at least some element of voluntary consent to people's payment of taxes to support the services the government supplies, as the occurrence of the American War of Independence should remind us.

If there is an element of volition in the payment of tax, it should also be acknowledged that there is sometimes an element of coercion in the way that charities operate. So, for example, the latter encourage people to make donations by automatic payment, make extensive use of telephone or face-to-face canvassing for funds, or give out highly visible flowers or small badges to people so that others will be aware of their charity and presumably will be motivated to imitate them.

Applying the concepts of merit and demerit goods also gives rise to difficulties, although the difficulties here are rather different. How does one know which goods are merit goods or demerit goods? Of course, it is completely plausible that there are goods that people tend to overvalue or undervalue, and, especially where there is a choice between immediate and deferred gratification, there has been some interesting psychological research that is relevant to the concepts of merit and demerit goods. For example, Ainslie (1992) suggests, on the basis of extensive research in operant psychology, that people discount future events using hyperbolic rather than exponential functions. The point of this apparently minor mathematical difference is that hyperbolic functions provide for reversals of preference as the future event draws near, while exponential ones do not. In this way one can account for why people might make a decision to follow some long-term goal but then reverse the preference later. For example, consider the case of Geoffrey who knows he is going to inherit $40 000 in six months' time when some money left him by his recently deceased aunt will become available to him. When he first hears the news, he may decide that when he obtains the money he would prefer to put it into saving for retirement. However, at the time when it actually arrives, his preference might reverse and he might end up buying a sports car.

Such theorizing is quite easy to use to justify government provision of old-age pensions. It is quite plausible that people might have a long-term goal to save for their retirement but that this goal is threatened by more short-term desires. One obvious way in which the threat can be overcome is by surrendering control over part of your money to an outside agency (such as the government) which effectively forces you to save. Of course, one does not necessarily need a government to do this, and Ainslie (1992) discusses how people make decisions of this kind in their private lives. For example, if Geoffrey knows that he has a weakness for sports cars, he could decide well before he gets his $40 000 to take out a short-term loan to buy into a superannuation fund with the knowledge that he will then be under pressure to repay it when his inheritance arrives.

Education and health insurance are also sometimes thought to be examples of merit goods. It is certainly plausible that people might skimp on health insurance, feeling that 'it could never happen to them' or that they might be reluctant to invest in the expensive education that would secure themselves or their children good jobs. Obviously such behaviour would provide a rationale for government intervention in education and health. The difficulty is that a rationale for government intervention can also be made starting from a quite contrary assumption. Some aspects, at least, of education and health spending could plausibly be seen not as merit but as demerit goods.

For example, it is commonplace that jobs that previously were filled by non-graduates are now filled by university graduates, sometimes university graduates with postgraduate qualifications. In some cases the university training probably does prove really beneficial in doing the jobs – and, of course, it might be beneficial in other non-job related ways. In other cases, however, the suspicion arises that we are observing qualification inflation, and that the real purpose of the education is to serve as an indication of underlying ability. If this is true, it is easy to see that society overall, and many individuals in it, might benefit from some kind of restriction on the acquisition of education, as the resources used in providing it could be put to some better use.

A similar case can be made that at least some types of health spending goes on demerit goods, particularly for conditions where there is no recognized cure. Consider, for example, people's attempts to rid themselves of cancers that have been pronounced incurable. Where the health system is run by the state, treatments for these conditions are often simply not undertaken, although individuals may then pursue various alternative treatments that will not be funded by the government.

As a rather minor example of this phenomenon, sufferers from severe tinnitus (persistent loud ringing in the ears) often spend money on a variety of ineffectual remedies that range from drugs to relaxation therapy (George and Kemp, 1991). This spending persists in spite of the virtually unanimous medical opinion that no cure is presently available except in a minority of reasonably well-identified cases. It is possible, then, that state intervention in health inhibits – if it does not completely prevent – the spending of money on pointless 'remedies'.

It is easy to raise objections to the arguments I have put forward for regarding some aspects of health and education as demerit goods, and it is certainly not my intention to maintain the argument that, overall, health and education are demerit goods. It seems to me most likely that education and health spending pay for bundles of services that contain both merit and demerit goods, as well as many goods whose value ordinary people are perfectly capable of assessing for themselves. Indeed, it would not surprise me greatly if in the end it was found out that overall education and health are merit rather than demerit goods. However, the essential point is that at present we do not really know one way or the other, and the argument for current government intervention on the grounds that they are merit goods is consequently dubious.

Practical problems are also troublesome when one considers government intervention to correct for externalities. The debate over the best way in which externalities should be dealt with – for example by regulation or by alteration of the market – has already been alluded to. Also problematic, however, is the measurement of the extent of externalities. For example, what is the real cost of air pollution in the Los Angeles basin, or of the Exxon Valdez oil spill, or of allowing the encroachment of industry or civilization into wilderness areas? In Chapter 5, where the method of contingent valuation is reviewed, it will become apparent that the accurate measurement of externalities is a rather debatable exercise.

BEHAVIOURAL MEASURES FOR INFERRING THE UTILITY OF GOVERNMENT SERVICES

Most psychologists and economists would agree in preferring direct behavioural measures of the value of government (or any other) services to introspective self-reports. The problem with the behavioural measures is that, as was discussed earlier, there are no direct behavioural measures for valuing most such services. However, for some of them at least, *indirect* behavioural measures of value can be found and where they have they have proved useful.

In general, such behavioural measures can be described as opportunistic and different types of measure have been suggested for different types of service or public good. As a start point, we might note that those people who make use of a service – for example, people who visit a park or have a free operation in a public hospital or send their children to a state-funded school – must perceive *some* value in the service that is provided. Otherwise, clearly, they would not use it at all. Hence simply finding that a service is used shows that it is not worthless. The question in this case then becomes whether the value they obtain is worth the cost of providing the service to them. This is important because otherwise the resources that go into providing it might produce greater value if they were diverted to provide some other service.

In some cases the use of the good or service has an expense attached to it and this expense can serve as at least a rough measure of the value of the service. For example, one indirect measure that has sometimes been suggested for establishing the value of recreation areas is to measure the travel costs that people actually pay to visit and use them (Clarke, 1998; Font, 2000; McKean *et al.*, 1996). These travel costs appear to provide at least a lower limit on the perceived value of the area.

Brookshire *et al.* (1981), in their attempt to measure the value of unpolluted air in the Los Angeles basin, made use of differences in property values between areas with relatively clean air and those with relatively dirty air. The idea is that if, say, a house in a clean air area costs an average of $1000 a month in mortgage and other costs while a similar house in an area with dirty air costs an average of $850 then one can infer that people are willing to pay around $150 a month to have clean air.

The obvious drawback of this kind of method – and one which Brookshire *et al.* readily acknowledged – is that it is extremely sensitive to what is often called the third variable problem (for example, Haig, 1992; Meehl, 1970). Obviously, neighbourhoods differ on more dimensions than air quality. For example, they differ in the level of crime, view afforded from the house, general greenness of the area, distance from work and centres of entertainment. The statistical technique of multiple regression can be used (and was used, in Brookshire *et al.*'s study) to try to account for and to remove the influence of such variables, but it is always possible (and indeed likely) that some other variable has been overlooked or not measured for some other reason, in which case the actual influence of clean air on property values in this instance is likely to have been overestimated. (A small appendix at the end of this chapter introduces the statistical techniques of correlation and multiple regression.) It is also possible, on the other hand, that statistical control of other variables in the technique of multiple regression might lead one to underestimate the true value of clean air. For example, houses with good outlooks are also likely to have clean air because they tend to be above the worst of the pollution. If one attempts to remove the possible influence of the outlook one also removes part of the correlated influence of the clean air. In general, it does not appear to be possible to estimate accurately and hence remove all possible contaminating third variable effects using statistical techniques (Meehl, 1970).

A further problem with indirect behavioural measures of value is that they appear to be easier to find for certain sorts of government service or public good than others. The comparison of property values seems to be a reasonable, although possibly imperfect, measure for inferring the value of clean air. The value of the police could be at least approximately inferred from people's use of private security firms in areas where policing is poor. The actual usage of roads and public hospitals provides some indication of their value. For example, few would disagree that a highways authority should widen and upgrade a much-used road before working on one in similar disrepair that receives little use.

But, on the other hand, it is not easy to think of a behavioural measure of the value of defence, particularly in times of peace. Indeed, advocates of defence spending often claim, not altogether unreasonably, that the lack of observable warlike behaviour is a good sign that defence spending is worthwhile. A similar argument applies to the provision of prisons or a department of immigration. One purpose of the latter is to restrict the flow of immigrants into a country. This function is likely to be valued more by the citizens of the country who make no direct use of departments of immigration at all than by the immigrants who are compelled to deal with it. Finally, it is not easy to find suitable behavioural measures that value transfer payments, for example unemployment benefits or old-age pensions, from wealthier to poorer members of society. (As an aside, it is frequently found that not all eligible recipients of such transfer payments apply for them, indicating that even the possible beneficiaries do not always value them sufficiently to make use of them. See, for example, Craig, 1991; Storer and van Audenrode, 1995.)

Thus, we see that behavioural measures are not at all easy to find for some services, and where these behavioural measures are available they may be quite different for different kinds of service. The obvious implication is that while such measures may often be extremely useful for doing a cost–benefit analysis of a single service, they are not often likely to be suitable for comparing the relative values of different types of service. So, for example, it is not easy to see how behavioural measures might be used to decide between the value of adding a squadron of fighter aircraft to a country's airforce and the value of a new state-run hospital complex.

A possible measure of value that can be applied to all government services – indeed all government activities in a democratic society – is that of voting, and there have been a number of attempts to show how measures of the value of different government services might be obtained from the way people vote in elections (for example, Schram, 1990, 1991; Schram and van Winden, 1989). The exercise is complicated by not knowing how actual individuals vote, but the electorate can be stratified into different occupational or other interest groups, and the numbers of each group in each electorate or polling booth area are known (or at least estimable). From this information, one can derive the preferences of each group for each party, and knowing the political platforms of each party one can estimate the support for each policy element of each group. Some of the inferential problems entailed in deriving preferences and values from votes are considered further in the following chapter where the connection between the political process and provision of public goods is discussed.

In the present context, one might also question to what extent voting should be regarded as a behavioural measure at all. On the one hand there is obviously a sense in which voting in an election or referendum has consequences that simply completing a survey questionnaire or answering an interviewer's questions does not. On the other hand, the consequences of any one person's vote are so small that researchers have questioned why people bother to vote at all (for example, Tullock, 1967). Moreover, the response called for in voting is more similar to (although typically rather simpler than) the response called for in a survey than it is to the behaviour of moving from an area of the city with polluted air to one with clean air or of travelling to a particular recreation area.

APPENDIX: CORRELATION AND MULTIPLE REGRESSION

Many of the results reported in this book assume a little understanding of the concepts behind the statistical techniques of correlation and multiple regression. Readers who are unfamiliar with these techniques might find this section useful, but I should warn that I cover only some of the most basic points here.

Measures of correlation measure the degree of association between two variables. The most commonly used such measure is the Pearson correlation coefficient, often simply written as *r*. The size of *r* can vary from –1 (perfect negative correlation) at one extreme through 0 (no correlation at all) to +1 (perfect positive correlation). Negative correlations arise when one variable decreases as the other variable increases. For example, as the fitness of athletes increases so the time they take to run 1000 metres will decrease, and we would expect a negative correlation between the two variables. Positive correlations arise when the scores on the two variables increase or decrease together. For example, we would expect a positive correlation between the fitness of athletes and the speed with which they run the 1000 metres. In general the larger the number in a correlation coefficient (positive or negative) the stronger the association between two variables. Zero correlation means that there is no association between the variables, or alternatively that they are completely independent of each other.

Finding a strong association between two variables does not necessarily imply that they are causally related. As students in psychology and other disciplines are repeatedly told, correlation does not necessarily mean causation. For example, if we measured ice cream consumption in a city every day over a period of a year and also the number of people who go swimming each day, we would probably find quite a strong positive correlation between the two variables. However, in this case neither variable causes the other. Going swimming or watching swimmers does not produce a desire for ice cream and eating ice cream does not incline people to go swimming. Instead, the correlation arises because of a *third variable*, heat of the day. On hotter days people are more likely both to eat more ice cream and to go swimming (Meehl, 1970).

The third variable problem is very frequently encountered where the researcher cannot manipulate the independent (or possibly causing) variable directly, but instead is reduced to observing it and its possible effects. One way in which researchers try to ameliorate the effect of the third variable problem (most believe there is no way to eliminate it completely in non-experimental contexts, for example, Haig, 1992; Meehl, 1970) is to try to measure and control for the possible effects of such variables. A frequently used technique that is used in the attempt to disentangle these effects is multiple regression. In multiple regression there is an equation of the form:

$$y = \beta_1 x_1 + \beta_2 x_2 + \ldots \beta_n x_n \qquad\qquad (2.1)$$

where y is a dependent (possibly caused) variable; the x_i are the independent (possibly causing) variables; and the β_i are called beta weights. (More sophisticated readers will note here that these variables have been described in their standardized forms. That is, for all the variables all the values have had their mean subtracted from them and been divided by their standard deviation.) For example, y could be the runners' speeds, x_1 their fitness levels and x_2 the degree of their training. The critical point of multiple regression is that we would expect x_1 and x_2 to correlate: people trained in running will also be fitter. The trick of the technique is to get a measure of correlation between each of the individual independent variables and the dependent variable that takes account of all the other independent variables in the equation. So, for example, we should like to know what the correlation would be between speed and fitness if we were able to hold the runners' levels of training constant. The beta weights (so β_1 in this case) are precisely these measures.

The beta weight linking two variables is usually smaller than the correlation coefficient, but also ranges (usually!) from -1 to $+1$. In general, the larger the number, the more important that independent variable is as a predictor of the dependent variable.

Multiple regression also supplies measures of the combined predictive power of all the different independent variables used in the regression equation. The most commonly used such measure is the proportion (sometimes percentage) of the variance in the dependent variable that is accounted for. This is often written as R^2. For simple regression with only one independent variable the proportion of variance accounted for simply equals the square of the Pearson correlation coefficient (r) between the two variables. A more complex formula is used in multiple regression. The value of R^2 can range between 0 (where the independent variables combined have no predictive power at all) to 1 (where perfect prediction is obtained).

Multiple regression is subject to a number of limitations. An obvious one is that if you have not been able to identify all the independent variables and include them in (2.1) then they will not be controlled for. So, in our example, we have not measured the runners' motivations, a variable that will probably affect the runners' speeds and their fitness levels. Another one is that the technique assumes a linear relationship between the variables (although more complex types of regression can handle non-linear relationships).

In fact, there is a vast variety of types of regression analyses. These different types make different mathematical assumptions and are used in a host of different applications in the social and behavioural sciences. Certainly, multiple regression and other techniques related to it are widely used by both research economists and psychologists. One consequence is that there is a huge number of books on the subject if the reader would like to learn more about it (for example Harris, 1985).

3. Government Spending in Democracies

> In a capitalist democracy, there are essentially two methods by which social choices can be made: voting, typically used to make 'political' decisions, and the 'market' mechanism, typically used to make 'economic' decisions. (Arrow, 1963, p. 1)

When money is allocated among the different services supplied by a national or local government it is necessarily subject to a political process. This chapter sketches some of the ways in which political scientists and economists have thought this process might operate. We concentrate on the notion of the median voter, which has been an influential account of how democratic processes might regulate and allocate resources. In this chapter, the outlines of the theory are presented, followed by some of the theoretical difficulties. We then evaluate its predictions in the light of some of the survey research that has looked at people's preferences. Finally, we look briefly at how other political systems, particularly direct democracy, might fare.

THE MEDIAN VOTER

The median of any collection of numbers is the middle value when the collection is ordered from biggest to smallest. So, for example, the median of the five numbers 4, 6, 10, 11 and 12 is 10. The median voter is thus the voter who occupies the middle position on an issue which can be ordered on some dimension. So, for example, if the issue were how much money should be spent on the health service, there would be as many people wanting to spend more than the median voter as there would be people wanting to spend less.

The theory of the median voter appears to have had its genesis in work done by Bowen (1943), Black (1958/1987) and Downs (1957). We begin by reviewing some of Black's account of how committees work.

By way of example and to get some kind of feel for the theory, we start by considering a decision that is to be made by a committee of five people. The decision concerns how much of the committee's funds should be spent on a present for their secretary who is leaving the organization because she has just obtained a post elsewhere. The secretary is absent, and all the committee's decisions are made when a motion is passed by a simple majority. Suppose that Adam and Brenda favour expenditure of $5, Clarissa wants to spend $10 and Daniel and Erica want to spend $15. Obviously there is no majority in favour of any one amount, and the outcome will then turn out to depend on what the preferences of the committee members are if they cannot get exactly what they want.

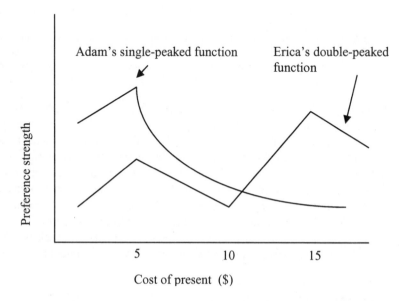

Figure 3.1. Two examples of hypothetical preference functions

Black's analysis hinges somewhat on the preference functions of the members of the committee. These functions are simply descriptions of the relative preferences each person gives to spending the different sums of money, and two examples of such functions are shown in Figure 3.1. Black's initial analysis assumed that all the committee members have single-peaked preference functions. If a preference function is single-peaked, then the member has a single favourite amount of spending and the further away an amount is from this favourite amount in either direction the less the member will like it. So, for example, if Adam's preference function is single peaked (as in the figure), his first choice is to spend $5. But if this is not possible, he will prefer to spend $10 rather than $15 and $3 rather than $2.

In the example I have just presented, it is clearly intuitively plausible that a motion to spend $5 on the present is likely to be rejected because a majority will regard it as too cheap, while a motion to spend $15 will probably fail because a majority regards it as too expensive. We would therefore expect that Clarissa's motion is quite likely to pass. Black formalized this problem and, subject to a number of assumptions, showed that this intuitive expectation is mathematically predictable. Formally, his theory predicts that only the motion of the median voter (in this case Clarissa) will get a simple majority over any other motion that is proposed.

It is important to note that the theory hinges on assumptions that need not be true, and hence there are good reasons why the will of the median committee member might not prevail. In political decisions generally, different procedural rules may produce quite different decision outcomes. For instance, suppose that in our case each motion tabled required a seconder at the outset, and that amending the amount of money specified in a motion was not permitted. In this case, Clarissa's motion would never have the chance to be put and hence could not be passed.

Although at first sight, the assumption that preference functions should be single peaked may appear to be obvious and uncontroversial, a little thought will suggest quite plausible scenarios in which preferences will not be single peaked and in which the will of the median committee member may not be the final outcome. Indeed, Black did consider other possibilities here. In our case, suppose Adam and Brenda want to use the money to buy the secretary a $5 bunch of flowers while Daniel and Erica want to buy a $15 bunch of flowers. There may be no $10 bunch of flowers for sale – this is sometimes known as a supply problem (Holcombe, 1989) – and Clarissa's preference is to give the secretary a $10 book voucher. It is easy to imagine that Erica might find her second choice to be the $5 bunch of flowers rather than the $10 book voucher, her preference for flowers in this case overriding her preference for a more expensive present. On the dimension of money she would then have a double-peaked preference function, with peaks at $5 and $15 and a dip in between at $10 (as shown in Figure 3.1). And, of course, it would not be surprising if in this situation the committee ended up voting for one or other of the bunches of flowers rather than Clarissa's book voucher.

Yet another major set of complications arises because committees typically make more than one decision, and the different decisions and the processes of making them tend to influence one another. So, for example, Daniel may agree to support Adam and Brenda with regard to the secretary's present because they are willing to vote with him on some other issue that is important to him or because they have supported him in the past or because they belong to the same political party. This kind of coalition formation, sometimes known as log-rolling (for example, Tullock, 1976) is extremely common in politics and is a well-known mechanism by which minorities can obtain favorable treatment on issues which are important to them.

Incidentally, although the example I have taken – like many of those that appear in the published work on this topic – considers people's preferences to be ordered on the dimension of money, the dimension does not have to be financial. The theory works equally well if, for example, the debate or differences occurred with respect to the maximum length of a gaol term for a crime, or how many members a sub-committee should have.

So far we have considered only the decision processes of a small committee. Obviously the politics of how an elected national government or even an elected local body responds to the financial wishes of the electorate are much more complex. One cause of the increased complexity arises because most modern societies are largely representative rather than direct democracies. That is, the voters do not directly make most of the decisions; rather, they vote for the people who do. Hence the influence of the median voter on some particular issue can only be exercised indirectly. Nonetheless, here too there are reasons for believing that the will of the median voter should be decisive.

A frequently used approach (for example, Stigler, 1972; Tullock, 1967, 1976) is to start from the assumption that politicians and parties are largely motivated by the will to power. Downs (1957), who made an early attempt to analyse this problem, pointed out that it became more tractable if one assumed that party members 'act solely in order to attain the income, prestige, and power which come from being in office' (p. 28). Given this basic assumption and the existence of majority voting it turns out that one would again expect the median voter's choice to be crucial: politicians who wish to preserve power in a democracy should follow the wishes of the median voter.

As a corollary it turns out to be rational, in a two-party system, for both parties to adopt positions that are very close to those of the median voter (for example, Downs, 1957; Stigler, 1972; Tullock, 1976). Ideally, this should occur for all the different issues on which the electorate has a range of preferences. So, for example, the wishes of the median voter should prevail with respect to the amount the government spends on the arts, the amount that is spent on the public health system, and the maximum (or mandatory) gaol term for burglary.

Incidentally, the assumption that politicians act in their own self-interest can also be applied to the voters themselves. An extension of this kind of political model is to try to infer the preferences of voters from the political parties they vote for at elections, as was briefly discussed in Chapter 2.

THEORETICAL ISSUES AND THE MEDIAN VOTER MODEL

In a review of the place of the median voter model in the theory of public choice, Holcombe (1989) points to a tendency to overestimate the power of its prediction. '[I]ts modest claim that under some circumstances the median voter's preference will emerge as the collective preference in a majority rule election system often was taken to imply that the public sector produces what the median voter wants' (pp. 117–18). We have already seen that there are good reasons why the model might not describe the behaviour of a simple five-person committee. Many of these reasons apply with at least as much force to, say, the way the cabinet votes in a democratically elected government.

So, for example, log-rolling (Tullock, 1967, 1976) is commonly observed in practice, particularly where formal coalitions are made between different parties to form a government. A party which, say, has received 45 per cent of the vote and seats in the House of Representatives may make up a governing coalition with a party which has received 6 per cent of the vote and seats. In return for its support the minor party might require that some of its most fervently desired policies are put into effect. If, as may well happen, the minor party occupies an extreme position on one or more of these issues, the outcome may be a policy that is quite a long way from that of the median voter. For example, if a Green Party was the minor coalition partner, it would not be surprising to find the government spending more on environmental issues than is desired by the median voter. Note, too, that in this case it is quite likely that both coalition partners would be aware that their policy differs from that of the median voter.

Similarly it is possible to imagine plausible scenarios where double-peaked preference functions might emerge when government spending is concerned. For example, consider someone in a municipality who votes on the provision of public money for a new city university. He might well consider that 'if a job is worth doing, it is worth doing properly', and might consider it reasonable either that the city should allocate enough funds to have a reasonably full range of academic departments and a university open to a wide range of students or that the city might not fund a university at all. In contrast, he might have much less sympathy with the idea of funding a university that can only afford to teach a narrow range of subjects.

Olson (1982) analysed the way special interest groups organize and influence governmental decisions. He pointed out that such groups are likely to develop in stable societies and from relatively small groups (for example, where there is a small number of manufacturers of a particular product) or groups which are easy to organize. Such groups are most likely to devote their energy to increasing their share of the available wealth rather than increasing the overall wealth of the society. Indeed, Olson's analysis indicates that the proliferation of such organizations acts as a considerable check on economic growth. In the present context, it seems quite plausible that such groups could also have a considerable biasing effect on the pattern of government spending.

Log-rolling and susceptibility to lobbying can occur in either democratically elected governments or in a small committee that is responsible to no one else at all. However, there are also reasons for expecting the median voter model to fail which apply only when the case of government is considered, or at least with much more force to a government than to a small group. In general, there is an enormous gulf between the act of the voter and the provision of a particular level of a government service. Except in referenda, which in most countries rarely involve voting on particular items of a government's budget, electors vote either for a particular candidate or for a particular party. The party or individual may have some more or less well-articulated policy on the provision of particular government services. For example, political parties in New Zealand have occasionally included specific levels of the old-age pension in their policy platforms. Normally, however, party platforms are not nearly so specific, partly because politicians are wary of making specific commitments on government spending. This wariness is not always unwise nor is it badly intentioned. It is quite common for a recently elected government which has promised to increase public spending in some area to be faced with macroeconomic information that indicates it should hold spending. The government is then faced with the unpleasant choice of breaking its promise or damaging the national economy.

Parties, then, do not usually offer voters a choice between different spending levels on particular services, although a particular party may be thought to be more likely to favour one sort of spending over another. For example, parties of the left are usually thought by the electors to favour more spending on social welfare and less on defence. Nonetheless, it is questionable whether the voter can make much use of such knowledge or beliefs to derive any very specific expectations about the spending preferences of the different parties. For instance, believing that a party of the left generally favours increased social welfare spending is little guide to knowing which of the many social welfare programmes they are likely to spend more on or how much the party wants to spend on them. Moreover, the political history of many countries provides examples of parties of the left or right actually acting in unexpected ways on this kind of issue, especially when confronted with macroeconomic considerations. For example, a left-wing government might decide against increased social welfare spending if confronted with evidence that this would damage the economy as a whole.

Finally, and perhaps most obviously, in most countries each voter has one vote. This vote must suffice to record all of his or her decisions and preferences on government spending on a variety of different services and his or her preferences on a variety of different policy measures – for example, macroeconomic policy, social legislation or foreign policy. Common lore suggests that the single most important determinant of voting behaviour is the overall state of the economy – 'It's the economy, stupid' – and there is now a good deal of research from a number of countries demonstrating that, indeed, a key determinant of people's voting is the shape that they perceive the economy to be in (for example, Alvarez *et al.*, 2000; Kinder, 1981; Price and Sanders, 1995). Curiously, the key determinant may be how individuals perceive that the nation as a whole is faring rather than how the outcome might affect their own economic interest (Funk and Garcia-Monet, 1997).

Alvarez *et al.* (2000) have attempted to model the relative contributions of 'the economy' and individual issues, and their analysis showed that economic perceptions had a strong influence on election outcomes in the USA, Canada and Britain, and that these perceptions often dominate other issues. They went on to suggest that 'by paying attention to the most immediate and tangible items of the national news – the economy – voters may be letting politicians off the hook for the less newsworthy but ultimately more important functions of government such as the production of public goods' (Alvarez *et al.*, 2000, p. 252).

Even if voters were to concentrate on services supplied by governments, the problem would not be solved. When everything comes down to a single vote every three, four or five years, it is hard to see how the preferences of the individual with regard to specific levels of spending on each of a range of particular services could be recorded. As Kristensen (1982, p. 37) puts it: 'elections could not be used to transmit policy wishes on specific policies from the governed to the governors in any case, because of the huge number of policy decisions on which the preferences of the electorate may differ.' Harris and Seldon (1979, p. 68), in the process of arguing for the superiority of the market system, ask: 'What sovereignty does the voter exercise through the ballot box? In place of the daily choice between myriad suppliers, the voter has a single option between two or three political parties at elections every four or five years.'

This line of reasoning, which, I should make clear, is quite well known to those researchers who have worked on the median voter model, leads one to ask why voters would bother to have preferences about government spending at all. Why should they attempt to discover the real spending preferences of different political parties? Why, indeed, should they attempt to inform themselves about current government spending? Do they in fact even know what is currently spent on different services? In Olson's (1982, p. 26) words 'the typical citizen will find that his or her income and life chances will not be improved by zealous study of public affairs, or even of any single collective good'.

Indeed, some researchers have gone further and have begun to question why people bother to vote. This issue is rather outside the scope of this book, but the main focus of the research has been on why it might be rational for people to vote at all when their individual choice is likely to have such a minimal impact not only on the decisions that governments make but also on the choice of government itself. (For some discussions of this issue, see, for example, Blais and Young, 1999; Riker and Ordeshook, 1968; Schram and van Winden, 1991; Tullock, 1967, 1976.)

Some of the other questions are obviously relevant to the subject of this book, and are taken up and looked at in more detail in later chapters. In Chapter 8 we look at the question of how well or badly informed the public is about the costs of specific government services and how this knowledge, or lack of it, relates to their valuations of them. Chapter 9 presents research on people's sources of information about government policies and their concepts of government services generally. In the next section of the present chapter, we consider whether the theory of the median voter aligns with what is known about people's preferences for government spending.

TESTING THE MEDIAN VOTER MODEL

A number of studies based on surveys of representative samples of electors provide some kind of empirical test of the median voter model. A number of these studies have presented the respondents with examples of government-provided services and have asked whether people wanted more, the same, or less spending on each service. If the median voter model were applicable and if the survey method is a valid way to go about uncovering people's preferences, one might formulate two possible expectations, one weak and one strong. The weak expectation is that the median respondent (ordering them from those wanting less expenditure and proceeding through those wanting the same expenditure to those wanting more expenditure on a service) should always be located within the same expenditure category. The strong expectation would require additionally that the percentage of those wanting more expenditure and the percentage of those wanting less expenditure on the service should be about equal (Kristensen, 1982).

In fact, it has frequently been found that neither prediction holds true although, as one would expect, the strong expectation is violated rather more often than the weaker. For example, Table 3.1 shows results obtained by Ferris (1985) from a representative US survey conducted in 1973.

Table 3.1. Percentages of respondents favouring less, the same, or more expenditure on six categories of public spending (after Ferris, 1985)

	Less	Same	More
Public education	7.9	33.0	59.1
Public welfare	49.4	25.3	25.3
Public housing	19.4	28.6	52.0
Public health	8.1	32.2	59.7
Highways	23.1	44.1	32.9
Defence	41.5	45.3	13.1

For these data, it is clear that the strong prediction of the median voter model is approximately true for expenditure on highways; in addition the weak prediction holds for public welfare (just) and defence. The weak (and of course the strong) prediction fails for public education, housing and health. Overall, the wishes of the median voter do not seem to have been very well met. Incidentally, it is worth noting that there is also an overall tendency to favour higher expenditures, although this is not true for all the services. As we shall see below and in later chapters, this overall tendency is often but not invariably found when people are questioned about government spending.

Lewis and Jackson (1985) reported the results of a British survey that used the same kind of questioning but presented a greater number of government services. In the end, seven of the 14 services failed to confirm the weak prediction. For four of these services, the percentage of respondents wanting more spending was greater than 50 per cent (hospitals and health, 80 per cent; pensioners and care of the elderly, 66 per cent; schools and education, 66 per cent; housing, 55 per cent); for three, the percentage of respondents wanting less spending was greater than 50 percent (Common Market, 69 per cent; foreign aid, 62 per cent; nationalized industry, 53 per cent).

Data are also available from a 1981 Danish survey (Kristensen, 1982). The results were reported as the percentage of respondents favouring more spending on each of nine areas minus the percentage of those favouring less spending. These percentage differences range from +60 per cent for old-age pensions to –49 per cent for defence; all but two of the differences exceed 30 per cent in one direction or the other. These results contradict the strong prediction of the median voter model, but, without knowing the (unreported) percentage of same responses, it is unclear for how many areas the weak prediction holds (although it must be violated for old-age pensions).

Other surveys using this method or variations of it (for example, Ferris, 1983; Maital, 1979; Smith and Wearing, 1987) show a basically similar pattern of deviance from the predictions of the median voter theory.

Relevant empirical results have been obtained from other methods as well. The results from budget game studies – see Chapter 5 for more detail on budget games – are also often out of line with the theory's predictions. For example, when Dutch respondents were asked to allocate budget cuts so as to achieve an overall 10 per cent decrease in the budget, different areas were subject to greater or smaller percentage cuts. For example, cuts of greater than 10 per cent were preferred for defence, cuts considerably less than 10 per cent for police and justice (De Groot and Pommer, 1987, 1989).

Strauss and Hughes' (1976) study asked respondents in the US state of North Carolina to allocate a hypothesized surplus in the state budget among different services supplied by the state. The categories receiving most of the allocated additional spending were public schools and health. A similarly designed study in England and Wales (Hockley and Harbour, 1983) found that the desired additional spending on health, education, housing and law and order was considerably greater than on overseas services and administration. Interestingly, defence spending was about middle ranked.

Zanardi's (1996) analysis of the preferences of a representative Italian sample found that of seven categories of public spending, more than half the sample (71.5 per cent) favoured a cut in defence spending and increases in spending on education (61.2 per cent) and health services (50.2 per cent). A subsequent budget game established that the average preferred increases in the *amount* of spending on education (15.8 per cent) and health (17.4 per cent) were relatively small, but the average preferred decrease in spending on defence (40.2 per cent) was rather large.

On the other hand, Bondonio and Marchese's (1994) study of respondents in the Italian city of Milan found that the median preferred expenditure was very close to the median actual expenditure for 13 of 14 municipal services. Indeed, the authors remarked on the 'almost exact correspondence between the municipal budget and the median budget chosen in the game' (Bondonio and Marchese, 1994, p. 211). This study raises the intriguing possibility that municipal governments may be more responsive than national ones.

To summarize, the general finding from this research has been that the predictions of the median voter model often do not seem to meet up with the preferences of the median survey respondent when representative samples are examined. Quite why the difference arises, however, is not so clear. In the previous section we investigated a number of reasons why one might not expect the median voter theory to apply in practice, and it may be that the discrepancy arises for one or more of these reasons. If this is true, the model is simply wrong when applied to government (or at least central government) spending. However, we should also consider the possibility that the discrepancy arises because there is a difference between the 'attitudes' expressed in the surveys and the 'behaviour' demonstrated in actual political activity such as voting. In other words, perhaps the median voter and the median survey respondent are not the same person or do not behave in the same way.

It is not easy definitely to exclude an 'attitude–behaviour' difference as the explanation of the discrepancy in this case, but a number of considerations make it appear unlikely. Firstly, there is a good deal of consistency in the results we have just examined, and this consistency appears to apply across as well as within the different methods. Thus, we find quite similar discrepancies when the 'more, the same, less' method and budget games are used. (Indeed, we shall see in Chapter 6 that a similar basic finding emerges from a psychophysical scaling exercise.) Secondly, the discrepancies that appear from the survey data appear to be simply too large to be explained as an attitude–behaviour difference.

A relevant point to recall here is that in most democracies a number of political opinion polls (attitudes in the present context) are routinely taken round about the time people vote (behaviour) in general elections. There are occasions on which the results of the polls are out of line with the outcome of the elections but these differences, although sometimes crucial for deciding who forms the next government, are simply not of the order of magnitude of the discrepancies reported here. It is not readily conceivable, for example, that a reasonably conducted opinion poll showing 53 per cent of the sample supporting Party A and 8 per cent supporting Party B (see the public health row in Table 3.1) would occur at the same time as an election result that produces equal support for the two parties.

Thirdly, there are 'behavioural' studies which also suggest that the median voter model is not correct. Boyne (1987) examined the patterns of tax policy in a number of different English local and regional governments and correlated these with the different parties and political systems employed. The basic idea was that the variations in tax policy ought, according to the median voter model, to be related to the variations in the party preferences. In fact, the expected relationship was not found.

Another possible artefactual explanation for the discrepancy between the predictions of the median voter model and the survey results comes from considering the different nature of the government services investigated. Some of these – defence and highways are obvious examples – have a rather high public good component (using the economist's definition of public good); others, for example education and health, are often viewed as mostly private goods. We saw in the preceding chapter that in theory the rule for the efficient provision of public goods is rather more liberal than for the provision of private goods: marginal utilities for public goods are added up over beneficiaries; marginal utilities for private goods are not. Perhaps, as Harris and Seldon (1979) have suggested, people consider the utility to themselves of public goods such as defence as if they were non-additive private goods rather than the additive public goods they really are.

Following this reasoning we would expect that asking people how much they want to spend on a service or whether they would like to spend more, the same or less on it to undervalue public goods in the economist's sense, or at any rate government services with a larger public good component. Clearly this account would be consistent with some of the results we have just examined. In particular, it would provide an artefactual explanation for why so many people in different countries would like to see defence spending reduced.

There are, however, difficulties with this conclusion. In the first place, it is not at all clear what sort of utility people have in mind when they make the judgements about government services that they do. If their judgements are based largely on the benefit to themselves, Harris and Seldon's point has a good deal of merit, but if the judgements are based largely on the perceived benefits to society as a whole, the argument is harder to make. The point here is that if the latter were true, we should be averaging the individual measures of utility, as each would be a measure of utility for society as a whole, rather than adding them up over all the individuals. We return in Chapter 6 to the question of which of these is more likely.

In the second place, and more crucially, closer examination of the results simply does not support the hypothesis that 'true' public goods are systematically undervalued. Defence does seem to be given a low valuation in most countries, but this result was true for neither the British study of Lewis and Jackson nor the English study reported by Hockley and Harbour. In both these studies, defence was actually given a middling valuation. Indeed, in Lewis and Jackson's study, defence was the government service that most closely fitted the predictions of the median voter model. As defence is just as much a public good in the UK as in the USA or Denmark, although for some reason it appears to be a more desirable one in the UK, the anomaly is hard to explain on this account.

Most importantly, other public goods do not appear to be systematically undervalued. Spending on highways fitted the prediction of the median voter model quite well in Ferris's (1985) data. Most compelling of all, in most of the studies more respondents wished to increase spending on the police, justice, and law and order than wished to decrease it. These services, which would seem to be about as much a public good as defence, thus show no sign of having been undervalued.

The idea that 'public goods' are undervalued is not the only one that fails to describe the pattern of the survey data. Another possible explanation for the failure of the median voter model, suggested by Olson's (1982) theorizing, is that well-organized special interest groups might be especially equipped to obtain government spending for their cause even if there were not a corresponding level of support from the public at large. It seems to me that this would provide a reasonable explanation for why defence spending has tended to remain higher than most survey respondents in most countries appear to want it. Armies, navies and air forces are, after all, generally thought to be quite tightly organized. However, the explanation does less well when other services are considered. In many countries health and education workers are at least reasonably well-organized, yet clearly the public would like to see more spent on them than is currently the case. On the other hand, welfare beneficiaries are typically among the least well-organized members of society, but most surveys show less demand for increased spending on welfare than for health and education.

OTHER POLITICAL ALTERNATIVES

The existing research suggests that the critics of the median voter model are correct and that in practice representative democracies do not choose to provide the mix of services that the median voter would choose. Governments may not be wrong to do so. It is quite conceivable that governments might in many cases actually serve the interests of their electors better by not following all their wishes in detail, particularly if, as we investigate in later chapters, there is good reason to doubt whether the electors are very well informed.

One might also try to put the discrepancies between apparent preferences and actual spending in a wider context. This chapter has reflected the focus of the existing research, which has tried to explain and to investigate how democratically elected governments allocate money. This focus is, of course, quite appropriate. Most governments today are democratically elected, and since the 1950s, when the median voter model had its origins, most government money has been spent by such governments, because democracies tend to be the wealthier countries. Again, most of the researchers live and work under democratically elected governments. But, of course, governments need not be democratic.

The castles of Europe provide enduring examples of the uses that kings and other hereditary rulers have found for government money. Less visible but probably more expensive were a number of wars – for example the Hundred Years War – that were fought to fulfil the dynastic ambitions of kings and queens and other unelected rulers. These wars were often fought with the aid of public money raised through taxation. Nor are all the examples old ones. The late President Ceaucescu appears to have considered large statues in honour of himself to be an appropriate use for Romanian public funds. Dictators of even small, poor African countries often manage to accumulate sufficient wealth in their terms of office to support themselves in pleasant lifestyles when they lose power and are forced into exile.

Such anecdotal evidence suggests that non-democratically chosen governments do not do a particularly good job of meeting the aspirations of the median citizen or subject, and it seems probable that representative governments do better in this respect. One might then go on to ask whether including *more* democracy in the political process would lead to a better mesh between government spending and citizens' wishes. Most western countries occasionally hold referenda on issues of national importance, and there is no particular reason why such direct democracy, as it is sometimes termed (for example, Frey, 1994), cannot be used to decide on government budgets or major alterations to government spending allocations.

Intuitively, one might expect direct voting on financial allocation to produce a number of changes to the way government spending is allocated. Most obviously, one would expect to end up with a rather better fit between the desires of the average citizen and actual spending allocation. Secondly and more subtly, one might expect to see some change in the desires themselves. Under direct democracy, citizens would have more incentive to inform themselves better about allocation issues, because they would be voting on them. On the other hand, it is not clear how much difference the change would make. After all, even in quite small jurisdictions the influence of any individual voter on the final resource allocation outcome would still be minute.

We do not have to rely completely on intuition, as there has been some research on how people vote directly on financial issues. The data come mainly from regional jurisdictions in North America and Switzerland. For example, US school budgets are occasionally the subject of referenda (Ingberman, 1985). The Swiss data are perhaps the most interesting. Fiscal policy in Switzerland is quite decentralized and often rather small regions and municipalities have considerable financial discretion (Pommerehne, 1990). Some of the Swiss local bodies decide financial matters by direct voting (sometimes at town assemblies) and some of them by representative democracy (that is, budgets are voted on by elected politicians). Thus, it is possible to compare local bodies where decisions are made by direct democracy with bodies that use representative democracy.

The Swiss comparisons (see, for example, Feld and Kirchgässner, 2000; Frey, 1994; Pommerehne, 1978, 1990) show that participation rates under direct democracy are reasonably high (typically above 40 per cent). Levels of public expenditure and public debt tend to be lower in jurisdictions with direct democracy, and there is some evidence for lower rates of tax evasion and slightly higher gross domestic product per capita in them as well. Propositions that are to be voted on often generate considerable interest and it is likely that citizens are better informed about such issues in direct democracies (Feld and Kirchgässner, 2000), although I do not know of any empirical comparison of levels of financial knowledge between different types of jurisdiction. Frey (1994, p. 341) remarks that 'the more developed the institutions of direct voter participation, the better the voters' preferences for publicly supplied goods are fulfilled and the more strongly public expenditure is influenced by demand rather than by supply factors'.

The claim that voters' preferences are better fulfilled under direct democracy does not mean that they are necessarily more likely to vote in their own narrowly defined self-interest. Swiss voting patterns for redistributional programmes indicate that people often do not vote in self-seeking ways. Indeed, Frey (1997) suggests direct democracies might do better at cultivating civic virtues. A rather nice demonstration of altruistic voting in direct democracy comes from a study on a river channelization project in Roanoke, Virginia (Shabman and Stephenson, 1994). The referendum was for whether or not the community should support a bond issue that would pay for work to prevent future flooding. Some 5000 voters were directly affected by the project because they lived on the floodplain, another 5000 were somewhat affected because they worked at locations on the floodplain, and a much larger number (about 90 000) were not directly affected at all. Although those who lived on the floodplain were more likely to vote for the project, there was a good deal of 'altruistic' voting from those who were not directly affected. The clearest evidence for this was the eventual 56 per cent vote in favour of the bond issue.

In general, then, the existing evidence suggests that direct democracies might fulfil the desires of the citizenry better than representative democracies, and that these might in turn do better than more autocratic forms of government. However, the evidence is suggestive rather than decisive. Even within Switzerland direct democracies appear to be more common in communities with fewer than 20 000 inhabitants. How well direct democracy functions in a large nation-state has not really been tested since classical times, but the example of Athens suggests that there might be difficulties. The absence of democratic institutions from Plato's *Republic* must in part reflect the author's perception (however biased) of the failings of Athenian democracy. Thucydides' description of the politics that preceded the expeditions Athens sent out in the unsuccessful attempt to conquer Sicily is also discouraging.

An important point to bear in mind here is that different monarchies or different representative or direct democracies may have somewhat different political institutions and that variations within the three types of government we have considered might be of considerable significance. For example, how budgetary or other questions are phrased in referenda is an important issue (for example, McDaniels, 1996). The outcomes of referenda on American school budgets have been shown to be affected by whether the defeat of a proposal causes a reversion to the budgetary status quo or (in theory) no budget at all (Ingberman, 1985). Thus, it may be that some, but not all, types of direct democracy would produce a tighter fit between government spending and the wishes of the median voter.

4. Quality of Life

This chapter and the next review some of the introspective measures that might be used to estimate the value or benefit derived from government spending. We first consider a little of the nature of such measures. Then the rest of this chapter considers how one's quality of life might be influenced by government or health authority spending. We focus first on the measurement of people's happiness or subjective well-being and how this is affected by people's circumstances, and, second, on how quality of life measures have been used in decisions to do with people's health.

INTROSPECTIVE MEASUREMENT

It was remarked in Chapter 2 that an important difference between the goods and services produced under the market system and the goods and services supplied by the government is that people are free to choose how much or how little of the former they pay for and consume. Their behaviour in paying for and consuming different market goods then gives us a reasonable indication of how much they value them. By contrast, behavioural indications are more rarely available for the goods and services that governments supply and where they are available they are less satisfactory measures for such goods than they are for goods that are bought in the market.

In this case an obvious strategy is to turn to measures of benefit and value that are subjective rather than behavioural, and this chapter and the next focus on some of the subjective, introspective measures that have been used. These measures have usually been developed within the discipline of psychology, or at least with some input from psychologists, and hence they constitute a psychological contribution to the study of government spending.

Before discussing these methods in detail, it is worth briefly noting for the benefit of readers who are not psychologists that not all psychological measures are subjective, although the ones we are concerned with here are. Many, perhaps most, psychologists share the preference of economists for objective measures. For example, behaviourists often record the pecks of pigeons, cognitive psychologists make extensive use of reaction time measures, developmental psychologists observe children playing. Similarly, psychologists often share the reservations that scholars from other disciplines have about the truthfulness and accuracy of what people say about their own experiences, feelings and motivations.

In fact, scepticism about the validity of introspection has a long history in psychology (for example, Watson, 1930; Skinner, 1971). Probably the best known modern attack was mounted by Nisbett and Wilson (1977) who concluded, on the basis of an extensive review of a number of studies where behavioural or physiological measures were taken and compared to verbal reports of evaluations and motivations, 'that people may have little ability to report accurately on their cognitive processes' (p. 246). Moreover, 'when people are asked to report how a particular stimulus influenced a particular response, they do so not by consulting a memory of the mediating process, but by applying causal theories about the effects of that type of stimulus on that type of response' (p. 248). Nisbett and Wilson also showed that people were often unaware of the actual variables which seemed to be controlling their behaviour. Thus, they conclude that 'it may be quite misleading for social scientists to ask their subjects about the influences on their evaluations, choices, or behaviour' (Nisbett and Wilson, 1977, p. 247).

Nisbett and Wilson's conclusions have seemed too sweeping for many (for example, Smith and Miller, 1978; White, 1980). Smith and Miller make the point that it might be more interesting to ascertain *when* access to mental processes is veridical, rather than to instance occasions when it appears to fail. Novelty and interest, for example, are more likely to enhance awareness. They also suggest that reporting during the process might be more accurate than after the fact, a point also made by Lazarus and Smith (1988) with reference to emotions. Moreover, although introspected attitudes and behaviour are often loosely connected, there is evidence that when attitudes that are rather specific to a behaviour and the behaviour itself are investigated there can be quite a close correlation (for example, Ajzen and Fishbein, 1977). Then again, it is difficult to see how a number of areas of psychological research – for instance that of mental imagery (for example, Finke, 1989) – could be investigated at all if introspective reports were to be entirely discarded. Finally, it might be noted that most of Nisbett and Wilson's criticisms concern people's ability to introspect on the causes of their own behaviour. When people are asked to introspect about the quality of their lives, they are not being asked to introspect about why their lives are the way they are but about what they are. Similarly, when they are asked to introspect about the value of government services they are not really doing so in a causal way, although it must be acknowledged that they are not introspecting on an immediate sensation either.

However, one can also be sceptical about whether people are capable of introspecting accurately on their desires, values and feelings. Freud

(1901/1960) suggested that people's behaviour was often influenced by desires and motivations of which they were unaware. Psychotherapists often set themselves the task of helping people 'to get in touch with their emotions' (Rosenhan and Seligman, 1989), and there is at least anecdotal evidence that people's perceived utilities may be conditioned by their environment and expectations (Marshall, 1961), and that self-reports may resemble behaviour in being unable to escape this conditioning . The following story, taken from Julian Barnes's novel *The Porcupine*, illustrates the point:

> One day, these three worthy peasants were lazing beside the Iskur river and talking generally among themselves, as people are apt to in such stories.
> 'Now, Ghele,' said one of the others, 'if you were a king and had all the powers of a king, what would you most like to do?'
> Ghele thought for a while and finally said, 'Well, that's a tricky one. I think I would make myself some porridge and put into it as much lard as I liked. Then I wouldn't need anything else.'
> 'What about you, Voute?'
> Voute thought for quite a bit longer than Ghele, and eventually he said, 'I know what I would do. I would bury myself in straw and just lie there for as long as I please.'
> 'And what about you, Gyore?' said the other two. 'What would you do if you were a king and had all the powers of a king?'
> Well, Gyore thought about this for an even longer time than the others. He scratched his head and shifted around on the bank and chewed on a grassy stalk and thought and thought and got crosser and crosser. In the end, he said, 'Damn it. You two have already picked the best things. There isn't anything left for me.'
> (Barnes, 1992, pp. 90–91)

Most of us could probably come up with a better, or at least a faster, response to this question than Gyore did, but it is still questionable whether we could quickly come up with an accurate idea of what each of the many present or potential government services do for us or could do for us.

Although psychologists are often sceptical about particular introspective reports or about the use of introspection in particular circumstances, as a rule they are happier to make use of evidence based on introspection than economists. The main reason for this is probably that it is psychologists who are chiefly responsible for investigating the validity of introspective methods generally, and they are more likely to be trained to do so. The prudent economist, faced with controversies over the validity of introspection arising from this alien discipline, is likely to wash her hands of the matter and to wait until some sort of consensus emerges among the psychologists. Present evidence suggests this is unlikely to be any time soon.

The different introspective measures that we shall consider here all require people to make numerical estimates of some subjective quality. Obviously if there is any possibility of using subjective estimates to formulate policy or to make recommendations about government spending, we should like to use numerical estimates rather than rely on statements such as 'That policy seems worthwhile' or 'Well, I would be happy to see spending on this project cut back'. However, there are serious problems in interpreting the numbers that people assign to their introspective judgements, and these problems are reasonably well known to both psychologists and economists. Some of them are apparent when the estimates are obtained from an individual, some are important when we wish to compare individuals or average estimates over different individuals.

First, there is a problem in knowing what scale the numbers are on. Suppose I say that the knowledge that my country is well defended gives me two units of happiness and the knowledge that my country's hospitals are good gives me four units of happiness. It seems reasonable to conclude that the latter pleases me more, but does it necessarily please me twice as much?

Stevens (1946), in an influential paper on scale types, distinguished four types of scale: nominal, ordinal, interval and ratio. These types of scale are distinguished by the information that they provide. Nominal scales occur when numbers are simply used to discriminate among different individuals. For example, if I hold a raffle ticket with the number 20 and you hold one with the number 40, this does not mean, for example, that you (or even your lottery ticket) have twice as much of anything important as I do. Ordinal scales are used when the numbers denote an order among the individuals, but give no further information. For example, if you come first in a race and I come second, we do not know how much faster you were than I. Interval scales have the property that differences in the numbers separating individuals can be interpreted. So, for example, it makes sense to say that the difference in temperature between 5 and 10 degrees Celsius is less than that between 12 and 22 degrees Celsius. Finally, in a ratio scale (often called a cardinal scale by economists) it makes sense to say that something individual is some ratio of something else. For example, it makes sense to say that $10 is twice as much as $5. Length and weight are other examples of everyday ratio scales. Another feature of a ratio scale is that the zero means something: that there is none of the quality in question.

It is important to realize that many of the ways we use numbers do not produce ratio scales. For example, temperature, measured in degrees Celsius, is not, since 20 degrees does not really mean twice as warm as 10 degrees. Nor does 0 degrees mean no warmth at all. (Note, incidentally, that this is not true when temperature is measured on the absolute, or Kelvin, scale.) The numbers attached to football jerseys do not make up a ratio scale. What does a player who wears the number 4 have twice as much of as a player wearing number 2?

It is sometimes difficult to state precisely which of these four types a particular scale might fall into. Such is the case with category rating scales, which are commonly used in psychology. With these scales, people are asked, say, to indicate their happiness on a scale from 0 to 10. Rating scales are not normally ratio scales, because it is not necessarily true that a rating of 6 means that the same individual is twice as happy as when she gave a rating of 3. It is, however, often considered that such ratings form interval scales. (For views on this issue, see, Poulton, 1989; Wegener, 1982.)

Leaving aside the question of scale types for the moment, the numbers obtained from a category rating exercise are also likely to be affected by the context in which they are asked for (Poulton, 1989). For example, suppose I am asked to rate the value of a government service such as legal aid as part of a list that includes eating a small chocolate and finding a dollar in the street. Now suppose I rate the same service again in a list that includes inheriting $100 000 from a distant relative and eating my dream meal. Most people would not be surprised if I were to give legal aid a higher number in the first rating exercise, where the context is comparatively valueless items, than in the second.

A variation on this problem arises if we compare numerical estimates derived from different societies or from the same society at different times. Different societies or different times create different contexts. Numerical estimates of subjective well-being, in particular, are made more difficult to interpret because often estimates obtained in different contexts are compared. For example, well-being ratings are sometimes compared across countries or from one decade to the next.

Probably the most difficult problems arise when the values of different people are to be compared in some way. If you rate the value of legal aid as 7 and I rate it as 6 on a 7-point scale does this necessarily mean that you rate it as more valuable than I do? This is quite possible, but it could also be, for example, that I am more reluctant to use the extreme values of the scale than you are. In fact, when one examines people's ratings one does find individual differences of this kind. Some respondents will place most of their responses into the middle categories (3, 4, 5). Other respondents tend to use the end points (1 and 7) a great deal.

An instance with policy implications arises if I rate the value of an educational innovation as 5 and the value of improved defence as 4. You rate the value of the improved education as 3 and the value of improved defence as 5. Clearly the average value of improving education is 4 and that for improving defence is 4.5, and simple averaging would suggest the latter should be the preferred policy. But because of the different way you and I use numbers it is possible that the 'real' benefit to me of improving defence is less than the real benefit to you of improving education. This kind of problem often turns out to be a rather a nasty one, as we shall see when we look at how decisions might be made regarding medical interventions. Note also that this is not simply a problem of whether the ratings are on an interval scale or not. It could be that both of us have internalized interval scales of rated value but that our scales are not calibrated in quite the same way.

Many economists have taken the view that interpersonal comparisons of utility and averaging utilities over individuals are essentially unscientific (for example, Robbins, 1938) or meaningless (Arrow, 1963). Historically, this view has acted so as to reinforce the preference for ordinal measures of utility that can be inferred from people's choices.

The various merits and problems of using the method of category rating are discussed in more detail in the next chapter. However, in the meantime it is worth noting that the difficulties caused by measurement problems with category rating and other scales turn out to be more important for some evaluation decisions than others. Hence, some of them are discussed in more detail in particular contexts throughout the remainder of this chapter.

SUBJECTIVE WELL-BEING

It is easy to imagine an apparently reasonable strategy for evaluating a new government programme. One could assess citizens' well-being at some point, then introduce the programme, and some time afterwards, when the programme has had a chance to influence people's lives, come back and evaluate the effect of change on the citizens' well-being.

There are, of course, a number of possible variations on this approach. One might only be interested in a particular sub-group of the citizenry – indigenous peoples, for example. In some circumstances, it might be possible to have some of the citizens affected by the programme and others not. Indeed, in the New Jersey income maintenance study, households were randomly assigned to different programmes (Kershaw and Fair, 1976). Obviously this would be a very powerful research strategy; equally obviously it is not often going to be possible to implement it. Alternatively, as a rather weaker research strategy, one might opt to gain a more immediate picture of the likely effects of changing a government programme by investigating the correlation between whether other communities have or have not adopted similar programmes and the level of subjective well-being in those countries.

Although these methods are quite different (for a discussion of their relative advantages and disadvantages, see, for example, Cook and Campbell, 1979), they have in common that they investigate the effect of policy on people's well-being. Now it turns out that we know something about people's well-being and what influences it. This is because, over the past 30 years or so, there has been a reasonable amount of research on the concept of well-being and the factors that affect it by psychologists and others. We now consider this research.

Most psychologists draw a distinction between well-being and happiness. Of the two, well-being is thought to be the more important, perhaps the morally worthier, concept. To see why such a distinction might be drawn, consider someone who with apparent honesty reported an hour after hearing of the death of someone who was close to him – his mother or his wife or one of his children – that he was perfectly happy. Most people, including psychologists, would consider that, even if this person was really telling the truth about being happy, he would not be in a state of well-being, and one would suspect, for example, that his happiness was chemically induced or that he had some kind of mental disorder.

Brodsky (1988, ch. 1) defines well-being by the presence of positive emotions, the substantial absence of negative emotions, and general satisfaction with one's life. In his view, which is fairly representative, well-being has four characteristics. First, it is subjective and emotional – hence, the usual use of the term *subjective* well-being to define it (for example, Diener *et al.*, 1999). Second, it is a state, implying that it will vary over time for most people. Third, it is thought to be the result of personal striving. Fourth, it is not simply described by the absence of negative feelings and the avoidance of conflict. Epicurus's notion that the aim of life is the avoidance of pain is thus not enough.

There have been suggestions that different types of well-being, for example, objective versus subjective, material versus spiritual, cognitive (satisfaction) versus emotional (happiness), might be distinguished (MacFadyen, 1999). Diener *et al.* (1999) suggest that pleasant affect, unpleasant affect and life satisfaction are different components of well-being that tend to separate over time – life satisfaction being, unsurprisingly, the most stable. (On a point of terminology, non-psychologists might note that psychologists often refer to feelings as 'affects'.) One might speculate here that some of these components might be more susceptible to manipulations of the supply of government services than others. For example, the ideology of improving the lot of the worst off would suggest that one might focus on changes to negative affect, although I know of no research which has looked at this.

As one would anticipate, there have been a number of different attempts to produce scales of well-being and its different components, but the use of simple category rating scales – for example, rating positive affect on a scale from very happy to not too happy, or life satisfaction on a scale from completely satisfied to completely dissatisfied – has probably been the most common approach.

There has been a good deal of research into the variables that influence people's well-being, mainly but not exclusively by psychologists. (See Diener *et al.*, 1999, for a recent readable and expert review of this work.) Much of the research has considered the impact of psychological variables, such as personality traits or coping strategies, but there has also been attention paid to the effect of more 'objective' – or at least more economically related – variables such as wealth, income and health. In brief, the general finding is that such variables do have an association with people's well-being, but as a rule the association is quite limited.

So, for example, Diener *et al.* (1993) found a correlation of 0.12 between income and subjective well-being for a representative US sample, with most of the effect apparently arising because those in the lowest income brackets had somewhat lower levels of well-being. Although those in the highest income brackets had higher well-being than those in the middle brackets, these differences were small. The suggestion that the relationship between income and well-being mostly arises because of low levels of well-being among the poor is strengthened by the finding from between-nation studies of a moderate correlation between GNP per capita levels and average well-being levels in a country (Diener *et al.*, 1993, 1995). On the other hand, one should also bear in mind when one evaluates this result that poorer countries are often less free, less democratic, and offer fewer interesting work opportunities, so that the cross-national differences in happiness may not really be caused by differences in income at all (Diener *et al.*, 1999; Lane, 1991). Similarly, the greater happiness of richer folk within a society may come about because of their more interesting work or their higher status. Certainly, there is very good evidence that being unemployed reduces people's happiness in ways that are not all connected with loss of income (for example, Jahoda *et al.*, 1933; Winkelmann and Winkelmann, 1998).

Another way to investigate how income affects subjective well-being is to consider changes in income. At a national level, the last 50 years have seen a considerable increase in the disposable incomes of the average person in the United States and Europe. This income increase, however, has not been matched by a corresponding increase in average well-being scores (Diener and Suh, 1997). At an individual level, people who have had quite large increases or decreases in their personal income over a decade do not generally report corresponding changes in well-being (Diener *et al.*, 1993). There are various possible reasons for this lack of relationship. For example, there is some evidence that the rapid acquisition of a higher income is associated with increased stress. Another possibility is that people adapt fairly rapidly to changed circumstances (Diener *et al.*, 1999). At any rate, it is clear that large improvements to people's material or financial position do not produce measurably large improvements to their well-being.

Individual differences in income do not account for much of the variation in well-being between individuals. In fact, differences in other types of 'resource' available to individuals are as a rule also poorly correlated with differences in well-being. So, for example, most studies have found little or no correlation between subjective well-being scores and measured intelligence (Diener *et al.*, 1999). Although university students who are physically attractive tend to be happier than those who are not, the size of the effect is small (Diener *et al.*, 1995).

Most surprising, perhaps, is that objective measures of people's health are also often not very highly correlated with subjective well-being, despite the fact that people often claim that good health is the most important contributor to well-being (for example, Breetvelt and van Dam, 1991; Diener *et al.* 1999). An explanation for all these phenomena that is frequently given is that adaptation occurs to many changes of objective situations, and people often adjust to lower or higher levels of income and health (Helson, 1947). On the other hand, if one is going to consider the possibility of adaptation to one's changed life circumstances, equally one might consider the possibility of adaptation to a different level of well-being itself rather than to the circumstances which might affect it. Thus, it might be that an improvement in one's health or income actually does produce a sustained increase in one's level of well-being, but that this sustained increase is not necessarily apparent from measures of well-being. My rating of my own well-being might be subject to context effects arising from my perceptions of the well-being of people around me.

Frank (1997) suggests other reasons why increases in income might not produce much improvement in subjective well-being. For example, it might be that a well spent increase in income would produce greater well-being, but the increase might not be well spent because we fail to predict what the actual outcome of the spending will be. For instance a large new house might be more troublesome to maintain and less fun to live in than anticipated. He also points out that a number of goods are in limited supply and that a general increase in income for everyone will not necessarily produce improved access to them. For example, in countries or regions that have a limited supply of land, if everybody's income is increased, this will still not make it any easier for a particular individual to buy a house with a large garden. Nor would increasing everyone's income by a constant amount or a constant percentage produce changes to people's status.

Overall, the research indicates that personality differences are more important determinants of individuals' subjective well-being than objective circumstances, suggesting the possibility that happiness, or a predisposition to it, might be a personality trait in its own right (Costa *et al.*, 1987). It is also apparent that people with different personality types and different coping styles will deal more or less well with the different challenges to well-being that are put forward by changes in their objective circumstances. This is easy to see in practice – consider, for example, the likely reactions of your different colleagues to some disappointment at work.

Another determinant of personal happiness is one's goals and progress towards them. Diener *et al.* (1999, p. 283) state that theories at present indicate 'that the process of moving toward one's aspirations may be more important to well-being than the end-state of goal attainment'. It is better to travel hopefully than to arrive. An important point here, of course, is that goals and aspirations are determined by the individual rather than by the objective circumstances he or she is in.

Even this brief, selective overview of the research into well-being should make it clear why the research strategy outlined at the start of this section is not likely to be very successful. Personal well-being is not very sensitive to changes in one's circumstances, and one would not expect most changes in the way that governments allocate resources to produce major measurable changes in the subjective well-being of most of the citizenry.

Of course, it is conceivable that governments could act so as to produce significant effects. A government that decided to enslave a good proportion of its people or that launched a major war against a well-defended neighbour might well succeed in lowering the average citizen's subjective well-being quite noticeably. But these are not the kinds of policy change that are of everyday concern. Nor are most democratically elected (or even authoritarian) leaders likely to be in much doubt about their effects.

More realistically, imagine that the New Zealand government (for example) decided to privatize the universities, which at present are (more or less) state-owned. This would be a reasonably radical change in government policy, but one would still not expect a great deal of change to the subjective well-being of the majority of New Zealanders who are not currently employed at universities, studying at them, or supporting someone who is studying at them. Even those who are directly affected, unless they were actually made unemployed as a result, are likely to find that the changes are less important to their subjective well-being than, for example, major health setbacks or a divorce or the birth of one's first child. Moreover, we would expect, on the basis of past research, that most of the individuals concerned would simply adapt to the change and, after a while, continue to report much the same levels of subjective well-being as they had before.

To illustrate this point further, we consider in detail a study by Frey and Stutzer (2000) which is interesting as a rare example of an examination of the real-life effect of some political difference or change on people's happiness. These researchers had the idea of trying to evaluate the effect on one's life satisfaction of living in a canton in which direct democracy was more or less of a feature of political life. The empirical basis of the study was a survey of 6000 Swiss residents who were asked a range of demographic (for example, what is your age?) and income questions. The chief dependent variable was the response to a typical well-being question – 'How satisfied are you with your life as a whole these days?' – which was answered on a ten-point scale ranging from 'completely dissatisfied' to 'completely satisfied'. The average response was 8.2/10 on this scale, indicating that on the whole the Swiss are fairly content. Incidentally, this finding of average contentment is typical for western countries (for example, Brodsky, 1988, ch. 1).

The main focus of the paper was a regression analysis. In this, the satisfaction scores were regressed on the demographic variables, the income variables, and an index of direct democracy in each canton. The analysis produced a statistically significant effect of direct democracy, even when all the other variables were controlled for, indicating that, indeed, living in a direct democracy might be a more satisfying experience for people.

Obviously, such a result could also be explained by some other unmeasured variable. The researchers did control for a number of other variables (for example, languages are differ across the different cantons) but none of these removed the direct democracy effect. They also found that the direct democracy effect was considerably greater for Swiss nationals (who can vote) than for foreigners (who can not). This result clearly reinforces the idea that satisfaction is really increased by being able to vote on a range of issues. So, although the evidence from such data can never be completely conclusive (because of the third variable problem discussed in Chapter 2), it should certainly be taken seriously. (Of course, if you accept the conclusion, it is still unclear quite why the effect arises. It could, for example, be because of the feeling of control that arises from being able to vote, because more satisfying bundles of government services are obtained in direct democracies, or even because people enjoy the experience of talking with each other beforehand about the issues they are going to vote on.)

It is quite easy to find statistically significant effects when you have a large, representative sample and you use powerful statistical techniques intelligently (as these researchers did). But, as everyone who has studied statistics knows, statistical significance means that an effect is unlikely to have arisen by chance, not that it is necessarily of great real-world importance. Thus it is important to know the size of the effect. Overall in Frey and Stutzer's study, only around 9 per cent of the variance in life satisfaction was explained by *all* of the independent variables measured (demographic, income and political) acting together. Perhaps, then, day-to-day variations and personality differences were more important determinants of Swiss satisfaction than these kinds of variables.

As a measure of size of individual effects the authors estimated what difference a change in the independent variable made to the chances of an individual's receiving the completely satisfied score of 10. The most influential independent variable measured was whether an individual was unemployed. Being unemployed was calculated to reduce the chances of complete satisfaction by 21 per cent. Being a foreigner reduced them by 9.1 per cent. On the other hand, the chances of complete satisfaction were increased by 6.8 per cent if you earned 5000 Swiss francs or more per month, underscoring the finding noted above that having a high income tends to increase your happiness but not by very much. Living in a direct democracy increased your chances of complete satisfaction by 2.8 per cent. In sum, yes, it does make a difference to people's happiness, but the difference is small.

QUALITY OF LIFE MEASUREMENT IN HEALTH

Over the past few years many countries have witnessed a good deal of concern and debate about the provision of health services. This applies both in countries, like New Zealand or the United Kingdom, in which much of the health service is state-funded, and in those, like the United States, in which a large proportion of it is funded via various forms of health insurance. In part because of extensive advances in medical technology, demand for the services exceeds the supply, leading to the often-reported phenomena of lengthening waiting lists for medical operations in state-funded hospitals and escalating costs of health insurance in insurance-based systems. In Ubel's (2000, xviii) blunt words: 'We cannot have it all. We cannot afford to give every health service to every person who could possibly benefit.'

In neither a state-funded nor an insurance-based health system is the decision to undergo medical treatment made solely by the patient. Usually in both systems there is an attempt to assess medical need, and the decision is made at least partly by medically qualified personnel. Lengthening waiting lists and escalating costs also entail the involvement of funding authorities or health insurers in the decision. One aspect of their involvement has been an increasing desire to perform some kind of cost–benefit analysis on the decisions in an attempt to see that scarce health care facilities are directed to those patients and problems that are likely to gain most benefit from them.

A variety of different methods has been suggested and used to evaluate the relative cost effectiveness of different medical interventions, and there are a number of recent books that outline how to go about doing the evaluations (for example, Drummond *et al.* 1997; Gold *et al.*, 1996b; Sloan, 1995; Staquet *et al.*, 1998). Different evaluation methods seem to be more or less suited for answering different kinds of questions. For example, it is rather more straightforward to evaluate two different methods for lowering a patient's blood pressure than it is to decide whether a finite sum of money should be used to increase the rate of screening for cervical cancer or to provide hip replacements. As one might expect, the second type of decision tends to be more controversial, in part because it is often not only about which treatment to provide but also about who is going to receive treatment. One might note that the problem of who is going to be benefited also surfaces when governments decide which services to provide, so this kind of medical decision is the one of most relevance for the general problem posed in this book.

A commonly used approach to making decisions of this kind is to make an estimate of the cost of each QALY that different medical treatments might produce. QALYs are *quality-adjusted life years*, and seem to have first been suggested as a useful concept by Fanshel and Bush (1970). To estimate QALYs it is usual to estimate the patient's quality of life, normally on a scale that ranges from 0 (for death) to 1 (perfect health), for each future year. A single measure is then obtained by adding up over these years. Typically the main variable of interest is the change in QALYs that are expected after some treatment provided. At the end of the analysis, we can evaluate the cost per QALY of each treatment.

So, to take a simple example, suppose we have an elderly patient, Adam, who is in very poor health and who is currently expected to have one year of life at a quality of 0.5 and then to die. His present QALYs add up to $0.5 \times 1 + 0 + 0 \ldots = 0.5$. Suppose the treatment under consideration will give him a life expectancy of 5 years at an average quality of 0.7. In this case the QALYs we expect after the treatment are $0.7 \times 5 = 3.5$. This is an improvement of 3 QALYs $(3.5 - 0.5)$ on what he would have without the treatment. If the total cost of the treatment is \$30 000, we would then reckon that this treatment costs \$10 000/QALY (\$30 000/3QALYs).

The patient does not have to be facing death for QALYs to be worked out. As a comparison example, imagine that Brenda suffers shame and embarrassment from having crooked and discoloured teeth which reduce her quality of life to (say) 0.8. If she had them capped her quality of life might become 1.0. If she has a future life expectancy of 30 years, the resulting increment to her QALYs would then be 30×0.2 (i.e. $1 - 0.8$) = 6 QALYs. Indeed, if the cost of this treatment were, say, \$12 000, her treatment would cost \$2000/QALY. In this case our analysis would produce the conclusion that treating her – and people like her – would be a better use of health funds than treating Adam.

The comparison of these two cases illustrates both the strength and weakness of the method. The strength is that it does enable comparisons to be made between very different kinds of medical treatment offered to very different classes of patient, and, at the end, the method returns a single measure of cost effectiveness that is fairly easy to understand. The weakness is that one can end up with decisions that look simply wrong. In this case, Brenda's cosmetic operation has been preferred to saving Adam's life.

To some extent, this particular outcome arose because of the way I oversimplified the QALY calculation. Generally, as is true in other types of cost–benefit decision, future time should be discounted in the QALY method so that in the final years of Brenda's life we would assume less benefit from having her teeth capped than we would in the years after her operation. A standard way to do this is to use a discount rate so that year by year each succeeding future year counts for less in the present decision. What the actual rate of discounting should be is itself often debatable (Lipscomb *et al.*, 1996).

More important, perhaps, than the issue of time discounting is the fact that the three variables involved in calculating costs of QALYs – cost, years of life and quality of life – are rather difficult to measure. Of the three, cost seems at first sight most straightforward, since we should be able to get reasonable estimates of both Adam's and Brenda's treatments. But as Adam is elderly and Brenda is estimated to have another 30 years of life, should we not include the costs of treating other future related or unrelated diseases they may suffer? Obviously, this is not an easy issue to resolve.

The estimation of years of life produces another set of problems. In practice, it is not likely that the prognosis for the length of Adam's life after his treatment could be estimated with certainty and for many conditions and treatments, especially those which have only been recently developed, even probabilistic estimates are very likely to be unreliable. Where probabilistic estimates are available, it is, of course, possible and necessary to include them in the QALY determinations. So, for Adam's example, we might have considered a 10 per cent chance that the treatment would quickly kill him, and a 90 per cent chance that he would survive for 5 years with a quality of life of 0.7, giving an overall expectation that the treatment will produce 3.15 (0.9×3.5) QALYs. I should also add, at this point, that it is unusual in QALY analyses to use time spans as long as 30 years, as I did for Brenda.

The most controversial measurement problems relate to determining the qualities of people's lives and the way the measures are used to compare people in rather different categories. A good start point is to consider the nature of the scale that the qualities are supposed to be assessed on. The scale is supposed to be anchored by 0, which represents a state of death, and 1, which represents a scale of normal, good health. It is, of course, conceivable that people could be in states worse than death, so negative values are often allowable (for example, Drummond *et al.*, 1997; Kawachi *et al.*, 1990). Perhaps the most critical aspect of the scale is that it is supposed to be an interval scale (Gold *et al.*, 1996a; Kawachi *et al.*, 1990; Sloan, 1995), which implies that equal intervals on the scale imply equal differences in quality of life. This assumption has important practical implications. As Sloan (1995, p. 49) puts it: '[T]he difference between 0.2 and 0.3 (0.1 QALY if the duration is one year) must have the same meaning as the difference between 0.7 and 0.8. A treatment which boosts patients from 0.2 to 0.3 must be considered of equal benefit to a treatment which brings patients from 0.7 to 0.8'. In the example of Adam and Brenda, the implication might be that if we just saved Adam's life by raising his quality of life from 0 to 0.2, this would be of equal merit to raising Brenda's quality of life from 0.8 to 1 by capping her teeth.

A number of methods have been proposed for trying to achieve such an interval scale of quality of life. They have in common that people are asked to make quality judgements of some kind, but not necessarily of quality of *life* directly. In the standard gamble method, judges are asked to choose between two imaginary alternatives. In one alternative, there is a certain state whose quality of life we do not know, being permanently in a wheelchair for example. In the other there is a gamble. In this gamble with probability, p, the judge ends up in normal health (with a quality of life of 1) and with probability of $1 - p$ the judge ends up dead (with a quality of life equal to 0). Suppose the judge says she is indifferent between the gamble and remaining in a wheelchair if p is 0.4 (a certain amount of iterating is necessary to find the value of p that will induce the judge to be indifferent between the gamble and the certain state). The implication is then that the quality of life of being in a wheelchair is judged to be $p \times 1 + (1 - p) \times 0$. In this case, p was found to be 0.4, so the wheelchair quality of life for this person is assessed at 0.4.

The standard gamble method is based on the theory of decision making under uncertainty originally developed by von Neumann and Morgenstern (1944), and it appears to enjoy considerable prestige. Nonetheless, there is good reason to question its validity. In effect the method assumes that people have an internal scale of probability that is an interval scale, and this can then be 'borrowed' to produce an interval scale of the quality of life. Of course, an objective probability scale is an interval one, but whether human estimation and thinking about probability reflect this interval scale is much more debatable. In general, human beings do not appear to be very good at making probability judgements and their judgements have been shown to be subject to a number of different types of bias (for example, Tversky and Kahneman, 1981). If people are not good at assessing probabilities, we would not expect this method to produce better eventual estimates of quality of life than asking people to estimate quality of life directly.

Time trade-offs are also used. In these, judges are asked to choose between living, say, 10 years with a certain poor standard of health and a shorter period of time with normal health. Again, the point of indifference is normally sought. In effect whether the method, and in this respect it resembles that of the standard gamble, really produces an interval scale for quality of life depends on whether the judge has an interval scale for length of time. Does, for example, the judge regard the interval between the sixth and seventh year of life as equivalent to that between the first and second? This is at least questionable, and in fact the work psychologists have done on temporal discounting suggests that the proposition is false (see, for example, Ainslie, 1992).

On the other hand, although it seems dubious whether either method can be relied on to establish interval scales for quality of life, they can be defended on other grounds. It is worth remembering that, in some situations, time trade-offs or gambles are precisely the decisions patients are called on to make.

Probably the simplest method of obtaining quality of life estimates is to ask judges to rate different states (being permanently in wheelchair, for example, or being deaf in one ear) on a scale from 0 to 1. Scales of 0 to 100 or 0 to 10 may also be used, as may various visual analogue scales (for example Gold *et al.*, 1996a). In a visual analogue task, judges might be presented with a line with the endpoints 0 and 1, and sometimes intermediate points, clearly marked on it, and asked to mark a cross at a point on the line where they think a particular state or states should be placed. As we have already seen, ratings of this kind are subject to a number of different kinds of bias.

The methods we have just discussed present quality of life as a single dimension, but it could well be thought of as a multivariate construct, and some measurement approaches take explicit regard of this. For example, the EuroQol measure covers six domains of health: mobility, self-care, main activity, social relationships, pain and mood (Gold *et al.*, 1996a). The main psychometric reason for preferring multivariate measures is that, if quality of life truly is multidimensional, judges who are attempting to make a single global judgement may focus only on one or two of the relevant dimensions at the time they make their estimate. It is possible that they may focus on different dimensions at different times, leading to unreliability. As the existing research suggests that people are not good at aggregating over different dimensions (for example, Edwards, 1992), this is a real concern.

If one wishes to get quality of life estimates that are aggregated over individuals rather than true for a particular individual, then there is a question of who should be asked to make the judgements. Medical professionals may sometimes be asked, but the usual choice is between a representative sample of the population or a sample of those individuals who suffer from the condition or conditions being investigated. Clearly the former may not have a particularly good understanding of the implications of a particular disorder. On the other hand, it is sometimes feared that sufferers from a particular condition might exaggerate the problems they face – especially if they have reason to suspect that their judgements might influence the likelihood of their getting treatment. The research into subjective well-being, however, would lead one to quite the opposite expectation. If anything, we would expect that sufferers from a particular disorder would not report much deterioration in the qualities of their lives, perhaps in consequence of adaptation to the condition (for example, Breetvelt and van Dam, 1991; Kawachi *et al.*, 1990).

If QALY measurement is used as part of a health resource allocation decision, interpersonal comparisons of the Adam versus Brenda kind are inevitable. The logic of the method suggests aggregation across individuals so as to maximize the total number of QALYs provided by the system. Normally, 'aggregation across subjects is undertaken, using the common 0–1 (dead–healthy) scale and obtaining the arithmetic mean. The difference in utility between being dead and being healthy is set equal across people, and each individual's health is thus weighted equally within the health domain' (Kawachi *et al.*, 1990, p. 47).

Readers with a philosophical interest will recognize that this way of using the QALY method makes the ethical assumption of utilitarianism, which emphasizes the greatest good of the greatest number (Burrows and Brown, 1993). Although it is not my wish to argue for or against this philosophy, it is worth noting that there are competing ethical assumptions, and that these lead to different resource allocation decisions. For example, Rawls (1971) suggests that social policy generally should try to maximize the well-being of the worst-off members of society. The application of this principle to health resource allocation suggests that those who have lower QALYs to start with should receive treatment ahead of those who are better off (Garber *et al.*, 1996). In the example of Adam and Brenda, Rawls's suggestion would lead us to treat Adam before Brenda.

In fact, there is reasonable evidence that people are often not happy with the implications of ruthlessly utilitarian application of the standard QALY analysis. Many readers of the earlier part of this section must have felt a little uneasy with the implication that Adam should die rather than Brenda have to put up with uncapped teeth. In the late 1980s, following a much-publicized case in which a seven-year old boy was refused Medicaid for an expensive bone-marrow transplant, the American state of Oregon carried out a large-scale cost-effectiveness study in order to attempt to decide which medical treatments would be paid for by the state and which not. The study was carried out and calculations were made but, in the end, the priorities captured by the study were not used. It was felt – with some justice – that they did not reflect people's actual priorities (Sloan, 1995; Ubel, 2000). For example, on the basis of the study, dental caps were initially rated ahead of treating appendicitis (Russell *et al.*, 1996).

In general it appears that the QALY method appears to underestimate people's feeling that it is fairest to give priority to those who are badly off – for example, those who are disabled. There are, of course, various ways in which the method could be modified to take account of this preference. Ubel (2000, ch. 10) suggests that 'societal values', people's preferences for different interventions, should be used instead of quality of life determinations. One consequence of this is that these values could sum to more than 1 for an individual – Ubel indicates that this might occur if, for example, we wished first to save the life of an individual with paraplegia and then second to attempt to cure her paraplegia or alleviate it in some way.

Other changes to the QALY method that might discriminate in favour of the unfortunate are perhaps more debatable. For instance, a recent discussion paper submitted to the New Zealand government (Ashton *et al.*, 2000) points out that Maori (the indigenous people of New Zealand) on average have poorer health than non-Maori. The paper points out (although it does not recommend) that this difference could be compensated for by attaching weights of greater than one to the QALYs of Maori patients.

If the QALY method gives rise to problems, it should also be acknowledged that it has definite successes. Forcing people to think clearly about exactly what is going on when medical decisions are made is probably one of them. One distinctly useful practical application has been in the evaluation of the effectiveness of repeated screening. There are a number of disorders, particularly cancers, for which screening has been recommended. But how often should this screening take place? The application of cost-effectiveness analysis to screening for cervical cancer (Russell *et al.*, 1996) indicated that screening once every four years as opposed to not screening at all costs about US $10 000 for every life saved. On the other hand, screening once a year rather than once every two years costs over an extra US $1 million for every year of life saved. The method has also proven useful for pointing up cases where drugs used to treat similar conditions can have enormous differences in cost effectiveness (Russell *et al.*, 1996).

IMPLICATIONS FOR GOVERNMENT ALLOCATION OF RESOURCES GENERALLY

It would be a mistake to suppose that the QALY method outlined above is the only methodology available as an aid to making health care decisions. Some health economists have suggested the use of Healthy Year Equivalents (HYEs) in place of QALYs (see, for example, Garber, 2000; Gold *et al.*, 1996b; Staquet *et al.*, 1998). Contingent valuation (see Chapter 5 for a detailed discussion of this method), in which people estimate how much they would be willing to pay to relieve different conditions or receive different treatments, is also sometimes used (Gold *et al.*, 1996b).

Neither the QALY method nor HYEs can readily be extended to compare, say, the value of health spending with the value of improvements to the education system. Although the concept of quality of life is clearly relevant to any service the government might offer, most other services do not have a determinable effect on individuals' life expectancies. There is also another important difference between the way health services might be distributed and the way other government services might be distributed. For health services it is likely that much allocation decision making will be carried out by individual medical practitioners practising 'bedside rationing' (Ubel, 2000) rather than by politicians or administrators working with fixed rules.

It is easy to see why this should be so. Different patients have different needs. For example, suppose there are two drugs available to treat a particular condition and one is more cost effective than the other. It might still be the case that some patients should be treated with the less cost-effective drug, because they turn out to be unresponsive to the preferred one or have a bad reaction to it. This kind of decision is likely to be much better made by the patient's doctor than by a distant administrator.

To some extent decisions of this kind, which involve knowledge of the needs of particular individuals, are made in other areas of government spending too. In some countries, some social welfare benefits are left to the discretion of individual case workers or area administrators, but generally rules for making such decisions for government services other than health are quite formalized. For example, eligibility for old-age pensions often have fixed criteria relating to age and past residency in the country.

Earlier in this chapter reasons were presented as to why the measurement of change in the well-being of the citizenry is unlikely to be a good way to evaluate typical changes in government policy. In essence, subjective well-being is too global a measure and is too little correlated to objective circumstances to be sensitive to such changes. The quality of life measure used in the QALY methodology is not subject to this kind of problem, principally because the medical decisions made apply to a small number of people for whom the changes in quality of life (and sometimes subjective well-being) are often quite profound. By contrast many, although not all, changes to government policy (consider, for example, the decision whether to upgrade an airforce or to improve the teacher/pupil ratio in primary schools) affect a much larger number of people but few of them in such a marked way. Thus, neither quality of life nor well-being are likely to be sensitive enough measures of how people are affected by the provision of government goods, and some other dependent variable seems called for.

On the other hand, clearly the basic question of how to measure people's preferences or utilities is important for all government services. Moreover, a number of the other methodological issues are common for all the different methods. For instance, there is a common issue of how to aggregate responses over different individuals. A point to bear in mind here is that, by and large, thinking about these kinds of issues is at present a little more advanced within the field of health economics than it is in public economics generally.

We remarked that some of the QALY methods used to date appear to fail by not taking adequate account of those people who appear to be worst off. In fact, societies often attempt to relieve the plight of the worst off in a number of different areas. An obvious example is that many countries have social welfare systems to ensure that a minimum standard of living is available to all. A less obvious one is suggested by the dental caps example. State-run medical systems are probably more reluctant in general to improve the appearance of someone by fixing the orientation of their teeth than they are, say, to offer plastic surgery to someone whose face has been badly burnt. A possible rationale for such behaviour can be found in the well-being research. The effect of income on well-being appears to be most pronounced at the bottom end of the income distribution.

Another point of similarity is also important: there is a common discomfort with making allocation decisions of any kind. Ubel (2000) notes the reluctance of medical practitioners to admit that they are making any kind of rationing decision, even though, as he demonstrates, in reality they often do. Much of this reluctance is because of their understandable unwillingness to do anything that might not be in the best interests of their patients' health. Similar unwillingness is shown by administrators and politicians with respect to health care budgets. Few have much enthusiasm for cost-cutting measures that are likely to lead to people dying, and it is understandable that many should want to avoid thinking about the subject altogether.

Reluctance is also justified by the fact that the assumptions on which the QALY method are based – and other methods used to obtain cost-effectiveness measures of health or any other services – may be, and frequently are, debated. What is the correct way to aggregate over individuals? Is raising a person's quality of life from 0.1 to 0.2 really equivalent to raising it from 0.7 to 0.8, particularly when different measurement methods are likely to give us different numbers anyway? These questions do not as yet, and may never, have very definite answers.

But, and this is true for all kinds of service, if the QALY method or some other formal method is not used in decision-making, the decisions still have to be made, and in fact are made, normally according to political processes of different kinds. At least where the health sector is concerned, there is now a growing recognition that these decisions are currently being made and that making them is unavoidable. There is also a genuine interest on the part of many in trying to find better ways to make them.

5. Methods of Assessing Value

In the previous chapter, some of the methods used to assess well-being and quality of life were investigated. This chapter considers some of the introspective methods that have been used or that might be used to get some idea of the value people assign to the different things the government does. The chief difference is that here we are concerned with the attempt to evaluate a good or service or range of services rather than obtaining a global assessment of people's well-being or quality of life.

CONTINGENT VALUATION

Although, as we shall see shortly, there are good reasons to question whether contingent valuation is actually doing what it is supposed to, there is no doubt that it has been by far the most frequently employed and most intensively researched introspective method for attempting to evaluate public goods (see, for example, Hanley and Spash, 1993; Hausman, 1993; Mitchell and Carson, 1989; Spash, 1999). For this reason alone, it would deserve detailed consideration.

The basic idea of contingent valuation is that individuals are asked how much they would be willing to pay for some public good, using the term here in its broader sense, or, more rarely, how much they would be willing to accept as compensation for the discontinuation of the good. Usually there is no presumption that people really are going to be asked to pay for the good, and contingent valuation can be viewed as an attempt to estimate a shadow price by creating a hypothetical or contingent market for the good in question (Spash, 1999). Clearly, the method is dependent on people's ability to introspect.

Although the method can be used to value virtually any type of good or service, in practice it has been most frequently applied to the estimation of the value of environmental goods: wilderness areas, national parks, places of scenic beauty, pollution-free environments and the like. For example, an early application valued woodlands in the state of Maine (Davis, 1963). The increasing concern for the environment and conserving it in recent years has led to explosive growth in the use of the method (Spash, 1999).

72

Environmental issues have often been politicized, and, perhaps most notably as a consequence of the Exxon Valdez oil spill off the coast of Alaska, the perceived importance of these issues and the publicity accompanying them have brought about intensive scrutiny of the contingent valuation method itself. After the Exxon Valdez oil spill had taken place, the state of Alaska used contingent valuation studies to try to assess the environmental damage caused by it. For its defence, Exxon funded a good deal of work (see, for example, Hausman, 1993) which turned out to be critical of the method. The (American) National Oceanic and Atmospheric Administration subsequently convened a panel that suggested guidelines for the use of the method.

A number of contingent valuation studies have produced valuations that not only appear sensible but also are in reasonable agreement with those obtained from other methods. For example, Brookshire *et al.* (1981) assessed the value of clean air in the Los Angeles area using a variant of contingent valuation known as the iterative bidding technique. In this technique survey respondents were presented with a starting point, $1, $10 or $50 per month, and then asked whether they would be willing to pay this amount for air of a particular quality. (The qualities were specified using photographs that showed the same perspective with differing amounts of haziness.) Respondents saying 'yes' were presented with higher sums until they were unwilling to pay more; those saying 'no' were presented with lower sums until a sum was found that they were willing to pay. These results were compared with those obtained from analysing differences in property values as outlined in Chapter 2. Overall, the results moderately supported the validity of the contingent valuation technique. The size of the starting bid usually had a non-significant effect on the final sum arrived at. Contingent valuation produced estimates of clean air value that were lower, but not ridiculously lower, than the property values: the former were of the order of $25–30 per month; the latter were of the order of $50–100 per month. This difference seems reasonable when one considers that estimates based on property values are quite likely to be overestimates of the real values because of the possibility that other, confounding variables were overlooked in Brookshire *et al.*'s multiple regression analysis of the variables affecting property valuation.

As one might expect, there are a number of different techniques within contingent valuation, and these techniques are subject to different sorts of biases and do not always yield the same estimates. For example, Boyle and Bishop (1988) compared the use of three of these techniques – iterative bidding, payment cards and dichotomous choice – in valuing the scenic beauty of the lower Wisconsin River. Iterative bidding, as discussed above, requires giving the respondent start points, and it is likely that the start points provide anchors that indicate suitable prices to the respondent (for example, Shafir and Kahneman, 1999). Payment cards involve presenting respondents with a card – often tailored to the respondent's income bracket – which shows typical expenditure on other services and requires them to mark their desired spending level in the appropriate place. Dichotomous choice, the simplest but least informative method, simply presents the respondents with a single suggested sum and asks whether he or she would be willing to pay that amount for the service. The sum is then varied across respondents. In Boyle and Bishop's study, this third method produced rather lower value estimates than the other two. Incidentally, psychologists familiar with methods of determining thresholds might see parallels between the three techniques that Boyle and Bishop used and the classical or Fechnerian psychophysical methods of limits, average error and constant stimuli (Woodworth and Schlosberg, 1955).

Studies such as these suggest that contingent valuation produces monetary estimates of value that are at least reasonable. However, there are also good reasons to doubt the validity of the method.

Perhaps the most important of these is that, as Baron (1997, p. 74) points out, contingent valuation 'judgments are often remarkably insensitive to quantity or scope of the good provided'. One example of this insensitivity comes from the existence of an embedding effect, in which a good seen as part of a larger good is assigned a reduced value. For example, Kahneman and Knetsch (1992) asked one group of respondents about their willingness to pay for improved preparedness for disaster and another group about their willingness to pay for improved rescue equipment and personnel. The latter measure was embedded in the former: preparedness included equipment and personnel. People in the two groups nominated about equal amounts for the larger and the smaller good that they were willing to pay. However, when they were asked how much they were willing to pay for the smaller, embedded good directly after they had been asked about the larger one, the sums were considerably smaller. (See also M. A. Kemp and Maxwell, 1993.)

Related to the embedding effect is an adding-up effect (Baron, 1997). For example, Diamond *et al.* (1993) presented respondents with scenarios which suggested that a number of wilderness areas were to be exploited commercially and then asked them how much they would be willing to pay to prevent either another one or another three areas from being exploited. They found that the amount respondents were willing to pay was not related to the number of threatened areas. So, for instance, a particular respondent might be willing to pay $100 to stop either one or three extra areas from being exploited. If the contingent valuation method is taken at face value such a result indicates that the second and third extra areas had no worth whatever. Similarly, Schkade and Payne (1993) investigated the valuation of preventing waterfowl deaths that occur when the birds alight on ponds contaminated by oil spills. Their results indicated that people were willing to pay similar amounts of money to prevent 2000, 20 000, or 200 000 waterfowl deaths from this cause.

Some of the amounts that people report being willing to pay to prevent environmental damage imply unreasonably high valuations. Mead (1993) points out that one study of the threatened whooping crane produced a valuation for the life of *one* of these birds of US $3.7 billion.

Such studies show a suspicious insensitivity of the contingent valuation method to the quantity of the good that is provided. The other side of the coin, as Baron (1997) points out, is that the method seems to be overly sensitive to factors which do not appear to be related to the value of the good in question. Two of these factors are the perceived fair price of the good and, in the case of an environmental good, the cause of the threat to it.

People's willingness to pay often depends on their perception of the fair price for the good. Thus, Thaler (1985) showed that people's willingness to pay for a beer to be drunk on the beach depended on the outlet that it could be bought from. People were willing to pay more for beer from a classy resort hotel than from a store. Baron and Maxwell (1996) found that, when the benefit was held constant, people would pay more for a public good that was believed to be expensive. These results are problematic because they indicate that the valuations of the good are being heavily biased by one's knowledge or beliefs about its present price.

The cause of the threat, particularly whether it is natural or human, also affects willingness to pay to prevent environmental damage. For example, people are willing to pay more to save sea birds from an oil spill arising from human error than to save them from a new virus, or to save Australian mammals threatened by hunters rather than predators (Kahneman *et al.*, 1993). Again, if the value of sea birds is what is being measured, why should it matter what is threatening them?

Results such as these indicate that the amounts people say they are willing to pay for environmental goods are not 'pure' valuations of the good. Instead the amounts may be related to the 'warm glow' or feeling of having acted morally that comes from attempting to preserve it (Baron, 1997). As Daum puts it:

> If I am willing to pay $100 for a program to preserve a resource out of a sense of charity or a sense of duty to others or to show my support for the environment in general or for a good cause, the good that I am purchasing with my $100 is not the resource; it is, instead, the moral satisfaction that comes with making the contribution. (Daum, 1993, p. 396)

Of course, neither Baron nor Daum is suggesting that people should stop acting morally or charitably. Instead they are drawing attention to the fact that respondents who are asked to do contingent valuation may be confounding the value of acting in a particular way with the value of a particular good.

Another contaminant is that contingent values are heavily influenced by people's perceptions of the importance of the good. As importance may only be weakly related to the quantity of the good in question, they may then become insensitive to quantity information. Baron (1997, p. 76) points out that 'when people are asked which is more important, life or money, most confidently answer that life is. If they are then asked whether they would spend $100 000 (borrowing if necessary) to extend a random patient's life by 1 hr, they feel tricked.' Kahneman *et al.* (1993) found that amounts people were willing to pay to avert or remedy various threats were highly correlated with the rated importance of the threats.

A problem with contingent valuation that has received rather less attention arises from the nature of the dependent measure of value. The use of sums of money as the dependent variable does have distinct advantages. The measure is understood by respondents, and it is directly interpretable as a measure of value by researchers or others who wish to make use of the information. Money is also a well-developed ratio scale, as it makes good sense to say that $100 is twice as much as $50.

Aristotle in his *Nicomachean Ethics* may have been the first to remark that money is used as a means to compare and equate different things, and to have suggested that money equates different things according to the measure of human demand. Indeed, he claimed that '[m]oney makes all things commensurable, since everything is measured by money' (Aristotle, 2000, 1133b). If Aristotle were correct, then the choice of money as the dependent variable in contingent valuation would indeed be ideal. But there is a good deal of evidence that the philosopher was not correct. Money is not always seen as an appropriate measure of value, and there are a large number of objects and experiences to which people are very reluctant to assign monetary values. Perhaps the clearest evidence for the reluctance and the clearest demonstration that money is not a universal measure of value comes from research (Belk and Coon, 1993; Burgoyne and Routh, 1991; Webley *et al.*, 1983) into people's unwillingness to give sums of money as gifts in a variety of situations. Two simple thought experiments should make the issue clear. Imagine offering your spouse or lover a cash gift when his or her birthday next comes round. Imagine giving a banknote instead of a bottle of wine or bouquet of flowers to your hosts when you are next out for dinner. Of course, the appropriateness of money as a gift varies from culture to culture. For example, in some communities cash is an appropriate wedding gift, in others not.

There are other indications that money is not always a universal measure of value. For example, there appears to be a taboo against paying people for acts of friendship, although quite why this arises is not so clear (Kemp and Burt, 1999). More important in the present context, the reluctance to regard money as a universal measure of value can be seen at a societal and governmental as well as at an individual level. As Ubel (2000) notes in his discussion of medical decision-making, there is a general reluctance to assign a monetary value to human life. Few countries unashamedly sell justice or openly offer to sell their citizenship to foreigners.

In brief, most people do not regard money as a suitable measure of value for all things. In particular, it is often believed that money has a tainting influence and that many human interactions should be held above this influence. One might note in this respect that there have been theoretical attempts to try to describe and to account for the perception that money sometimes has a tainting influence, and for the way in which people appear to distinguish between different kinds of money (for example, Belk and Wallendorf, 1990).

The perception that money taints and that it is not a suitable measure for all human activities and desires creates problems for contingent valuation. I know of no advocate for the contingent valuation method who has seriously suggested that the method should be used to assess the value of, say, one's partner or of a corruption-free justice system, but the issue of the appropriateness of money as a measure of value surfaces even in the most frequent use of the method – when environmental goods are valued. Respondents in contingent valuation surveys do occasionally state that, for example, unpolluted air or areas of natural beauty are goods that should not be purchased, but held above and out of the money economy in some way. Baron (1997, p. 83) describes such people as having 'protected values'. A behavioural consequence of this feeling is that people in contingent valuation studies sometimes respond by being unwilling to pay anything for such goods. Hence, responses of zero are virtually uninterpretable (and are often treated as missing data) in contingent valuation studies. Do they mean that the respondent attaches a very high value to the good or no value whatever?

Finally, in contingent valuation respondents have usually been asked to consider how much they would be prepared to pay for a single good from their after-tax income. This is not, of course, the same thing as considering how much should be spent on each of a wide range of government-supplied services. In the latter case, there are more goods to be considered, and a good deal of the money to be allocated has in a sense already been handed over by the respondent to the government as tax. Thus, theoretical problems aside, the method of contingent valuation needs some modification to be suited for the task of valuing a range of government services. One such modification, considered a little later in this chapter, uses a budget game.

PREFERENCES FOR MORE, THE SAME OR LESS SPENDING

A basic approach to the valuation of government services, sometimes referred to as an attitudinal approach (for example, Ferris, 1983), is to present respondents with a list of government services or categories of government service and to ask them simply if they favour spending more, the same or less on each of the services or service categories. This method is the simplest in current use, and clearly this simplicity is itself an important merit. This advantage is probably responsible for its frequent use in opinion polls, but as we saw in Chapter 3 a number of published studies have also made use of it.

An obvious problem with this rather simple measurement system is that it does not indicate directly by how much people would like to increase or decrease expenditure. This in turn makes it difficult to order the different services on a dimension of value. For example, suppose a (very) small sample of five people who evaluate the two government-supplied services of raising kangaroos and providing gum trees for koalas to eat. The government has just enough money to improve one of these two services. Suppose three people want more spent on kangaroo raising while two would like to spend less on this service. On the other hand, one person would like to spend more on providing trees for the koalas while four are happy to spend exactly the same amount. It is not clear from these results which of the two services, if either, the government should spend more money on.

Maital (1979) has made some suggestions as to how this information might be inferred from the percentages responding in each of the three categories. His analysis assumes that for each service or category of service the respondent evaluates 'the difference between the marginal dollar of benefits he derives from an incremental unit of X and the marginal tax bill which that unit places on him' (Maital, 1979, p. 87). He then goes on to derive such marginal differences for each of a range of services. Maital's analysis assumes normal distributions, but, as he points out, the actual distributions could be fairly easily checked from the results collected. (For instance, the kangaroo and koala example quoted in the previous paragraph clearly violates this assumption.)

The simplicity of the 'more, the same, less' method has theoretical as well as practical implications. While it is not at all clear what cognitive processes respondents are using when they use the different kinds of valuation methods, it is quite likely that they could use a different and rather simpler process for the more, the same, less method than for contingent valuation. Most crucially they do not need to make any estimate of the likely effects of particular amounts of decreased or increased spending in the former method. They could, for example, respond by asking themselves only whether some people are at present in real need (implying the service needs more money), whether things seem to be running fairly smoothly (implying expenditure should be kept the same), or whether there are signs of waste (implying expenditure should be lowered).

BUDGET GAMES

Budget games resemble contingent valuation in that they ask respondents to estimate the amount they would like to see spent on a government service. They differ in that respondents are asked to make these estimates for a range of government services. Thus the respondents must perform a more complex task than simply stating whether they would like to see more, the same or less spending on a particular service. Indeed, in some variations (for example, Bondonio and Marchese, 1994) the initial stage of responding is the identification of those services or service categories on which the respondent would like to see more or less spent.

An early report of a type of budget game is provided by Strauss and Hughes (1976) who asked a sample in North Carolina to use movable penny coupons to transfer spending between different state budget categories, a technique also used by Hockley and Harbour (1983). In this method, each coupon showed the image of a penny, and so many coupons were assigned to each service initially. Changes that a respondent desired were recorded by moving one or more coupons from a less desired service to a more desired service. Using movable coupons is one way to ensure that the overall budget is maintained or, where it is changed, to ensure that respondents are aware that it has been changed and that changes to the tax revenue structure are also required. Another, and more modern, way to perform the task is to require the respondents to adjust their preferences on a computer. Zanardi (1996) reports a study in which a large sample was required to state their preferences for spending on the Italian budget.

A characteristic of Zanardi's study is that respondents were informed not only of the impact of the expenditure changes on the country's budget but also of the impact of the changes on their personal tax and income. Clearly, computerizing the budget game method, and using the level of programming sophistication one routinely encounters in present-day computer games like *Civilisation*, enables quite accurate and immediate presentation of the implications of particular choices, and it appears probable that Zanardi's approach will be used more extensively in future.

As an illustration of how a budget game might work in practice we consider a rather simpler example – that given by De Groot and Pommer (1987). In this, a sample of Dutch respondents was presented with nine categories of government spending: police and justice; primary and secondary education; higher education; services for the elderly; mental health care; in-patient health care; out-patient health care; culture and recreation; and defence and general government. Respondents were told that a 10 per cent budget cut was needed and they were presented with a sheet which showed the level of current government expenditure as a row of drawn coins. The 10 per cent budget cut equated to 20 coins, and respondents were told they could have a maximum 20 per cent budget cut on any one item. De Groot and Pommer's analysis showed the size of the cuts to vary with the service, the biggest cuts being in defence and general government, the smallest in public services for the elderly.

Finally, it might be remarked that the budget game approach resembles contingent valuation in its use of money as the key measure of value. It differs in two important respects. Firstly, in the budget game approach the respondents obviously value more than one government supplied service at once. Secondly, in most budget games the emphasis has been on reordering allocations to individual services, while the game specifies the total government budget. This contrasts with the usual approach in contingent valuation where respondents are essentially asked to think of their spending on a good or goods as being from their after-tax income.

PSYCHOPHYSICAL SCALING

The non-psychologist is likely to think of psychological measurement as mainly consisting of attempts to measure differences between people. Tests to measure personality or intelligence in which an individual's (or sometimes a group's) score is compared with that of some reference group are likely to come to mind. However, while it is true that the measurement of individual differences is an important part of psychology, it is also true that psychologists since the publication of Fechner's *Elemente der Psychophysik* in 1860 have been interested in measuring how people perceive qualities of stimuli – that is to say properties of the external world – as well as distinguishing the qualities of individual people (Murray, 1993). Such perceived qualities include, to take some frequently studied examples, the loudness of a sound, the subjective length of a line, or the seriousness of a crime. Obviously such qualities are subjective ones, although they often have objective correlates. For example, the loudness of a sound is closely related to its physical intensity; the subjective length of a line to its actual length; the seriousness of a crime to the length of the prison sentence convicted criminals incur for committing it.

A number of methods have been proposed over the years for measuring such qualities, of which the two most commonly used today are the methods of magnitude estimation and category rating.

The method of magnitude estimation was proposed by S.S. Stevens (1957, 1975). As an experimental method to measure the loudness of sound, for example, the experimenter first presents the subject or subjects a particular sound of a certain intensity and assigns this standard sound a standard loudness, 100 say. Further comparison sounds that differ in sound intensity (and sometimes along other dimensions as well) are then also presented, normally after pairing with the standard. The subject is told to assign numbers to each comparison sound according to how many times louder or less loud it is than the standard. So, for example, if she feels the sound is three times as loud, she should assign it a loudness of 300, if half as loud, she should assign it a loudness of 50, and so on.

It was Stevens' claim that the scale of loudness obtained by this method constitutes a ratio scale. This claim assumes, firstly, that people do have internal scales of this type and, secondly, that they can report on them reliably. Unsurprisingly, these assumptions have been the subject of ongoing research and debate ever since.

Stevens went on to examine the relationships between the subjective scales he obtained by magnitude estimation with the objective scales they were supposed to be correlated with. This examination revealed that in many cases the two dimensions, for example loudness and sound intensity, were related by a power law of the form:

$$\psi = k. \varphi^n \tag{5.1}$$

where ψ is the psychological magnitude (for example, loudness) and φ the physical magnitude (for example, sound intensity), k is a scaling constant, and n is an exponent. Typically the exponent is unchanged when the psychological and physical dimensions are unchanged, and, unlike k, it is not affected by changes in the value of the standard stimulus or in the units used to measure the physical dimension.

This relationship is often known as Stevens' Law, and it is widely reported and used in psychology. If logarithms are taken of both sides of the equation, the law predicts a linear relationship between the logarithm of the psychological magnitude and the logarithm of the physical magnitude, with the slope of the line equal to the exponent. It is common to plot the logarithmized measures against one another, with the expectation or hope of seeing an apparently linear relationship, and the correlation between the two logarithmized measures is often taken as a measure of the strength of the relationship and how well Stevens' Law describes it.

The size of the exponent, n, has a definite interpretation. If the exponent is less than one, as is found for most sensory dimensions (for example, Stevens, 1975), then the psychological dimension is a compression of the physical dimension. For example, an exponent of around 0.3 is usually found when loudness is related to sound intensity, and this implies that a tenfold increase in the intensity of a sound is experienced as a doubling of its loudness.

An obvious application of both the method of magnitude estimation and the law is to the measurement of value and the relationship between value and price, and, indeed, there has been some research which has investigated this. Galanter (1962b, 1974) used the method to measure the utility of sums of money, asking people to estimate the happiness they would experience from receiving different sums. The estimated utilities or happinesses were quite well related to the sums of money by a power function with an exponent in the range 0.40 to 0.45, indicating that the subjective utility scale is a compression of the money scale.

In at least two studies respondents have been asked to perform magnitude estimation on sets of non-monetary items. Galanter (1990) in a series of experiments asked respondents to estimate the pleasantness or unpleasantness of a series of positive or negative events, some of which could readily be assigned a monetary value. Kemp (1988) had samples of student and general public respondents estimate the 'desirability, value or usefulness to you' of each of a set of items available in the market place such as a new Toyota Corolla, a new colour television set, or a can of fruit juice. The value estimates were rather well related to the prices of the items, with high correlations between the logarithms of the estimated values and the logarithms of the prices of the items. More details of this study are given in Chapter 6.

There have also been a few studies in which the method of magnitude estimation has been applied to valuing the goods and services supplied by the government. Kemp (1988) had respondents estimate the value of a range of possible options for increased government expenditure, for example, removing all lead from New Zealand petrol and increasing the Family Benefit (currently $6 per week per child) by $10 per week for each child. These estimates, in contrast to those reported above for non-monetary items available in the market, suggested virtually no relationship between the perceived value of the option and its cost. Kemp (1991) had respondents estimate the utility of goods and services currently supplied by the German government, for example, police, environmental protection and defence.

Correlations between the estimated utilities of the services and their per capita costs were again weak.

The other commonly used psychophysical scaling technique, category rating, is, if anything, simpler to use than magnitude estimation. As with the latter method, there are a number of variants of it, but it is characteristic that the respondent or judge has a rather smaller selection of numbers to work with and these numbers have an upper bound. For example, in much of the research discussed in Chapters 6 and 8, respondents were asked to value on a scale between 0 and 10 where 0 denoted no value and 10 denoted very high or the highest value. Numbers greater than 10 or less than 0 were not permitted and nor were fractional or decimal responses like two and a half or 6.3.

When category rating of perceptual qualities has been performed it has often been found that, as with magnitude estimation, there has been a regular functional relationship between the rated categories of the subjective dimension (ψ) and a related physical dimension (φ). For this method, however, the relationship found is generally logarithmic:

$$\Psi = k \log(\varphi) \tag{5.2}$$

The relationship is often known as Fechner's Law, after its nineteenth century proposer Gustav Fechner (Fechner, 1860). It is common to plot the category rating against the logarithmized measure of the physical dimension and to see if the result is linear.

A little reflection should convince the reader that the numbers obtained from magnitude estimation and category rating of a subjective dimension such as loudness will not be the same. Nor is it likely that one can get from one set of measurements to the other by simply multiplying one set by a constant. The critical difference is that the category ratings are bounded while the magnitude estimates are not. It has also been suggested that (ideally) category rating produces an interval scale while magnitude estimation produces a ratio scale. In fact, it is often (although not always) found that the relationship between category ratings and magnitude estimates is logarithmic (Galanter, 1962a). If one takes the view that subjective qualities such as loudness, perceived line length, or crime seriousness are in some way essentially inherent in the person making the judgements, then it follows that at most one of the two types of judgement may correspond with this 'real' dimension. The other then does not, but is only a transformation of it.

This consideration has given rise to an ongoing controversy within psychology as to which is the 'truest' method of psychophysical scaling. So, for example, Parducci (1982, p. 89) claims that category ratings provide 'direct pipelines to the psyche'. Stevens (1975) argued the superiority of magnitude estimation because, he claimed, it gave rise to a ratio scale. Readers wishing to learn more about this controversy are invited to consult Algom and Marks (1990), Gescheider (1988), Krueger (1989), Poulton (1989) or Wegener (1982). My own current view, which has perhaps been rather biased by the arguments of Anderson (1990) and Poulton (1989) in favour of category rating, is that, while the fight is by no means over, category rating appears to be ahead on points, and that it is debatable whether magnitude estimation does supply a true ratio scale.

While this issue may eventually have implications for our understanding of people's inherent unidimensional construct of value – presupposing for the moment that they actually have one – it is not clear that the controversy has important practical implications for our present level of understanding of the value of public goods. The rank order of value between magnitude estimates and category ratings is unchanged. Although the relationship between value and costs is different for the two measurement methods, at present no measure of the value of government-provided goods has a close functional relationship of any kind with cost as we shall see in later chapters.

Perhaps most important, it has been found that the two kinds of scaling give closely related results when government services are valued. Kemp (1991, Study 2) asked respondents to value a range of government-supplied services using both magnitude estimation and category rating. Both for individual respondents and overall there was a high correlation between the category ratings and the logarithm of the magnitude estimates of value, in line with the findings for some other dimensions (Galanter, 1962a). Moreover, neither value dimension related very strongly to the costs of the services: the correlation between the logarithm of the median magnitude estimates and the logarithm of the costs was 0.44, that between the mean category ratings and the logarithm of costs was 0.42. These results indicate that the two measures are more or less interchangeable with the aid of a logarithmic transformation. Category rating, however, is perhaps a little simpler to use and, in this study at least, tended to be preferred by the participants. Fifty-seven per cent of the sample claimed category rating was the better scale; 20 per cent claimed magnitude estimation was better; the remainder had no preference.

Another issue, too, tends to favour category rating. Occasionally, respondents assign zero value to a service or an item of expenditure. Such values are meaningful and interpretable but they create analytical problems because you cannot take a logarithm of zero. Hence, such values must be excluded from a power–law analysis.

A final methodological point is worth brief comment. We would not expect to obtain a simple linear relationship between value and cost using either psychophysical method. Stevens' Law suggests there should be a linear relationship between the logarithm of the measures of value and the logarithm of cost; Fechner's Law that there should be a relationship between the rated value and the logarithm of cost. When Pearson correlations between value and cost are calculated, therefore, in the research reviewed in Chapters 6 and 8, the appropriate transformations are made. Thus, when magnitude estimates of value are correlated to cost, both variables are logarithmically transformed first; when category ratings of value are related to cost, cost is logarithmically transformed.

MULTIATTRIBUTE UTILITY THEORY

So far, all of the methods we have considered in this chapter have effectively taken it for granted that utility or value is a unidimensional concept. But, as was remarked in the previous chapter when quality of life was discussed, this need not be true, and it is quite plausible that government services are thought by people to serve a number of rather different kinds of value. If this were true then clearly it would be good to discover, firstly, what these dimensions of value were, and, secondly, how different services might be valued on each dimension.

There is a variety of means one might use to uncover different dimensions of value. For example, Kemp and Willetts (1995b) factor analysed the category rating valuations of a number of different government services (without discovering any factors of particular interest). Multidimensional scaling or cluster analysis might also be employed in this cause. The most obvious candidates for the task, however, would appear to be the methods that arise from multiattribute utility theory, as it is sometimes known.

Multiattribute methods are commonly used in decision-making, have been widely researched and written about (for example, Edwards, 1977; Fandel and Spronk, 1985; Jungermann and de Zeeuw, 1977; Keeney, 1977; Nelson, 1999; Pitts *et al.*, 1980; von Winterfeldt and Edwards, 1986), and make explicit reference – as their name suggests – to dimensions of value or utility. It is thus perhaps a little surprising to find that they have been rarely used to establish relative values for different government-supplied services.

Although multiattribute methods have in common that they assume the existence of a number of different dimensions of utility, they are otherwise extremely varied. Perhaps the most fundamental division concerns whether or not the different dimensions can be traded off against one another, the two types sometimes being known as compensatory and non-compensatory models (Nelson, 1999). In models of consumer choice, where multiattribute models have been most heavily used (for example, Carroll and Green, 1995; Nelson, 1999), it is quite plausible that either type of model might be employed. For example, one consumer might insist that a car she purchases be large enough to seat five people in reasonable comfort, and all cars that fail to meet this criterion would be rejected regardless of how excellent they are in other respects. Another consumer might be prepared to trade off size against some other attribute.

It is easy to conceive of analogies in how people might evaluate government services. For example, one person might insist on some criterion of fairness or tenet of social justice being met, while another would be prepared to trade this off for increased efficiency or all-round societal improvement. Indeed, those who have written on moral philosophy and social justice often do use different sorts of criteria. So, for example, the Rawlsian theory of distributive justice which emphasizes the utility of the least advantaged members of society might be contrasted with philosophies which emphasize the greatest good of the greatest number (for example, Singer, 1999).

Within compensatory models, the utility of a particular good, service or product is often calculated from a simple linear formula of the type

$$U_i = \Sigma \ W_j \ V_{ij} \qquad\qquad (5.3)$$

where U_i is the final utility score of good i, W_j is the value of utility dimension j, and V_{ij} is the value attached to good i on dimension j. (Σ means summing up, in this case over all the j utility dimensions.)

Of course, more complex formulae are sometimes used. Also, there is a variety of different ways of judging the particular values (the V_{ij}) and the relative weights (W_j) of the different utility dimensions. In general non-compensatory theories are modelled with decision trees rather than by a single formula. If a criterion is met for a particular good, the good can then proceed into the next stage of decision-making.

By way of illustrating how multiattribute utilities could be worked out and applied to the issue of evaluating government services, the procedure and results from Kemp and Willetts (1995a, Study 4) are briefly reviewed. No claim is made that the particular method used in this study – a simple compensatory one – was the best way of approaching the problem, and I imagine that many readers familiar with either multiattribute methods or the general problem of evaluating public goods could easily suggest improvements. The method we used was adapted from Edwards' (1977) SMART technique.

The first step in the analysis was the attempt to identify some possible dimensions (or attributes) of the utility of government services. For this identification 12 individuals of varying sex, age and occupation were visited at home on two separate occasions. During the first visit each was asked to make up a list of 20 factors the government might take into account when deciding what to spend money on. A few days later the lists were collected and examined for overlapping or repeated concepts and a list of 24 factors which seemed to cover all the issues raised by the 12 individuals was prepared. This composite list was then taken back to the identification group who were asked to rate each of the 24 factors on a scale from 1 to 5 as to how important they were for evaluating 12 government services. In a separate exercise, they were also asked to pick out what they thought were the six most important factors. As a result of these two exercises, seven factors were chosen for the main study: health and welfare; education; security and crime prevention; effect on the economy; long-term benefits; promoting employment; and fairness and equity.

In the main study 60 different respondents completed two questionnaires two weeks apart. For the first questionnaire they simply rated 16 government services according to the value they thought New Zealand people received from them on a scale from 0 (no value) to 10 (highest value). The reason for this initial questionnaire was to see if the ratings and estimations carried out in the multiattribute procedure itself affected the way that people thought about valuing government services, because a number of multiattribute theorists (for example Humphreys, 1977; Keeney, 1977; Pitz *et al.*, 1980) have suggested that the multiattribute process itself educates the users. According to these theorists, people are benefited by consciously using multiattribute procedures, which help them to make better, more considered decisions. It may also be that people are not very good at the subconscious calculation of equations like (5.3). Edwards (1992, p. 275) argues that 'machines are good at aggregating information, while people are good at providing that information in aggregateable form'.

The second questionnaire asked for the evaluation of the importance of the factors (W_j in equation (5.3) above). Health and welfare was given a score of 10, and the respondents were asked to evaluate the importance of the other dimensions using a form of magnitude estimation. So, for example, if they thought another factor twice as important they were to assign it 20. The questionnaire also called for the rating of each of the 16 government services on a scale from 0 (no value) to 10 (utmost value) on *each* of the seven factors (the V_{ij}). Finally, overall category ratings for each of the government services were obtained as in the first questionnaire.

When the importance scores were averaged over the respondents, the seven factors turned out to be of quite similar average importance, with means ranging from 12.5 for education down to 8.7 for long-term benefits. However, individual respondents sometimes produced very different patterns of importance. Overall multiattribute scores were then calculated using equation (5.3) for each service and respondent. It turned out that these scores correlated reasonably well with the first set of overall category ratings ($r = 0.74$ between the average service scores and ratings) and even better with the second set of category ratings ($r = 0.86$). The improvement in the correlations indicates that people did change their valuations a little between the first and second set of category ratings and that the second set was more like the results obtained from employing the multiattribute procedure. The implication of these results is that the multiattribute procedure did indeed have some educational role. Further and rather stronger evidence for this role appeared when the second set of category ratings was simultaneously regressed on the first set of ratings and the overall multiattribute scores. The β-weight of 0.36 that was obtained between the latter and the second set of ratings suggests that the multiattribute procedure did affect the second category rating. Thus, it appears that the overall valuations of respondents can be influenced by effectively forcing them to take into account a number of different value factors when they value government services.

An obvious final question to ask is whether the seven different factors of value really were conceptually different from each other. In fact, the seven factors all correlated quite highly with the overall multiattribute score, with correlations ranging from 0.53 for security and crime prevention to 0.96 for effect on the economy. These results suggest that in reality the seven factors were not conceptually very different, and hence that the way people think about the values of government service might not in fact be truly multidimensional. Thus,. the status of dimensions of value for government services is probably best described at present as being unclear.

MERITS OF DIFFERENT METHODS

Obviously the ideal method to establish the values of government services would be direct and behavioural, and would involve people doing something very similar to actually paying for the individual services they wish to consume. Equally obviously, the nature of government services precludes this option, and one is left instead to choose among various possible second-best options.

The clearest choice is between indirect, behavioural measures (such as using property values to infer the value of clean air) and direct, introspective measures such as contingent valuation or psychophysical scaling. Both types of measure have intrinsic defects.

The most obvious problem with the behavioural measures, already outlined in Chapter 2, is that reasonable measures of this kind appear to be more widely available for some kinds of government services and public goods than for others. Moreover, the types of measure are likely to be very different – and suffer from different specific problems – for different services, even where they are available. This implies that such measures, while useful for evaluating some specific services, are less suitable for comparing the valuations of a range of different services.

The second major problem with such measures is that they are all liable to suffer in some way from the third variable problem that was discussed in the context of evaluating clean air. This problem arises generally with behavioural measures to assess value, not just when trying to infer the value of clean air from house prices. Most seriously, it is known that the third variable problem can not be definitively solved using any kind of correlational or regression technique (Meehl, 1970).

If psychologists are likely to give a little more credence than economists to introspective reports, and are more willing generally to make use of research that is wholly or partly based on introspection, they also have a traditional distrust of correlational research strategies. The sensitivity of psychologists to the possibility of the third variable problem is partly the consequence of the repeated admonitions that 'correlation is not causation' that are made in undergraduate psychological research method classes.

The obvious solution to the basic dilemma in the choice of measurement strategies that we have here is to use more than one kind of measure – as Brookshire *et al.* did. In practice, however, this strategy is not always possible, especially when we are assessing the merits of a number of different kinds of government service.

As well as considering the larger issue of the merits of indirect, behavioural versus direct, introspective methods, there are also methodological choices to be made within these categories. Choices among the behavioural measures are most likely to be based on pragmatic, opportunistic criteria, because these choices vary markedly depending on the service or public good one wishes to value, and often may not be available at all.

On the other hand, there is a good deal of choice among the different introspective methods. Some of the differences have been hinted at above and can be briefly summarized here. The multiattribute approach differs from all the others (including the behavioural methods) in supposing value to be inherently a multidimensional rather than a unidimensional construct. At present, there seems to be little evidence that people do evaluate government services on a number of quite different dimensions, but the sparseness of the evidence may reflect mainly the sparseness of the investigations that have sought it. Certainly, there does seem to be a need for future research to look at this question in more depth than has been managed to date.

Of the unidimensional measures, contingent valuation, psychophysical scaling and the more, the same, less method can be thought of as ordered on a continuum that differs mainly in the nature of the dependent variable that is used. The monetary measure used in contingent valuation is clearly a ratio scale; asking people whether they wish to pay more, the same or less is clearly a crude ordinal scale; the psychophysical methods appear to produce scales that fall somewhere in between these extremes. On the other hand, the use of sums of money as the dependent measure in contingent valuation raises problems of its own. Finally, budget games can be seen from this perspective as an adaptation of contingent valuation that attempts to value a range of services or goods rather than a single one.

More biases and potential defects have been discovered with the method of contingent valuation than the other methods, but this difference may be mainly because the method has been more heavily scrutinized than the others. This heavier scrutiny, in turn, has probably arisen because of its heavier use and because of the political controversies that have surrounded its application to valuing environmental goods, rather than because of the deficiencies of the method. Certainly, as Baron (1997) points out and as is discussed further in Chapter 6, at least some of the anomalies in the results that have been obtained with contingent valuation appear to have parallels in the results that are obtained from psychophysical methods.

In this context it is worthwhile considering what assumptions – explicit or implicit – the different introspective methods outlined above make about the relative worth of people's utilities. In this respect budget games and contingent valuation are alike in using the money scale. Clearly average, median or other monetary measures aggregated over the sample or population are then interpretable as indications of how people would like money to be allocated or reallocated. Whether or not such aggregations of notional sums of money bear much relation to aggregated individual *utilities* is much more questionable, especially when one bears in mind the various biases and other problems with contingent valuation outlined earlier.

This question is related to a more theoretical question that is often posed, not only when utilities are measured, but when the measurement of any subjective dimension is attempted. The question is: Are the qualities additive? So, for example, is the measured utility of a health system comprising, say, hospitals and free supply of pharmaceuticals equal to the sum of the utility of hospitals and the utility of pharmaceuticals measured separately?

There are a number of good reasons why this property of additivity is highly desirable in any measurement system. Think for a moment what it would mean if it did not apply to the way prices are calculated. It would mean that each item would have a different price depending on what other items were bought. But where evidence is available for the measurement of utility, it suggests that utilities, like other psychological magnitudes, cannot be simply added.

This is most obvious for the method of category rating where the ratings have an upper bound of, say, 10. If hospitals were rated as having a value of 9 and pharmaceuticals are valued as 8, then the rating of health can still only be 10 or less, not 17. The method of magnitude estimation has no upper bound but, as Stevens (1975, ch. 2) concedes, additivity is not normally found there either. Perhaps the best documented case of this is in loudness scaling: usually the loudness of two sounds combined is less than the sum of their separate loudnesses (see, for example, Kryter, 1985).

Intuitively one would expect additivity to apply to values obtained from contingent valuation since this method makes use of the normally additive scale of money. But in practice here too additivity often fails, as we saw in more detail earlier in the chapter. In general, then, it appears that people's concept of utility does not include additivity, however desirable it might be if it did, although it is possible that some as yet untried method might entice judgements that are genuinely additive from respondents.

Another issue that needs addressing is the question of averaging over respondents. The frequent use of the Pareto optimality criterion by many modern economists arises in part because of their reluctance to make judgements about trade-offs between two people's utilities (for example, Arrow, 1963). If a governmental policy increases Sally and Teresa's utility but reduces Ursula's, how can we know whether the benefit to Sally and Teresa outweighs the loss to Ursula?

As we saw, Pareto optimality sidesteps this issue completely by emphasizing changes or transactions in which no one is made worse off, but in practice, governments often do institute changes that make some people worse off, or at least enforce changes that some people would not voluntarily accept. The most obvious cases of this occur when people are unwilling to leave their homes to make way for some construction project like a new motorway despite apparently fair offers of compensation, but further consideration suggests that the phenomenon is quite general. Consider, for example, increases in particular marginal tax rates, the privatization of government-held assets, changes to social welfare benefit structures, or changes to eligibility for state-funded medical operations. For all of these cases there is at least an implicit belief that people's utilities can in some way be weighed against one another. Nor is it easy to imagine how any government could accomplish very much if it could only institute changes when no one dissented. Thus, whatever the theoretical difficulty of making interpersonal comparisons, the decisions made by governments do, in effect, assume they are possible.

When utilities are averaged or when a median is calculated over different individual people, the usual implicit assumption is that all individuals count equally. This assumption seems a reasonable one to make in any society which stresses the equality of individuals and, as a rule, the equality of the votes they cast. One might debate whether this really should be the case, and of course, it is possible to have averaging procedures which do not weight individuals equally, but in general this seems one of the less problematic methodological assumptions.

With both the more, the same, less method and psychophysical scaling it is important to take into account what is actually being asked of the method in each context. The problem of aggregating responses to the former method has already been discussed above, but in practice such aggregation has rarely been called for. When the method has been used to test the predictions of the median voter model (see Chapter 3) the problem does not arise.

The problem of aggregating results obtained from psychophysical scales has been widely recognized (for example Stevens, 1975; Poulton, 1989). Thus, for example, when the category rating method is employed, it is well known that if George rates a value as, say, 7 (where the range is 0 to 10) and Percy rates it as 6, it is not necessarily true that George rates it as more valuable than Percy. They could simply be using the numerical scale in different ways.

The tendency for different people to use psychophysical scale numbers in different ways may be countered in two ways. Firstly, one can perform a reasonable proportion of analysis within individuals rather than across them. For example, if George rates a lemon as having 7 units of value and an orange as having 6, while Percy rates the lemon as 6 and the orange as 5, there is no great difficulty in concluding that the sample of two perceives the lemon as the more valuable, or even in concluding that they both rate it a little rather than a great deal more valuable. Hence, much of the data analysis originally conducted for the studies reviewed in Chapters 6 and 8 below involved investigating patterns of response within individuals and then examining the aggregate statistics of the patterns instead of averaging the individual ratings for each individual and looking for patterns that describe the relationships of these averages. For example, the relationship between rated value and the logarithm of cost (cf. Equation 5.2) can be calculated for each individual and the aggregate results of these calculations examined. This supplements analyses where the average rated value is regressed on the cost measure. Multiattribute utility measurement also takes this issue of individual differences in number use seriously: recall that in the example discussed, different values of the W_j and V_{ij} were obtained from each individual.

Secondly, when large samples are taken and averages compared, individual differences in the use of numbers are averaged out so long as they are not correlated with the independent variable of interest. Thus, intergroup comparisons are usually not prone to the interpersonal comparison problem.

There has been controversy over whether or not averaging of this kind is valid if one is not sure (as in category rating) whether the scale is truly an interval one. However, recent analysis suggests that the process of averaging is valid provided that the different individual scores are symmetrically distributed about the mean with approximately equal variances for different subgroups, as they generally appear to be when the distributions of value ratings are examined. (For a technical discussion of the issue of averaging in this way, see Maxwell and Delaney, 1985.)

Much of the research discussed in the rest of this book makes use of psychophysical scaling methods, particularly that of category rating. However, there seems no *a priori* reason for expecting such methods to provide results which are more valid as a measure of the economic construct of utility than those obtained from different introspective measures. Perhaps a better justification for their use is that a good deal is now known about these methods as a way of investigating psychological constructs, and thus they seem suitable methods to use if value or utility is to be investigated as a psychological construct in its own right.

A further justification can be added. In practice, people do often attempt to convey to others the quality or worthwhileness of particular goods and services using psychophysical scaling, particularly category rating. Consider, for example, the grading of hotels or the way in which films may be rated by reviewers as having one, four or five stars. The frequency of this practice suggests not only that such grading is in some sense a natural thing to do, as Parducci (1982) suggests, but also that such ratings provide a reasonable means of communicating quality. Furthermore, while hotel gradings can be at least partly tied to objective measures (for example size of bedroom, availability of particular services), this is clearly not possible for film ratings. In the latter case, ratings are used to convey a crude numerical assessment of a quality which is almost entirely subjective.

6. Psychophysical Scaling of Value

The major theme of this chapter is the summary of some of the work that my co-workers and I have carried out asking respondents to value government-supplied goods using the methods of magnitude estimation and category rating. The earlier work mainly used the method of magnitude estimation, the later used the method of category rating.

As reported in the previous chapter, the psychophysical methods of magnitude estimation and category rating have been extensively used to try to build subjective scales and on occasion to relate these scales to objective ones. It therefore seems an obvious tactic to ask respondents to estimate utility and value and then to attempt to relate the scales so obtained to the 'objective' scale of price or cost of the items.

In the first study of the series (Kemp, 1988) the method of magnitude estimation was used to value items that were consumed personally and had item prices. Respondents were asked to imagine that they did not have to pay for any of the items personally and different respondents were asked to assess their value relative to one of two standards: 'dinner for two at the Sign of the Takahe' (a moderately expensive and well-known local restaurant) which was assigned 10 units of value; or 'a new colour television set' which was assigned 100 units of value. They were told that if they felt another item was three times as valuable they should assign it 30 (or 300 if the television standard was presented) units of value, if a tenth as valuable they should assign it 1 (10) units of value, and so on.

Respondents were then given a list of items that could be consumed personally, for example, 'a new Toyota Corolla', 'a can of fruit juice', 'winning a cash prize of $200 in a sports club raffle' and asked to estimate their value. Except for the cash items, such as winning the raffle, they were not informed of the item prices but the majority of the items were commercially available and could be priced.

It was a reasonable expectation that the values given the items would obey Stevens' Law, which predicts a power function between value and cost (5.1), and this is what was found. Figure 6.1, which shows the results obtained from the 'dinner for two' standard and the general public sample, clearly indicates a power–law relationship between the medians of the magnitude estimates of value and the costs of the items. (Remember that a power–law relationship is indicated if the relationship between the two logarithmized measures is linear.) The results for the different groups of respondents featured power–law exponents in the range 0.33 to 0.46, which were in reasonable agreement with those found previously when utility has been related to sums of money (Galanter, 1962b, 1974, 1990). Exponents of this size indicate that the range of people's values is rather less than the range of the actual monetary costs, something which is also evident from the figure. Another way to put this is to say that the subjective scale of value is a compression of the more objective monetary scale. The figure also indicates rather a good fit between the median values and the costs, and this was confirmed by finding quite high correlations, varying between 0.94 and 0.95, between the logarithms of the costs and the logarithms of the median values. In short, Stevens' Law provided a good description of the relationship between the perceived value of these items and their costs.

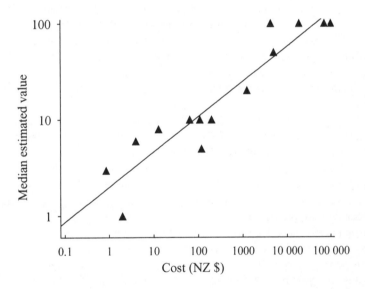

Figure 6.1. Median estimated value of market-supplied goods as a function of their price (adapted from Kemp, 1988, Fig. 1, General public sample, Standard 10). The line of best fit implies a power–law exponent of 0.37. Pearson r = 0.94

Psychophysical methods offer the possibility of valuing items which naturally have prices, such as a Toyota Corolla or a can of fruit juice, side by side with items which do not, such as fine weather next weekend or (for the student sample) receiving an A grade in a psychology course. Having obtained estimated values for these items one can then work backwards, with the aid of the relationship established between value and price for those items which do have prices, and obtain a kind of shadow price for the unpriced items. For example, if the method of magnitude estimation has been used, the values for the parameters, n and k, in equation (5.1) can be estimated for the items which are valued and which have known prices. If one then has a median value estimate for an unpriced item, it is straightforward to calculate a 'price' for it from the equation. For example, in the Kemp (1988) study, the median value for the A grade pass translated to an estimated price of around NZ $6000. The median value for fine weather next weekend translated to around $100 for the student sample and around $500 for the general public sample. These values seem reasonable.

A similar procedure can be followed when category ratings have been obtained using equation (5.2). The opportunity of obtaining such shadow prices in this indirect way seems to be an advantage that the psychophysical methods of valuation have over the simple 'more, the same, or less' method. On the other hand, unlike contingent valuation, psychophysical methods do not require respondents to use a monetary measure of value themselves, so the 'tainting' problem discussed in the previous chapter does not arise. Galanter (1990, p. 458), who also saw that psychophysical methods could be useful in this way, describes them as producing a 'universal solvent' for value.

In theory at least, the value of unpriced or uncostable items of government or public policy – for example, corruption-free government or democracy or support for some moral issue in foreign policy – could also be obtained using much the same procedure. In practice, as we shall see, the worth of such measures is seriously vitiated in this case by the consistent finding that value estimates of government services are rather poorly related to the cost of their provision.

Kemp (1988) asked the same student and general public samples who had estimated the values of consumer goods to value a group of policies that were either followed by or had been suggested to the New Zealand government. Examples of these policies included 'Increasing Family Benefit (currently $6/child) by $10 per week for each child' ($252 million annually); 'Removing all lead from New Zealand petrol' ($54 million annually); and 'Providing another 100 police nationally' ($4.5 million annually). The result was quite different to that found with the consumer goods: correlations between the logarithms of the estimated values and the logarithms of the costs of the policies were low or negative, ranging from 0.01 to –0.27. As Figure 6.2 shows, there was no evidence for a power–law, or indeed any other type of simple functional relationship, between the magnitude estimates of the value of these items and their costs.

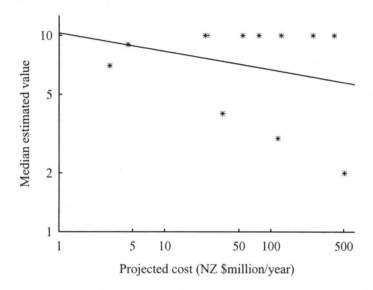

Figure 6.2. Median estimated value of suggested changes to government services as a function of their projected cost (adapted from Kemp, 1988, Fig. 2, General public sample, Standard 10). The line of best fit implies a power–law exponent of – 0.09. Pearson r = – 0.2

It seemed odd that the relationship between value and costs would be so much poorer for the government- than the market-supplied goods, but there were a number of possible explanations for it. For example, it could be that people's tastes for different government services are highly variable, and that only by taking a representative sample of electors would one find a strong relationship. Another possibility, particularly applicable to the results just discussed, is that the changes to the services and service expansions that were presented to the respondents in this study were not appropriate for the analysis. Perhaps it would have been better to present existing whole services (for example, 'the police force' rather than 'providing another 100 police nationally'). Accordingly the next set of studies asked people to value services that were currently provided.

Kemp (1991) asked German students and members of the general public to use magnitude estimation to value services currently provided by the German government for which costs were available. In Study 1, the respondents estimated the value of 15 services like old-age pension insurance

(DM 2923 per capita per year), defence (DM 847), or street lighting (DM 24) with respect to a standard service – schools and preschool education (DM 837). Respondents were assigned to one of four conditions. The *control* group were asked to ignore the costs and simply to estimate the value to German people as a whole; a *costs* group were told the costs of the measures but were otherwise similarly instructed; the *allotment* condition required respondents to allot money in proportion to the standard (but were not informed of the actual costs); and a *loss* group was asked to estimate the loss to German people if a service was discontinued.

The important results were, firstly, that respondents in the four groups made very similar estimates, and, secondly, that in no condition were high correlations between median estimated value and actual costs obtained. Correlations in this case were positive, but ranged between 0.27 and 0.52. In comparison, when the same subjects estimated the value of market-supplied items, a correlation of 0.93 between the median estimated values of such items and the actual item costs resulted, a result similar to that obtained in the earlier study (Kemp, 1988).

I wondered if the magnitude estimation procedure might be a little complicated for the respondents. Thus, the second study of this paper requested respondents from the general public to perform both magnitude estimation and category rating on the same set of government services. The critical result, already mentioned in Chapter 3, was that the two sets of measures were highly correlated, but most respondents found category rating easier to use. Hence, most of the subsequent work used category rating rather than magnitude estimation. However, values and costs were still not very highly correlated.

The low correlation between respondents' valuations of the services and the cost of the services implies that there are services which are indicated to be high in value but on which little government money is spent, and services which are perceived to be rather low in value but which are quite expensive to provide. However, none of the samples used so far, although adequate for answering methodological questions, was really representative of a national population, and one would not expect that a group of students or any other non-representative group would value government services in the way that the population as a whole might.

Kemp and Willetts (1995b) asked a representative sample of 563 New Zealanders to value 27 services provided by the New Zealand government. The survey was carried out by a market research firm – this seemed to be the best way of carrying out such a survey – and the respondents used category rating, and rated each service on a scale from 0 (the service is worthless) to 10 (extremely worthwhile and useful). The average results of the survey are shown in Figure 6.3.

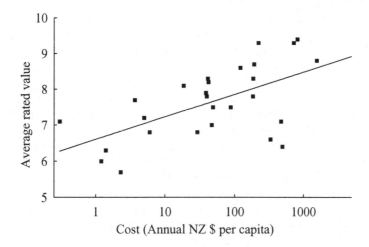

Figure 6.3. Average rated value of New Zealand government services as a function of their per capita cost (adapted from Kemp and Willetts, 1995b, Fig. 1)

Three important results are obvious from the figure.

Firstly, although there was quite a variation in rated average value, no service was rated as very low in value. In part this result was a consequence of valuing each service one at a time. The interviewers began by selecting a random example of the services, asking for a valuation of that and then proceeding to another service and so on. In contrast, most of the other studies asked the respondents to look through the list of all the items first before valuing them. The more common method has the advantage of spreading out the values of the services but it is not possible then to consider these values as being in any way absolute. Indeed, as mentioned above, it is known that category ratings are affected by precisely this kind of context, so that the values cannot be generalized from one study to another. In the Kemp and Willetts (1995b) study, however, the context was effectively randomized across the respondents, because of the different starting points they were given. (Readers who have some knowledge of different types of bias in rating scales will probably note that the random choice of starting points also has a corresponding disadvantage. Many of the services were given very high average ratings, so that a ceiling effect arose in this study. Thus it is difficult to draw valid conclusions about differences in value between services like police, hospitals and schools.)

The finding that all the services, even defence, were perceived in this study to have a value of greater than 5 when valued in this way underlines a point made in Chapter 3. A democratic government might not produce exactly the mix of spending that the median voter desires, but almost all of the spending is perceived as having some value.

Secondly, as indicated by the spread of the points about the line, the correlation between the rated average values and the costs of the services is not particularly high. In fact, the correlation between average rated value and the logarithmically scaled costs of the services is 0.62. (One would expect a logarithmic relationship – cf. Equation (5.2) – between value and costs here and, indeed, a logarithmic relationship was found to be the best of a number of simple alternatives.) Overall, the numbers indicate what can be seen in the figure: while there is an average tendency for the more expensive services to be rated as higher in value, the tendency is hardly consistent. This result can be seen as a close parallel to the 'insensitivity to quantity' in contingent valuation that was noted by Baron (1997).

Thirdly, there are services which are rated as relatively high in value and are relatively inexpensive. These services appear above the regression line in the figure. Similarly, there are services which are relatively expensive and rated as relatively low in value. These appear below the regression line. Table 6.1 below identifies the 27 different services and shows their annual per capita actual costs, their average rated values and the value that would be predicted from their costs using the logarithmic function. The final column (which orders the rows of the table) shows the difference between the rated and predicted values – a positive number indicates relatively high value for the cost, a negative number relatively low value for the cost.

For the average New Zealander at the time of this survey, the police force seemed to provide the greatest perceived value relative to its cost, closely followed by hospitals, schools and the Hillary Commission (an organization which subsidizes gifted athletes). On the other hand, defence provided the lowest perceived value relative to cost, with Domestic Purposes Benefits (a benefit paid to single parents with dependent children) and Unemployment Benefits also scoring poorly on this criterion.

These findings are similar in implication to some of the results that were discussed in Chapter 3. The results from many of the surveys conducted in other countries using the more, the same and less method indicated that respondents wanted to see more money spent on education, health and the police, and less on defence. These results are quite compatible with the results of this New Zealand study that indicated that people valued the health, education and police services very much more highly than they did defence. On a more theoretical level, the existence of services that are rated as relatively low in value but that are relatively expensive to provide is another indication of the apparent failure of the median voter model that we noted earlier.

Table 6.1. Average rated value, annual per capita cost, value predicted from the equation, Value = 0.65log$_{10}$(Cost)+6.54, and the difference between the rated and predicted values of government services (Data from Kemp and Willetts, 1995b)

Service	Rated value	Cost (NZ $)	Predicted value	Difference
Police force	9.3	220.00	8.1	1.2
Public hospitals	9.4	811.30	8.4	1.0
Primary & secondary schools	9.3	713.50	8.4	0.9
Hillary Commission	7.1	0.30	6.2	0.9
Universities	8.7	189.50	8.0	0.7
Polytechnics	8.6	120.40	7.9	0.7
Environment conservation	8.3	41.00	7.6	0.7
Customs Department	8.1	18.50	7.4	0.7
Kindergarten & childcare subsidies	8.2	41.90	7.6	0.6
Pharmaceutical Benefits	8.3	184.50	8.0	0.3
National Library	7.9	38.50	7.6	0.3
Government old-age pension	8.8	1556.20	8.6	0.2
Ministry of Agriculture	7.8	39.50	7.6	0.2
Meteorological Service	7.2	5.00	7.0	0.2
National Archives	7.1	3.70	6.9	0.2
Subsidized work schemes	7.5	48.50	7.6	−0.1
Family Support	7.8	182.00	8.0	−0.2
Prisons	7.5	87.50	7.8	−0.3
Legal aid	6.8	29.00	7.1	−0.3
Ministry of Women's Affairs	6.3	1.40	6.6	−0.3
Access Courses (for unemployed)	7.0	46.80	7.6	−0.6
Arts Council	6.0	1.20	6.6	−0.6
(State) Housing Corporation	6.8	29.00	7.5	−0.7
NZ Symphony Orchestra	5.7	2.30	6.8	−0.9
Unemployment Benefits (dole)	7.1	467.40	8.3	−1.2
Domestic Purpose Benefits	6.6	329.40	8.2	−1.6
Defence	6.4	489.50	8.3	−1.9

Another important result from the Kemp and Willetts (1995b) survey concerned the effect of demographic variables. We investigated the effect of a number of these variables on the ratings assigned to each of the 27 services. The variables we used included the respondents' sex, age, political party voted for in the last election, marital status, employment status (employed versus not employed), highest educational qualification, whether they had dependent children, and personal and household income. There were a few statistically significant effects, as one would expect from a sample of this size. (See Kemp and Willetts, 1995b, for details of the analyses actually carried out.) For example, the value of the Ministry of Women's Affairs was rated higher by women (average 6.7) than by men (average 5.7), the old age pension (paid to all those who were 60 or over at the time) was rated 8.4 by those under 35, 8.8 by those aged between 35 and 59, and 9.2 by those aged 60 or over. Overall, however, the demographic variables, taken either singly or together, had very little predictive power in relation to the value ratings.

This was a rather surprising result, since our naïve expectation was that, for example, women would assign a much higher value to women's issues, and older respondents would value the government old age pension much more highly than younger respondents. Where we found effects, they were generally in the predicted directions but they were small.

But when we came to check it out, we found that this result, too, was in line with those found by previous researchers using somewhat different methods. De Groot and Pommer (1989) found that the responses in their Dutch budget-game procedure were poorly predicted by the independent variables they considered. Tan and Murrell (1984) found that evaluations of American city services were not closely related to the mix of demographic and attitudinal variables that they used as predictors. So, once again the results from this survey are in line with those obtained from other methods in other countries.

Perhaps the result should not have surprised us. While, say, the existence and operation of the Department of Women's Affairs are probably more important for women than for men, it is not hard to believe that the provision of decent health services or an effective police force might be more valuable for both women and men than such a department.

MARGINAL AND TOTAL VALUE

Economics makes much of the differences between marginal and total utility and between marginal and total costs, and much of economic theory is concerned with the analysis of marginal utility and marginal costs. The chief reason for this concern, as I see it, comes from mathematical considerations.

Utility in economics, as we have seen, is usually thought to be an immeasurable concept and, while it is assumed that there is a functional relationship between utility and the quantity of some good or service that is used or consumed, the nature of the function is normally believed to be unknown. Nonetheless, and this seems to me to be a critical insight in microeconomic theory, it turns out that we can still find out some interesting results even if we do not know the nature of this relationship. In particular it turns out that we can uncover interesting results about marginal utility.

One such result is that for a consumer the marginal utility per unit cost of all the goods that she consumes ought to be the same. Let us consider what this means in very simple terms. To return to an example that was used in Chapter 2, suppose for the moment that the only two goods I consume are red wine and white wine and I spend all my money on these two. Suppose, too, for the moment, that the cost of each bottle of red or white wine I drink is about the same. In general I might prefer red wine to white wine, and so I would drink perhaps ten times as much of the former (and, of course, I would spend ten times as much on it as well). Now suppose someone gives me a wine token one day for a birthday present, enough for one bottle of wine of either type. What type of wine am I likely to buy with my token?

The obvious answer to this question is to say 'red', because this is what I drink most of, but in fact the microeconomic theory predicts that I am equally likely to choose red or white. In the terms of this theory the marginal utility to me of an extra bottle of red or white wine is the same. The basic reason for this is simply that I must be indifferent between the two at the point when I receive my present, for if I was not then I would have already altered my consumption patterns before receiving the token, and, for example, cut down my white wine purchase and consumption even more and bought more red from my own resources.

It is important to be clear about what is and what is not being said here. The theory says that I am indifferent between red and white wine when I come to consider an extra bottle over and beyond the normal amount I consume within my budget. On the other hand, the theory does not say that I generally derive equal pleasure or utility from drinking red and white wine. Indeed, the normal presumption would be that on average I get more value from drinking a glass of red wine than from drinking a glass of white wine, and this is why I drink more of it. Hence, it is clear that marginal utility, the utility from a little bit more than my 'usual' consumption, and average utility, the utility from a typical unit of consumption of a good, are not the same. Moreover, and more obviously, one would expect that the total utility I get from all the red wine I drink is greater than the total utility I get from all the white wine I drink.

The difference between marginal and average utility is sometimes explained in terms of satiation. The idea is that one derives most utility from the first part of the good or service consumed and then progressively less thereafter, a process sometimes known as diminishing marginal utility. Colloquially we might call it the law of diminishing returns (Samuelson et al., 1975). Figure 6.4 shows how this might operate for my example of the red and white wine. This proposition makes intuitive sense, and indeed is in line with a good deal of psychological evidence.

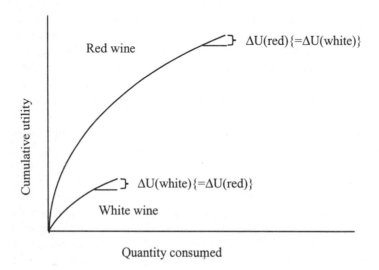

Figure 6.4. Hypothetical figure showing utility as a function of consumption of red and white wine. Marginal utilities are shown as ΔU(red) and ΔU(white)

The theory can be complicated in various ways. A more realistic description of my consumption would recognize that I occasionally purchase non-alcoholic goods. But no matter how many goods I purchase and consume, their marginal utilities should all be the same for given unit costs. Nor need the marginal costs of all the products be the same: if red wine is more costly than white, a slightly more complex version of the theory results. In this case, I should allocate my expenditure so that the utility gained from the last dollar (or whatever currency unit) spent on each good is equal.

There have been very few attempts to test this interesting and counter-intuitive proposition of microeconomic theory, perhaps because it is hard to find a conclusive way to do so. One such attempt – we make no claim that it is conclusive – was made by Kemp, Lea and Fussell (1995). The attempt is interesting in the present context because it used the category rating method.

In brief, we selected a number of consumer goods and services that all cost about the same and asked people to rate the value they thought they would receive if they were simply given a small unit of the good. So, in a $1 condition, the respondents were asked to rate the value of seven goods, including the value of being given a chocolate bar or of coming across a small box of fruit juice in the refrigerator. In a $20 condition, they rated, for example, the value of being sent two cinema tickets or of being given a $20 book token. Effectively, we were asking respondents to rate the marginal utilities of the products. We also asked the respondents how often they consumed the good in question.

The microeconomic theory makes two predictions. Firstly, the ratings of value for similarly priced products ought to be approximately equal provided that the respondent occasionally consumes it. Secondly, the ratings of value should not be related to how often the product is consumed by someone, so long as there is some consumption. Rather to our surprise we found both predictions were fulfilled (Kemp *et al.*, 1995, Study 1). On the other hand, the rated values of the $20 items were clearly higher than those of the $1 ones, and, as both theory and common sense would lead us to expect, the different items were valued more highly by users than non-users. A follow-up study (Kemp *et al.*, 1995, Study 2) found that when people were asked to rate the average utilities of the different products (for example, the average value you get from drinking a bottle of wine) these utilities *were* correlated with the amount of consumption. Furthermore, while the average and marginal utilities for the different products were correlated, the correlation was far from perfect. Overall, somewhat to our surprise, we were forced to conclude that the microeconomic theory had been well supported by the results.

So far we have considered the concepts of marginal and total utility only as they affect goods supplied by the market, but the concepts are equally applicable to the goods and services that the government supplies. An obvious point to make in this regard is that asking people to value the current services supplied by a government, using either the method of magnitude estimation or that of category rating, seems to be requesting an estimate of their total or average utility. What would happen if we were to ask for an estimate of their marginal utility?

Kemp and Willetts (1995a, Study 1) asked a sample of general public respondents to estimate the value of 16 different services supplied by the New Zealand government in different ways. Each respondent was asked to complete either a *dollar value* questionnaire or a *total value* questionnaire. Within each questionnaire, two sets of ratings were called for: a *current utility* and a *marginal utility* rating.

In *dollar value* questionnaires they were asked to estimate the value or usefulness to New Zealand people per dollar spent on each of the services.

Current ratings then asked how much value New Zealand receives from each dollar the government currently spends on the item; marginal ratings asked how useful or worthwhile it would be to spend an extra dollar on each of the services. In the *total value* questionnaires, respondents were asked to estimate the value they thought New Zealand obtained from each service. Current ratings then asked for the present value or usefulness of each service, marginal ratings asked the value of the government increasing spending on the service by 5 per cent.

On the basis of the microeconomic theory, we could make a number of predictions about the results that should be obtained. In the first place, the four (2 × 2) average ratings should all be rather different. That is, they should correlate moderately rather than highly. Secondly, the marginal dollar ratings should all be similar for the different services and show no correlation with current spending on the different services. In this respect, they should differ from, say, the current total value ratings, as it would be expected that the more expensive services should provide the greater total value.

The actual results did not bear out most of these predictions. The four sets of average ratings were highly correlated, with correlation coefficients ranging from 0.93 to 0.99. There were also substantial differences between the ratings for the different services under all instruction sets, including the marginal dollar ratings. Finally, all the ratings, including the marginal dollar ratings, showed moderate correlations with the logarithmically scaled costs of the services, and there were no great differences in the strength of the relationship between value and cost. Overall, the results suggest that people do not distinguish marginal and total utility for government services as they do for personally purchased and consumed items. Rather they suggested that there was a single simple dimension of value that all the ratings tapped in a similar way.

One practical implication of these results is that they help us to understand the connection between the valuations of the services and people's views as to what additional funds should be spent on them. The fact that the services which receive the highest average values are also those which receive the highest marginal values indicates that any of the measures can serve as an indication of where people want the government to allocate money. Thus the high value for money given to services like health in the Kemp and Willetts (1995b) study is also an indication that people would value more money spent on the health system.

The results of the two studies we have just reviewed also indicate that people think about the utility of personally purchased and consumed items and about the utility of government-supplied services in rather different ways. People appear to have separate (although obviously related) concepts of marginal and total utility for items that are bought in the market place. They do not appear to have separate concepts for services supplied by the government. However, it is not so clear just why this difference arises. One possibility, which we take up again in Chapter 8, is that the difference might arise because people know very little about what it costs to supply government services. Another possibility is that at least some of the difference arises because government services were not itemized in the way that market-supplied goods are. Respondents rating government services were asked to rate the value of hospitals or primary and secondary schools rather than the value, say, delivered by a single operation or a primary school teacher. On the other hand, respondents rating the value of goods bought in the market were asked to rate the value of, say, a chocolate bar or two bottles of wine rather than, say, the value of confectionary or alcohol.

Hence, Kemp (1998b, Study 1) asked respondents to rate both government services and classes of goods and services supplied by the market. The latter were chosen as some figures were available for total New Zealand spending on classes of market-supplied goods (for example, total spending by all New Zealanders in a year on food or on clothing), and it was thought desirable to try to match government services as closely as possible with classes of market goods of similar total costs.

As a first step, a pilot study determined eight government services (for example, state schools, the police, subsidized work for the unemployed) and eight classes of goods and services supplied through the market (for example, home heating and electricity, clothing, fruit) that could be paired so as to be approximately matched on total value and cost. In the main study (Kemp, 1998b, Study 1), general public and student respondents were presented with lists of the 16 items in which the market and government items were mixed and randomly ordered and were told that some of the items were supplied by the government and others they purchased themselves. Two different questionnaires were used, each asking the respondents to use category rating to value the 16 items twice.

In answering the *total/personal* questionnaire, respondents estimated, firstly, the value that New Zealand people as a whole got from each item in a year and, secondly, the value that 'you expect to get from each of the items in your lifetime'. (The change of times here was so that, for example, younger people could still record some personal value for the government-funded old age pension.) In the *total/marginal* questionnaire, there was an identical request for total valuation and a request for rating the marginal value, defined as the value New Zealand people as a whole would get from an extra dollar spent on each of the items. (The order of the two tasks was varied across the questionnaires.)

As we should expect, the two different total valuations were much the same across the two questionnaires, and on average the government and

Public Goods and Private Wants

market items received similar total valuations. (This has no real significance in this case, because of the way the services and classes of goods were chosen.) There was no difference between the average ratings of the student and the general public respondents, a result that echoes the common finding mentioned above that people's valuations are not closely related to their demographic characteristics.

Table 6.2. Mean ratings of total and marginal value to NZ (total/marginal questionnaires) and total and personal value (total/personal questionnaires) for selected government services and market goods (after Kemp, 1998b)

Questionnaire: Valuation Type:	Total/Marginal		Total/Personal		Item cost ($/head)
	Total	Marginal	Total	Personal	
Government Items					
State schools	8.0	7.8	8.4	8.0	686
The police force	7.9	7.5	8.1	7.3	218
New Zealand universities	7.3	7.0	7.1	7.8	171
Government Retirement Income	6.8	6.8	6.6	5.3	1425
Unemployment Benefits	5.7	4.4	6.1	4.0	298
The National Library	5.4	5.2	5.6	4.8	15
Subsidised work for unemployed	5.2	5.3	6.1	3.9	46
Department of Women's Affairs	4.8	4.2	4.4	3.4	1
Average government	6.4	6.0	6.7	5.6	
Market Items					
Home heating and electricity	7.6	6.2	7.7	8.2	341
Private housing	7.2	5.0	8.0	7.7	2106
Private transport e.g. cars	7.1	4.5	7.1	8.0	1350
Clothing	6.8	4.2	7.9	6.8	367
Children's shoes	6.1	3.9	6.2	4.0	15
Fruit	6.0	4.5	6.8	7.4	126
NZ holiday accommodation	5.2	3.6	5.7	4.9	67
Carpets & floor covers	5.0	3.4	5.4	5.5	58
Average market	6.4	4.4	6.8	6.5	

Table 6.2 shows some of the results relating to the comparisons between the total and personal ratings and the total and marginal ratings on the two types of item. For the market items, ratings of value to New Zealand were the

same as ratings of value to oneself personally and these average ratings were similar to those obtained when the value of the government items to New Zealand were considered. Ratings of the value of the government items for oneself, however, were significantly lower. (For the details of statistical significance testing, see Kemp, 1998b, Study 1.) Thus the study provided an indication that people's ratings of the value of government-supplied services are to some extent based on altruism as well as their own personal wants, a theme we shall return to shortly.

The comparison of marginal and total ratings is also instructive. As examination of Table 6.2 shows, marginal and total ratings were barely distinguished for the eight government services, but they were quite different for the eight market-supplied items. (Correlations between the two sets of ratings confirmed the result of visual inspection.) Thus, the general finding we noted earlier that the two types of utility are distinguished for government but not market-supplied items held up quite well even when classes of market-supplied goods were compared with government services.

ALTRUISM

A powerful reason for government intervention in the economy is to redistribute resources so as to benefit those who appear to be most in need. Hence, we would expect that when people consider the value to be obtained from government services they consider not only the benefits they expect to gain themselves but also the benefits for others. In other words, we would expect to find altruistic as well as selfish motives in the way that people value government services.

A number of the results already reported in this chapter indicate that people's valuation of government services contains a component of altruism. In the previous section, it was noted that Kemp (1998b, Study 1) found that the rated value to respondents personally was smaller than the rated value to New Zealand people as a whole for a sample of government-supplied services while similar ratings were obtained for a sample of market goods. It should also be noted that many of the rated values in the other studies make very little sense unless some degree of altruism is assumed. For example, all respondents in these studies were too old to derive any immediate personal benefit from future government expenditure on schools, although, of course, their children or grandchildren might. Only unemployed people derive any immediate benefit from unemployment benefits.

Similar conclusions can be drawn from some of the results discussed in Chapter 3. The survey results reviewed there indicate concern by adults in many countries that governments should spend more on education. Funk and

Garcia-Monet (1997) suggested that voters' perceptions of how the economy as a whole is doing are more important as a predictor of voting than how the individual is prospering. The outcome of the Roanoke referendum reported by Shabman and Stephenson (1994) indicated that many of the voters wanted their fellow citizens to be protected from flooding.

It seems reasonable, then, to suppose that there is at least some element of altruism or perhaps civic virtue in the way that people value government services. But how big is this element? Is it the same for all government services? Such questions raise another: how could we go about measuring it?

Hudson and Jones (1994) have suggested a rather simple way of doing this. The basis of their approach was to assume that people's general attitudes to government services (denominated TA^g in their paper) might be a weighted average of their perception of their own self-interest (TA^s) and their perception of what is in the public interest (TA^p). They suggested a simple additive model:

$$TA^g = \alpha TA^p + (1 - \alpha)TA^s \qquad (6.1)$$

The averaging constant, α, is denominated a 'coefficient of altruism', which can range from 0 to 1. If $\alpha = 0$, then people's general attitudes would be determined exclusively by their perception of their own self-interest, if $\alpha = 1$, their general attitudes would be determined wholly by their perception of the public interest.

Hudson and Jones then gave their British respondents three alternatives (which could be coded on a single three-point scale): reduce tax and social spending; hold tax and social spending; and increase tax and social spending. Social spending in this case was defined as spending on health, education and social welfare. Their respondents then chose among these three alternatives under three different choice conditions. First (in order of response) they were asked simply which alternative they favoured. Second, they were asked which they thought was in their own self-interest. Third, they were asked which they thought in the public interest. The results from two separate surveys were subjected to regression analysis and these yielded coefficients of altruism of 0.66 and 0.73. Thus their results suggested a rather large component of altruism in public spending preferences.

Kemp and Burt (1999, Study 1) extended this method to include a range of government services. General public respondents in New Zealand were asked to use category rating to value 10 government-provided services three times using the same three instructions (and in the same order) as Hudson and Jones. They were also asked to make a general rating about whether they favoured tax cuts or increased government spending under the three instructions.

The coefficients of altruism (α) obtained from the study varied from 0.34 for the state-subsidized New Zealand Symphony Orchestra to 0.96 for schools. Taken over all ten services a coefficient of altruism of 0.75 was obtained. Another and simpler way to measure the similarities of the ratings is to compare the mean ratings. The average ratings of both the separate services and the overall tax versus spending preference under the public interest instructions were higher than those under the self-interest instructions. Moreover, and in line with the coefficient of altruism results, the averages under the public-interest instructions were close to the general value ratings.

There is clearly a strong indication from this research that people's valuation of government services has a large component of altruism. Initially, one might think that this component should be limited to goods and services supplied by government, if only because they are often funded in such a way that less well-off members of society have good access to them, which is not true for many of the goods and services supplied by the market. But further reflection suggests that market-supplied goods, too, might have some altruistic component. Many companies pay at least lip service to the ideal of customer service and their mission statements often stress some aspect of service excellence rather than maximizing the return to the shareholders. For example, Honda's recent mission statement reads: 'We are dedicated to supplying products of the highest efficiency yet at a reasonable price for worldwide customer satisfaction' (*Pocket Strategy*, 1998). The phenomenon of gift-giving, although often involving a strong element of reciprocation, suggests some degree of altruism on the part of the giver (for example, Belk and Coon, 1993; Burgoyne and Routh, 1991; Caplow, 1984). More generally, many people derive pleasure from watching complete strangers enjoying themselves.

Thinking along these lines suggested that it might be worthwhile to use Hudson and Jones's method to compare a small sample of market and government goods and services. Hence, Kemp and Burt (1999, Study 2) asked general public respondents to rate the values of five government services (police, universities, the National Library, old age pensions, and subsidized work for the unemployed) and five classes of market-supplied goods (home heating and electricity; clothing; private transport; children's shoes; and holiday accommodation) under the three instructions sets used earlier. The particular services and goods were chosen on the basis of previous research (Kemp, 1998b) to have approximately equal average ratings on the general value measure.

Some of the average results are shown in Table 6.3. The self-interest ratings were substantially lower than the public-interest ratings for the government services but a little lower for the market goods. The overall coefficients of altruism, however, were fairly similar. Perhaps more striking than the average results, however, was that there was considerable variation within both the market goods and the government service items sets. Coefficients of altruism for the government services varied between 0.93 (for old age pensions) and 0.40 (for universities). For the market goods, αs varied between 0.77 (for children's shoes) and 0.27 (for home heating and electricity). It would be unwise to read too much into the results obtained from such small samples of goods and services, but at the least it seems clear that government services do not have a monopoly on altruistic components, and that there is some variation between different goods and services on the size of these components.

Table 6.3. Mean ratings for five different government services and five different market services and the average preference for spending on government services as opposed to tax cuts for three different conditions in Kemp and Burt, 1999, Study 2. Coefficients of altruism (α) are also shown

Valuation condition:	General	Self interest	Public interest	α
Government services				
Police	8.6	7.2	8.3	0.69
Universities	8.1	7.0	7.3	0.40
National Library	7.5	4.8	6.6	0.61
Superannuation	7.3	4.2	7.0	0.93
Subsidized work for unemployed	5.4	2.8	5.4	0.77
Average government	7.4	5.2	6.9	0.56
Market services				
Home heating and electricity	8.5	8.4	8.4	0.27
Clothing	8.1	7.9	7.5	0.74
Private transport	6.4	8.0	6.7	0.62
Children's shoes	6.6	2.1	6.2	0.77
NZ holiday accommodation	5.3	4.3	5.2	0.33
Average market	7.3	6.1	6.8	0.67
Preference for government spending	3.0	2.3	3.1	0.55

CONCLUSIONS

In subsequent chapters we consider in more detail how people's valuations relate to what they know about the costs of government services, and this consideration will shed more light on some of the results reported in this chapter. However, in the meantime some conclusions can be drawn from the results we have just reviewed.

In the first place we should note that many government services are highly valued, a result that echoes the finding reported from the previous chapter that respondents would often like to see more spent on some government services. Indeed, these values seem to be quite commonly held across different demographic groups. A reflection of this result is that quite similar patterns of valuation emerge when small and rather unrepresentative samples have been used.

Second, it is clear that people do not think about and value government services and the goods and services supplied by the market in quite the same way. The most obvious demonstration of this is in the failure to distinguish marginal and total utility for government services. This finding has a problematic implication. If the two types of good are not really thought about in the same way it is not likely that people will be very good at making judgements of the 'how much of the market goods are we prepared to sacrifice for more of this particular government service' kind. Overall, the research we have looked at, especially with respect to marginal and total utility, suggests that people think about government services in a way that is simpler than the way they think about goods and services supplied by the market.

Third, while much of the economic theory has proceeded by assuming that people think only of their own immediate self-interest when they decide about the quantity and allocation of government spending, this assumption does not appear to be tenable. This, of course, is not to say that people's valuations are entirely altruistic. Rather, they appear to be a mix of self-interest and altruism. Interestingly, there is some evidence that it is not just the provision of government services which is considered in part from an altruistic standpoint.

There are a number of implications of the finding that people do think altruistically – or at least in part altruistically – about government services. One of them is that we cannot really get an estimate of the total value of government services by adding up over the whole population or over the possible beneficiaries and treating the sum as the sum of all the individual benefits. In fact it probably makes more sense to think of each individual's value ratings, even though they may be biased by self-interest, as their estimate of the value for the whole country.

7. Taxation and its Relationship to Spending

Previous chapters have mainly focused on valuing the effects of government spending, and on how the values of the different services relate to how much is spent on them. In this chapter we take into account the other side of the equation – how government spending is funded by the taxpayer. We consider first some aspects of the psychology of taxation. Then we go on to a brief discussion of some of the previous work on the way people perceive the relationship between spending and taxation, focusing particularly on the possibility of fiscal illusion.

PSYCHOLOGY OF TAXATION

The first requirement of any taxation system is that it should bring in revenue to fund the government's activities. It is also obvious that there are a number of quite different means of collecting a given amount of revenue, and that some of these different means will be better than others. Lewis (1982) identifies and discusses four characteristics that appear to be important in a tax system.

First, the tax system should be simple. A complex system raises genuine doubt in the taxpayer's mind as to how much he or she should be paying, and as a rule people are not enthusiastic about paying more tax than they believe they should. The issue of compliance cost is also important here. Complying with tax demands costs people and businesses time as well as money and it is obviously desirable to make these costs as low as possible. Small business owners, in particular, report that it takes quite lengthy periods of time to complete taxation formalities. It seems that this time is often something of a deterrent to their being in business at all, and clearly it is undesirable if the tax system is so complex that it prevents people from carrying on with otherwise worthwhile and productive business activities (Mackenzie, 1998).

Second, tax systems should be equitable. Two forms of equity seem to be of particular importance. In the first place it is important that a taxpayer can see that other potential taxpayers are bearing what he or she perceives to be their appropriate shares of the tax burden. Secondly, there is the question, of particular importance for the main theme of this book, of exchange equity. Do taxpayers feel they are getting a reasonable return from the government for the tax they are paying?

Third, the tax burden should fall more heavily on those who are better able to pay. This is partly because of considerations of fairness and equity: few people would like to see Georgina deprived by taxation of the necessities of life while Henry pays little tax and can afford luxuries. But there is also a practical consideration. Too high a tax rate might actually produce damage to the tax base and lead to lower returns in the long term. As the Roman Emperor Tiberius is supposed to have remarked to his governors, tax should shear the sheep as a good shepherd does, not skin them (Suetonius, 1951, Tib., 32.2).

Finally, the tax system should be efficient. This desideratum has received considerable attention from economists (for example, Musgrave and Musgrave, 1984; Stiglitz, 1988). The basic problem is that a tax system might discourage people or businesses from producing goods and services which are actually desirable, and distort patterns of consumption or labour supply. For example, a high tax on books might reduce the literacy or general level of education in a society. A high rate of personal income tax might make people reluctant to take on demanding but socially necessary jobs. At the level of the economy as a whole, and particularly in periods of recession, it is often feared that too high a level of taxation might produce an overall lowering of demand so that fewer goods are produced and fewer people employed than is optimal.

At least three of these principles – simplicity, equity and efficiency – are foci for psychological as well as political and economic research. The question of how tax forms and procedures can be made simple is a natural one for the cognitive psychologist or ergonomist to investigate. The perception of equity and fairness has frequently been studied by social psychologists. Finally, the effects of different kinds of reward systems on people's behaviour have been investigated by psychologists from a wide variety of backgrounds.

The existence of a psychological component in an area that is traditionally seen as the concern of the economist, the accountant or the political scientist is no guarantee that it will actually be studied by psychologists. However, as it happens, there has been a reasonable amount of psychological research into taxation. No doubt, this has been brought about mainly by academic interest, but it is also true that tax collecting authorities have often been willing to fund this kind of research. In particular they have been interested to find out how intentional or unintentional tax evasion might be reduced.

In thinking of tax evasion it is important to remember that, although the taxpayer is required by law to pay the appropriate amount of tax, the requirement is not always easy to enforce. If a tax becomes very unpopular, it may be virtually impossible to collect, as the British discovered when they attempted to tax their American colonies in the 1770s. More recently, the imposition of a poll tax to fund British regional government in 1989–90 produced such widespread protest and non-compliance that the tax was quickly abandoned.

At an individual level, it is impossible for tax authorities to check that everyone is paying the taxes they ought. The probability of an individual being audited by a tax inspector in any one year is small. Moreover, in many countries, for example the Netherlands, fines for evading taxes are in practice rarely imposed because of the difficulty in distinguishing intentional tax evasion from genuine misunderstanding of the often complex tax codes (Elffers, 1999). It is worth remembering in this context that, while there is a clear theoretical distinction between (legal) tax avoidance and (illegal) tax evasion, even experts may have difficulty with the distinction in practice. Thus, finding ways to motivate people to pay tax, or at least not to evade it, is an important consideration for tax authorities.

The 'rational' economic model of tax evasion of Allingham and Sandmo (1972) proposed that the crucial parameters are, on the one hand, the probability of being detected in evasion and the punishment that is incurred if one is detected and, on the other hand, the financial rewards of evasion. This model has the merits of simplicity and testability but there is good reason to question its validity. As Elffers (1999) points out, as the probabilities of detection and the scale of fines are often low, it is hard to see why more people do not evade. Moreover, it has been empirically difficult to find evidence that these parameters do have much influence on tax evasion (for example, Webley *et al.*, 1991). The model also has difficulty with explaining individual differences in willingness to pay tax. Parameters such as the probability of detection should be similar for all self-employed builders (for example), but not all self-employed builders will evade tax.

Hence, models which attempt to explain tax evasion by incorporating psychological variables have been proposed (for example, Cullis and Lewis, 1997; Groenland and van Veldhoven, 1983; Weigel *et al.*, 1987). In Weigel *et al.*'s approach, tax evasion is thought of as an uncooperative act in a social dilemma, so that it is similar, for example, to a fisherman using a fine-meshed net in an over-fished area or someone driving a car with a faulty exhaust in a city that is prone to air pollution. Key elements of the model are the social conditions and psychological conditions. Social conditions divide into situational instigations, such as one's financial circumstances and social norms, and situational constraints, such as the opportunity to evade and legal controls. Psychological conditions reflect social conditions and in turn divide into personal instigations, for example one's perceived financial difficulties and how self-serving one is, and personal constraints, for instance one's perception of the risk and opportunity and one's own beliefs about the morality of tax evasion and the desirability of government goods.

Finding evidence for and against the different models has proven difficult, because there are serious practical difficulties involved in researching tax evasion. One can use official sources to estimate the extent of tax evasion. In some cases one can go even further and use such sources to identify known tax evaders – in Australia and New Zealand, for example, lists of them are published in the newspapers. If one can identify people who been caught evading taxes, one can then compare the characteristics of the known evaders with people who have not been caught in evasion. Another approach is to survey random samples of the population, assure the respondents of anonymity, and then ask them a variety of questions, including questions about the extent of their tax evasion. This stated measure of evasion can then be related to, say, their scores on personality tests or demographic factors. Finally, one can run experiments in which people take part in games to increase their wealth or run computer simulated businesses. In these games the individual or business has to pay tax. The research question then is how much 'tax evasion' takes place when one manipulates the variables of interest (for example, Friedland *et al.*, 1978; Webley *et al.*, 1991).

It is easy to think of problems with each of these types of method. The first is not likely to produce very accurate measures of non-evasion. Most tax evaders are not likely to be caught, and one has to ask what might be different about those that are. Results obtained from the second method are obviously likely to be biased by self-serving or fearful non-cooperation from the respondents. Note that even if the respondent trusts the interviewer's assurances of anonymity, he or she has no great incentive to tell the truth. For instance, it would not be in any of the evaders' interest to alert the researcher to what is going on if there was widespread evasion within an industry. The third method relies on participants responding in the experiment as they would in real life, rather than as if they were in the game that they are actually in.

These problems would matter less if the results actually obtained from the different kinds of method were consistent with each other. Elfffers *et al.* (1987) carried out a study in which information on tax evaders obtained from the Dutch authorities was combined with self-report data from the same individuals. The study featured elaborate safeguards of anonymity and produced surprising results. First, there was virtually no correlation between documented and self-reported evasion. Second, the two 'kinds' of evasion were predicted by rather different sets of variables, documented evasion being better predicted by personality variables (including a self-serving orientation index), self-reported evasion by attitudes towards evasion and subjective norms. These findings are somewhat disconcerting, but the pattern has been replicated in an American study (Kinsey, 1988).

Probably the most relevant aspect of the research into tax and tax evasion for this book concerns people's perceptions of fairness and equity. A series of experiments carried out by Webley *et al.* (1991) found little effect on the amount of tax evaded when the amount of tax paid by others was manipulated in a simulated business situation, but these authors did not conduct experiments that attempted to investigate exchange equity. Nor is it clear that such a manipulation could easily be set up as a simulation experiment.

Falkinger (1995) produced a theoretical analysis of the effect of perceived equity between taxpayer and government on tax evasion. The point of the analysis is the demonstration that 'evasion decreases with perceived equity if and only if the tax payer's risk aversion is an increasing function of equity' (p. 71). Thus, people are more likely to take the risk of being caught if they are annoyed with the government, or, alternatively, people are more likely to acquire a bad reputation or a bad conscience if they evade tax when the government is seen as fair.

Falkinger's conclusion is obviously a reasonable one, and in line with the general principle that people are more likely to comply with rules if they perceive the rules as equitable (for example, Adams, 1963; Thibaut *et al.*, 1974). It is supported by some empirical findings. It is obviously in line with extreme cases of taxpayer revolt such as the American War of Independence and the British resistance to poll tax. There is also some evidence that tax evasion tends to be reduced in Swiss jurisdictions with direct democracies (for example, Feld and Kirchgässner, 2000).

On the other hand, it is easy to see why those who evade tax might justify their behaviour by citing the real or imagined failings of the government, and research into the relationship between personality differences and tax evasion suggests that this may happen. For example, Hessing *et al.* (1988) found that documented evasion was predicted by individuals' alienation. Moreover, surveys on whether tax evasion is associated with perceptions of inequity have provided mixed results, some studies (for example, Wärneryd and Walerud, 1982) finding such a relationship, others not (for example, Mason and Calvin, 1978).

Of course, whether or not a tax is perceived to be fair and whether the government is seen as giving value for money are important for other reasons besides tax evasion. The various taxes with which small businesses in New Zealand are expected to comply are often perceived as unfair, and this perceived unfairness may act as a considerable disincentive, not only to paying the tax but also to being in business at all. Interestingly, the perceptions of unfairness appear to be stronger for taxes which take considerable time to comply with the official form-filling but do not actually lead to much money being handed over, than for the taxes which generate most revenue (Mackenzie, 1998).

There is, then, reasonable evidence that perceived equity or fairness is an important variable in understanding the government–taxpayer relationship. One can go on to ask whether people's perceptions of how much they pay in tax and what they perceive to be the cost of providing government services might also be important. In fact, it has often been suggested that people do not have a particularly firm grasp of fiscal reality. That is to say, they may not know how much money the government receives, and they may not have the sense of a strict relationship between what is paid and the services that are provided.

FISCAL ILLUSION

The issue of whether people have particularly well-founded notions of how much they really pay in tax and what they get from the government in return has probably been debated since the beginning of organized society. A common theme mentioned in modern writing on this issue has been that people are often subject to a *fiscal illusion*, which leads them to underestimate the tax they pay, partly because such tax may be indirect and therefore hidden and partly because there are numerous different sources of tax and some of them may be overlooked (for example, Clotfelter, 1976; Heyndels and Smolders, 1995; Misiolek and Elder, 1988; Sorensen, 1992; West and Winer, 1980). The implication is that complex or invisible tax-gathering methods may lead people to underestimate the real tax burden and hence to favour higher government spending because they perceive government services to be cheaper to provide than they really are (Pommerehne and Schneider, 1978; Wagner, 1976). In practice, the distinction is usually drawn between indirect taxes such as sales tax, which are built into the price of products in most countries, and direct taxes, such as income tax. Particularly where indirect taxes are variable between products – for example, there is often a high tax on petrol – it is hard to know exactly how high this tax rate is, while wage and salary earners are often informed when they are paid as to how much they have had deducted in income tax.

An early recognition of the possibility of fiscal illusion comes in the writing of John Stuart Mill who, in a discussion of the relative merits of direct and indirect taxation, remarks that some people 'contend that the very reason which makes direct taxation disagreeable makes it preferable. Under it, every one knows how much he really pays; and if he votes for a war, or any other expensive national luxury, he does so with his eyes open to what it costs him' (Mill, 1848/1909, p. 864). Mill's observation finds support in more recent research. For example, Cullis and Lewis (1985) found in a British survey that people's knowledge of income tax was higher than their knowledge about other taxes as it was direct and visible.

Mill himself was unconvinced by this argument for the superiority of direct taxation, not so much because he thought it invalid, as because he felt that the tendency to underestimate the amount people pay in indirect taxes was smaller than the tendency to underestimate the benefits produced from government supplied services. After listing some of the useful services provided by British governments of his day – education, efficient justice, compensating people for the emancipation of slaves – he remarked:

> Every one of these things implies considerable expense, and many of them have again and again been prevented by the reluctance which existed to apply to Parliament for an increased grant of public money, though … the cost would be repaid, often a hundred-fold, in mere pecuniary advantage to the community generally. (Mill, 1848/1909, p. 866)

So, do governments spend more than people want because we underestimate what we pay in tax? Alternatively, are governments too reluctant to undertake spending which people want and which would really be beneficial? Both sides of the debate are readily recognizable in more recent writing. West and Winer (1980, p. 607) remark that '[t]he basic idea [of fiscal illusion] is that complex payments structures induce underestimation of the tax-price of public expenditure, and therefore result in voting behavior favoring relatively large public sectors.' They go on to point out that the way taxes are collected is the product of political and bureaucratic processes, and that politicians and bureaucrats benefit from their collection. It is thus in their interest to maximize the tax take and hence to make it as invisible as possible. The researchers' theory proposes that 'the illusion is the result of attempts by utility maximizing public managers (politicians or bureaucrats) to direct the resources of the community toward themselves' (West and Winer, 1980, p. 617).

On the other side, an eloquent case that American government spending tended to be too low was made by J.K. Galbraith (1969) in *The Affluent Society*. Galbraith claimed that usually it is the value of increased private production that is stressed, while goods and services supplied by the public sector tend to be regarded as a drag on the economy. This leads to some 'interesting contradictions … Vacuum cleaners to insure clean houses are praiseworthy and essential in our standard of living. Street cleaners to insure clean streets are an unfortunate expense. Partly as a result our houses are generally clean and our streets generally filthy' (Galbraith, 1969, p. 128).

In Galbraith's view, this difference in attitude has a number of causes. In the first place, 'traditional' essentials like food and clothing are, he claims, better produced privately, but, when these wants are satisfied, other goods, like education, become of greater importance and these are better produced in the public sector. Thus, to some extent our present attitudes are influenced by past scarcities. Additionally, the private sector makes greater use of advertising to promote desire for its goods. He noted, too, that the attitudes of American business tended to be hostile to government spending and intervention in the economy generally.

Galbraith saw the increased supply of private goods as leading to social imbalance and he thought balance should be restored by increasing public spending. He points out that it 'is scarcely sensible that we should satisfy our wants in private goods with reckless abandon while in the case of public goods, on the evidence of the eye, we practice extreme self-denial' (Galbraith, 1969, p. 229). Galbraith remarks that on the whole private industry invests in material capital while the public sector invests more in human capital. Thus, the social imbalance produces an investment imbalance, in which too little is invested in human capital. In Galbraith's view, this imbalance can have moral as well as material effects. The moral problems of the young are enhanced by greater opportunities to consume private goods, and 'in an atmosphere of private opulence and public squalor, the private goods hold full sway' (Galbraith, 1969, p. 227).

A number of objections might be made to Galbraith's analysis. He was describing a particular society (the USA) at a particular time (the 1950s and 1960s), and one might remark, for example, that governments have now discovered advertising. It is also true that many on the economic right – Margaret Thatcher was a good example – have shared Galbraith's enthusiasm and concern for education, but would prefer to see more of it supplied through the private sector.

Smith and Wearing (1987, p. 65), who reviewed Australian preferences regarding public spending, conclude, as Mill did about the British governments of the nineteenth century, that Australian 'governments have ignored public demand for welfare, sometimes for decades'. This comment seems quite consistent with the research we reviewed in Chapter 5, as well as with some of the findings reported in Chapter 6.

Clearly there is a lively theoretical and ideological debate as to where the balance between the sizes of the public and private sectors should be struck, and what role fiscal illusion plays in the current practice. There have also been a few attempts to find empirical evidence for or against the existence of fiscal illusion. Misiolek and Elder (1988) recorded the per capita tax revenues in the different American states as well as measures of how complex the state's tax system was, what proportion of its tax take came from more visible sources, and a variety of other variables. They then performed a regression analysis using the tax revenues as the dependent variable. If there were fiscal illusion, one would expect that, when the other variables were taken into account in the regression, the tax take would be higher for states with more complex systems and where less of the tax was visible. In fact, however, no significant relationships of this kind were found.

Sorensen (1992), in a paper entitled 'Fiscal illusions: nothing but illusions', found that Norwegians were generally poor at perceiving the costs of providing different public services, but he found no overall tendency to underestimation of these costs. He also noted that the government services he examined seemed to have low price elasticities (see, also, Bergstrom and Goodman, 1973), a result which suggests that, even if people did underestimate the real costs, this would have little consequence for their demand for these services. Overall, the result implies that people may not take costs into account very much.

On the other hand, Winter and Mouritzen (1998) found that providing information about the actual costs of government services did have the effect of making people more cautious about local government spending. He also found that providing this information considerably reduced the number of people responding 'don't know' to questions about their spending preferences, a result which is important although unsurprising.

Winter and Mouritzen's study is one of several that have reported a phenomenon that has sometimes been linked to fiscal illusion: a tendency for people to 'want something for nothing' (Citrin, 1979). Readers of A.A. Milne may remember a visit that Winnie-the-Pooh paid to Rabbit one day. '[W]hen Rabbit said, "Honey or condensed milk with your bread?" he was so excited that he said, "Both", and then, so as not to seem greedy, he added, "But don't bother about the bread, please"' (Milne, 1978, p. 23). It is quite common to find that when respondents are asked whether they would prefer to have lower taxes or more spending on welfare services such as health or education that they too ask for both, without apparently being too concerned about where the money is to come from.

Although the phenomenon is fairly well documented, the reasons for it are not so well understood. Furnham and Lewis (1986, p. 229) state that '[t]he majority of individuals are relatively unaware of what we can term the "fiscal connection" between taxes paid and benefits received from government spending'. They go on to point out that '[t]he mass of results from the UK, USA, France, Germany and Denmark over the last 15 years (and before) show majority preferences for reductions in taxation but increases in public expenditure especially on favoured items such as provisions for the sick, the old and for schools'. One contributing cause is thought to be fiscal illusion, so that people underestimate the actual costs of providing government services (for example, Pommerehne and Schneider, 1978; Wagner, 1976).

It is easy to claim that someone who favours both increased social spending and decreased taxes is simply ignorant of economic reality because they apparently do not understand that whatever money is spent must somehow be received. Hence the use of the term 'fiscal illusion' to describe their perceptions. But in fact the connection between government expenditure and the tax take is more complicated than that. Note first that many people do want to see spending on some services reduced (although usually not by enough to balance the increases they would like to see elsewhere). It should also be noted that it is quite possible for some people to receive both the benefits of a decreased tax take and the benefits of increased government spending. This might occur if, for example, a government acted both to raise the level of social spending and to reduce tax on poorer members of society by taxing the rich more.

This last consideration suggests that people who favour decreased tax and increased spending might be self-serving rather than ignorant. In this context, Winter and Mouritzen (1998) hypothesized and indeed found evidence for a tendency for users of social services to favour increased spending on these services. To what extent people are actually self-serving in their preferences for government spending is, however, debatable. For example, Kemp (1998b, Study 3) found that New Zealanders with higher preferences for overall government spending were actually more likely to favour *lowering* the top marginal tax rate (a tax rate that is not paid by those on low incomes or those receiving considerable welfare assistance). The research we reviewed in the last chapter suggests quite a large component for altruism in the way people think about government services. Mouritzen (1987) has claimed that in a relatively socially homogeneous country like Denmark, government spending preferences are more driven by ideology than by self-interest.

Finally, one might question whether people who simultaneously favour increased spending and lower taxes should necessarily be viewed as either self-serving or ignorant. Governments and economists from the late 1980s onwards have tended to regard balanced budgets as desirable, if not positively virtuous, but it is worth remembering that this has not always been so. Up until the middle of the 1980s, many western governments were quite happy to follow the Keynesian prescription of running fiscal deficits to attempt to maintain aggregate national production and reduce unemployment. Indeed, as we saw in Chapter 2, such stabilization has long been thought to be an important element of public economics. The consequence is, as Galbraith (1969, pp. 232–3) points out, that public services have often been voted on because of their apparent urgency, while tax policy has often been decided on the basis of the current level of economic activity. Clearly, if government budgets are to contribute to the stabilizing production by manipulating demand, one can no longer expect a close match between the tax take and the level of social (or any other government) spending.

It is not my intention here to enter into the murky field of macroeconomic theory, and still less to attempt any recommendations about it. My point is simply that in the 1970s it seems to have often been thought fiscally respectable for governments to run budget deficits, and at that time the practice was not widely condemned by economic experts. It would therefore be scarcely surprising if many lay people were influenced into believing – correctly or incorrectly – that increases in social spending need not be paid for by increased taxes. The really critical point here, of course, is that it is not easy to say that someone who believes that she might be able to benefit from an increase in social services without *anyone* having to pay more tax is really being irrational or subject to some kind of illusion in this belief.

8. Valuation and Knowledge of Cost

The research into fiscal illusion suggests that most people do not have a good understanding of how much they pay in tax to the government and do not have particularly well-developed ideas about the relationship between taxation and overall government spending. One might also ask how much they know about what the government spends on each specific service. This chapter focuses on what people know about the costs of providing individual government services, and how this knowledge, or lack of it, relates to people's valuation of the different services.

Clearly if people were to attempt to work out the value for money of different services they would need to have some kind of information or beliefs about their costs. This is one reason for studying what information they have, but there is another. There is also the possibility that people's estimates of the intrinsic value of different services might be influenced by their knowledge or perceptions of their prices. In the field of consumer research there is good evidence that price is sometimes used as a cue to product quality (for example, Rao and Monroe, 1989) and it is at least conceivable that people might use their knowledge or beliefs about costs as a cue to the value of government-supplied services.

We consider first the question of what people could know about the costs of government services, then we consider what they do know and how their knowledge relates to the values they put on different services. Finally, we consider briefly what happens if the cost information that people are given is manipulated experimentally.

INFORMATION ABOUT THE COSTS OF GOVERNMENT SERVICES

Before we look at what people know or believe, it is worthwhile to consider briefly how much they *could* reasonably be expected to know about government spending. After all, government offices do not normally display prices in their windows as many stores do. Thus, a critical question here is: how do the media portray government spending? Kemp and Crawford (1999, Study 1) examined newspaper articles to do with government spending.

All the issues of *The Press* between 1 September 1998 and 31 December 1998 were searched and 181 articles on planned or suggested items of New Zealand (central) government spending found. (*The Press* is the sole daily newspaper published in Christchurch, New Zealand, and it contains local, national and world news.) A small, comparison sample of 29 articles on (national) government spending from *The Times* (London) was also obtained by searching issues between 29 October 1998 and 21 November 1998.

The articles covered a range of different areas of government. For *The Press* sample, health, education, defence and social services each had more than 10 per cent of the total mentions; for *The Times* sample, the categories of health, social services, agriculture and transport were each the subject of more than 10 per cent of the total articles.

The principal analysis concerned how real or proposed amounts of money were portrayed in the articles. Six different points were considered:

1. Was there any *numerical analysis* in the article at all?
2. Was there mention of *total spending* in an area of government in the article? As an example, on 4/12/98, *The Press* reported that total spending on mental health was expected to rise to $848 million by the year 2004.
3. Was there mention of a *specific change* in spending (either increase or decrease) in an area? For example, the same article reported that an extra $59 million per year was to be spent in each of the next five years.
4. Was there mention of a *percentage change* in spending (either increase or decrease)? As an example, on 11/12/98, *The Press* reported that international travel expenses for the spouses of former MPs had increased by 47 per cent in the last financial year.
5. Was there mention of an *individualized* per person or item amount? For example, on 25/11/98, *The Press* reported that government funding for tertiary education had been cut by $603 per student.
6. Did the article describe a new *package* with its own specific amount? For example, on 23/11/98, *The Press* reported government plans to spend $28 million on the redevelopment of Princess Margaret hospital.

Percentages of articles containing each of these kinds of information are shown in Table 8.1. Note, firstly, that the two newspapers presented government financial data in roughly comparable ways. Secondly, the newspapers tend to provide more information about the costs of change to policy (specific or percentage increases and decreases; costs of new packages) than about the ongoing costs of government services. We could say that they tend to report marginal rather than total costs. Thirdly, the majority of the articles from both newspapers included at least some kind of numerical data. Indeed, some articles mentioned more than one type of spending. This is an important if rather unsurprising result. It shows that these two newspapers actually do make cost information about government services available to people, and particularly cost information about actual or projected changes to government services. Thus, people could know a reasonable amount about what it costs to provide individual government services without elaborate espionage and even without having to wade their way through official statistics.

Table 8.1. Percentages of articles from each newspaper mentioning different types of figure

	The Press	The Times
Type of mention:		
Spending increase	64	62
Spending decrease	22	21
Reallocation (no incr. or decr.)	7	3
Change in taxation (incr or decr)	7	14
The policy change was:		
Actual	57	41
Suggested	43	59
Any numerical analysis?	73	86
Total spending mentioned?	18	7
Specific change mentioned?	34	59
Percentage change mentioned?	11	3
Individualized amount mentioned?	23	31
Package amount mentioned?	17	24

ESTIMATING THE COST OF GOVERNMENT-SUPPLIED SERVICES

If, as the results reported in the previous section indicate, a reasonable amount of financial information is available to people, what use, if any, do they make of it? An obvious question to ask is whether they take it in and remember it. A second issue to consider is what influence their knowledge of this information has on their valuation of government services.

Kemp and Burt (2001, Study 1) investigated both these issues. The study employed two samples, one of working respondents from the general public and one of students. All the respondents were asked to use category rating to estimate the total value of 16 government-supplied services. Half of them did so in the absence of cost information; these respondents were also asked to estimate what the government currently spent on each of the services per capita per year. The other half of the respondents were given accurate information about what was spent on the services.

Table 8.2. Actual and median estimated costs of government services by a general public sample (Kemp and Burt, 2001, Study 1)

Service	Actual cost	Median estimate	% within factor of 2
Government health spending	1471	700	35
NZ Superannuation	1389	500	28
Primary and secondary schools	768	500	37
Domestic Purposes Benefits	414	200	28
Unemployment Benefits	359	550	23
Police force	208	500	14
Universities	178	200	23
Prisons	67	220	16
Subsidised work for job-seekers	36	40	21
Immigration	15	50	30
National Library	14	20	30
NZ Symphony Orchestra	2.70	10	30
Department of Women's Affairs	1.35	50	12
Hillary Comm. for rec. and sport	1.22	20	7
NZ contribution to WHO	0.43	20	0

Note: Costs in NZ $ per New Zealander per year. The third column shows the percentage of respondents accurate within a factor of 2 (i.e. between a half and double the actual cost).

In brief, the table shows that the respondents were quite inaccurate at estimating the actual expenditure, although the median results did show that the respondents as a whole had a reasonable idea of which the more expensive services were. Individuals frequently made estimates that were either far too high or far too low, and there was a consistent tendency to underestimate the costs of expensive services and to overestimate the costs of inexpensive ones. Probably the most interesting result shown in Table 8.2 is the finding that respondents were quite routinely out in their estimates by more than a factor of two. For example, 65 per cent of the sample stated that the cost of running the health system, whose actual cost was $1471 per capita per year, was either greater than $2948 or less than $735. Interestingly, the students, who generally pay little or no income tax, made poorer cost estimates than the working respondents, a result that suggests actually paying tax might make one slightly more sensitive to the costs of providing government services.

People obviously were not very well-informed about the actual costs of the different services. What effect might this have on their valuations? In fact, telling people about the actual costs of the services did not affect their value ratings very much. Moreover, both the respondents who were informed of the actual services costs and those who were not displayed moderate correlations between their rated values and the logarithm of the actual costs: averaged over the respondents, the correlations were 0.38 and 0.34 respectively. Thus telling people about the costs of the services made little difference to the relationship between value and costs. Certainly, telling them of the costs did not produce any spectacularly different valuations.

In addition, those respondents who estimated costs displayed rather low correlations (averaging 0.15) between their rated values and the logarithm of their own estimates. Thus, the relationship between respondents' own cost estimates and their valuations of the different services was even weaker than the relationship of their valuations to the actual costs. This result may well reflect an awareness on their part that they do not know what the services cost (an issue we turn to again in Chapter 9). It also suggests that respondents did not make much use of their cost beliefs when they valued the services.

An obvious question to ask here is whether similar results have been found in countries other than New Zealand. In fact, at least two studies conducted in other countries have looked briefly at what people know about the costs of government services and found much the same result. Sorensen (1992), in a Norwegian study devoted largely to investigating fiscal illusion, found no trend to overall underestimation, but did find that his respondents had a rather poor idea of what it cost to provide the few individual items that he included (day nurseries; primary and secondary schools; old-age institutions). Harris and Seldon (1979, pp. 123–6) asked British respondents to estimate government spending on seven different areas and also obtained wildly variable estimates. On average they found that the costs of the expensive items (for example, education) were underestimated and the costs of relatively cheap items (for example, unemployment benefits) overestimated, a result very similar to that found by us. Thus, it does not appear that the results we obtained are caused by some problem that is unique to New Zealand. Indeed, the rather simple structure of New Zealand government and its funding system would suggest that the problem might often be worse in other countries.

Harris and Seldon used their findings to support their preference for the provision of goods by the market rather than the government. In their discussion of the results, they claimed that 'this ignorance is not a criticism of the people but primarily of government, which destroys information by dispensing with the pricing system' (Harris and Seldon, 1979, p. 125). We attempted to investigate the validity of their claim with our next two studies.

Table 8.3. Average value ratings, actual costs and median estimated costs (in NZ $) of 16 market items from Kemp and Burt (2001, Study 2)

Item	Average rating	Actual cost	Median estimate	% within factor 2
'Scratch and win'	2.3	1.00	1	94
One Kg long-grain rice	3.3	1.50	2	78
1-litre carton of fruit juice	3.1	2.00	2	95
Cinema ticket to film of choice	4.8	10.00	9	98
Paperback book of choice	4.9	20.00	20	85
Compact disc of choice	5.1	34.00	30	91
Home telephone rental for a month	4.2	38.39	39	92
Concise Oxford English dictionary	4.2	75	30	33
Dinner for 2 at 'Sign of the Takahe'	4.7	140	100	72
Year's subscription to *The Press*	5.1	255	200	61
New 21-inch television set	5.1	530	600	87
Simpson HD washing machine	5.9	900	1 200	78
Return air ticket to London	8.8	2 300	2 100	93
Computer (HP Pavilion 6327)	7.3	2 999	2 999	96
Toyota Corolla (Manual 1600 GL)	7.9	23 500	23 000	83
Average Christchurch house	8.5	154 000	150 000	93

Note: The final column shows the percentage of respondents whose estimate was within a factor of two of the actual price.

The next step we undertook was to ask whether people are any better at estimating the costs of goods available in the market place, and whether the costs of such goods relate any better to their valuation. Kemp and Burt (2001, Study 2) gave general public respondents a list of consumer items that could be purchased in the market, and asked them to estimate the cost of each of the items. They were also asked to value each item using the category rating method. As Table 8.3 shows, the respondents were generally rather accurate in their estimates of the costs, even though it is very unlikely that most of the sample had purchased many of the items in the recent past. Note especially the generally high percentage of respondents who were accurate to within a factor of two. Also, we found that their estimates of the value of the items were quite highly correlated with the logarithmized actual costs. The average of the individual correlations was 0.56. The correlation between the average value and the logged costs was 0.92. The finding of reasonable correlation between the category rated value and the costs of such items parallels previous findings, noted in Chapter 6, that the magnitude estimates of their value and their costs are quite well described by Stevens' Law (Kemp, 1988, 1991).

This study established that people are better informed about the price of items purchasable in the market place than they are about the cost of supplying government services. But why does this difference come about? The most obvious answer is that people have more experience at actually paying for the market goods, but a glance at some of the items listed in Table 8.3 suggests that most respondents are unlikely to have bought many of the items recently. Indeed it is likely that most of the respondents had never bought a return air ticket to London or a new Toyota Corolla.

Alternatively, it could be that the difference arose because people become better informed about individual item prices than they do about annual per capita spending, and the market goods had item prices rather than annual per capita costs. An obvious way to research this suggestion would be to ask people to estimate the prices of specific items that the government spends money on, and to compare how accurately people estimate these with how accurately they estimate the prices of the market goods. Unfortunately, this is problematic. Many government services, because they are not supplied through a market system, do not have item prices, since there is no real need for them. Indeed, often these are simply unknown. In such cases, it is clearly impossible to measure how accurately the public might estimate them.

There was, however, an alternative way in which government-run services and market-supplied goods could be placed on an equal footing. This is to compare how well people estimate annual per capita spending on market-supplied goods with their estimates of annual per capita spending on the government goods. This was more straightforward because there was New Zealand statistical information available on average per capita spending on a reasonable range of classes of market-supplied goods. For example, there were statistics on total annual spending on home heating and electricity, fruit and children's shoes. Thus, the third study in this series (Kemp and Burt,

Public Goods and Private Wants

2001, Study 3) asked general public respondents to estimate the annual per capita spending in New Zealand on eight items of current government expenditure and eight classes of market goods.

Table 8.4. Average value ratings, median estimated annual per capita expenditures and actual annual per capita expenditures on government services and market goods from Kemp and Burt (2000, Study 3)

Item	Average rating	Actual cost	Median estimate	% within factor 2
Government provided goods and services				
State schools	8.1	686	750	21
Police	8.0	118	500	19
Universities	7.7	171	775	21
The National Library	6.9	15	100	16
NZ Superannuation	6.8	1425	800	20
Unemployment Benefits	6.2	298	800	22
Subsidised work for unemployed	6.1	46	275	9
Department of Women's Affairs	5.7	1.35	75	8
Average government	6.9			17
Market goods and services				
Home heating & electricity	7.7	341	700	37
Clothing	7.7	367	500	39
Private homes & rent	7.5	2106	4000	34
Fruit	7.4	126	250	36
Children's shoes	6.8	15	100	10
Owning/running private transport	6.5	1350	1500	45
Carpets & floor coverings	6.3	58	150	21
NZ holiday accommodation	5.9	67	200	11
Average market	7.0			29

Note: The final column shows the percentage of respondents whose estimate was within a factor of two of the actual price.

Some results from this study are shown in Table 8.4. As can be seen in the table (and was confirmed by the statistical analysis), there is a tendency for spending on market goods to be slightly better estimated. Probably this reflects respondents' ability to make calculations like: 'I/we spend about so much per week on fruit, hence so much per year, hence I guess the average person probably spends a little less, because we really like fruit'. More noticeable, however, is that generally spending on these classes of market goods is not well known either. Compare, for example, the percentages of respondents estimating accurately within a factor of two between Tables 8.3 and 8.4.

The results of this study provide partial support for Harris and Seldon's contention that it is the absence of prices which is responsible for people's lack of knowledge about the costs of providing government services. The study suggests that it is prices that people remember, not per capita costs, and it is possible that if government services were priced people would remember the prices. On the one hand, even if they did know item prices for government services this would not necessarily be a great help in working out per capita costs of government services: although people generally have a good knowledge of market prices, they do not seem to use this knowledge to generate particularly good knowledge of the per capita costs of classes of goods supplied by the market.

The reader might also have noticed another difference between Tables 8.3 and 8.4. By and large the rated values of the individual market items appear to be closely related to the costs shown in Table 8.3. In Table 8.4, however, the rated values of the classes of market goods are not closely related to the per capita annual spending on the classes of goods. In fact, the average of the individuals' correlations between the rated value and the logarithm of the annual costs of the eight market-supplied goods was quite low ($r = 0.15$), indeed lower than the corresponding average correlation for the eight government-supplied services ($r = 0.22$). This is a much weaker relationship than that obtained between the rated value of individual market-supplied goods and their costs.

This difference raises another and more subtle issue. So far, all the studies we have investigated in which people have valued goods and services supplied by the market, whether using category rating or magnitude estimation, have found a strong relationship between the values assigned to the items and the costs of the items. All of the studies we have reviewed in which people have valued government services have found a weak to moderate relationship between the values assigned to the services and the costs of providing them. Does the difference in the strength of the relationship arise because of the difference between item prices and annual service costs?

The fact that the relationship between the values of classes of market goods and their annual per capita costs is also weak to moderate rather than strong is a strong pointer that it does. This conclusion is also strengthened by a theoretical consideration. Just as we can distinguish total and marginal value, so we can distinguish total and marginal costs. The annual cost of a government service or people's average annual expenditure on fruit is clearly most like a total cost; the cost of a specific item is most like a marginal cost. In general, economic theory leads us to expect a rather close relationship between marginal value and marginal cost and a rather weaker relationship between total value (or marginal value) and total cost, and this is generally what the results of the different studies have shown.

There are, however, a few complications here. As we noted in Chapter 6, people do not really distinguish total and marginal value for government-supplied services although they do appear to make this distinction for market-supplied goods. Again, the first study on valuing government services using magnitude estimation described in Chapter 6 (Kemp, 1988) did require people to value additions to services, and this study found no relationship at all between value and cost, even though in this study it is arguable that marginal values and marginal costs were being measured. In general, as has just been remarked, the issue is made difficult to test because of the difficulty of finding prices for most individual items of government expenditure.

One possibility available in New Zealand arose because it turns out that the cost of different state-supplied medical operations is calculated by health authorities. These costings are not used as a basis for charging patients – the operations are supplied free of charge if they are done in the state health system at all – but to aid in the contracting out of different medical procedures to different hospitals and other health care providers. It proved possible to obtain a list of a number of these services and their associated costs, that is, the amount paid by the Health Funding Authority to a hospital for each such operation. Two samples – one of 29 members of the general public, the other of 34 people employed as medical professionals – were then asked to rate the value obtained from each of these operations using category rating. Some of the results obtained are shown in Table 8.5.

Examination of the table suggests a number of conclusions. The first and most obvious feature of the ratings is that all the operations, with the exception of circumcision, were rated as having fairly high average value. The straightforward interpretation is that, as we would hope, generally the Health Funding Authority is funding worthwhile operations. This result can also be seen as complementary to the finding mentioned in Chapter 6 that a representative sample of New Zealanders rated all the services provided by the New Zealand government as having some value.

Second, it is evident that there is a reasonably strong relationship between the rated values of the operations and their costs. Averaged over the respondents, the correlation between the rated value of the operations and the logarithm of the operations' costs was 0.48 for the medical sample, and 0.53 for the non-medical sample. Thus the relationship between value and cost was rather stronger for the operations than we have generally found for government-provided services, although not quite so strong as the relationship that we found between the rated values of items supplied by the market and their costs. Thus, as economic theory suggested, the relationship between marginal (item) value and marginal cost for these medical operations was quite good. Curiously, the value–cost relationship was actually a little stronger for the non-medical than the medical sample.

Table 8.5. Cost (in NZ $) of operations funded by the Health Funding Authority and their mean value as rated by a medical and by a non-medical sample

Operation	Cost	Medical mean rating	Non-medical mean rating
Kidney transplant	16 459	9.6	9.2
Coronary bypass	14 746	9.5	9.6
Cardiac pacemaker	12 868	9.2	8.7
Knee replacement	12 452	8.2	7.8
Hip replacement	9 480	9.1	8.2
Angioplasty	7 964	9.4	8.9
Hysterectomy	3 639	8.0	7.3
Hernia operation	2 458	7.2	7.4
Cataract removal	2 220	8.4	8.0
Varicose veins	1 501	6.1	5.0
Tonsilectomy	1 276	6.3	6.4
Carpal tunnel	949	7.4	7.2
Circumcision	841	3.2	2.5
Ear grommets	644	8.1	6.8
Colonoscopy	558	7.8	6.8
Gastroscopy	368	7.2	6.1

Note: Descriptions actually given to the respondents were more detailed than those shown here.

Two tangential aspects of this study are probably worth remarking. One might ask if it makes a difference whether the respondent worked in the medical sector or not. In fact the average value ratings for the two samples are quite similar ($r = 0.97$), indicating good agreement between the two samples on the value of the operations and suggesting a reasonable knowledge of the practical implications of the procedures on the part of the non-medical sample. It seems improbable that many non-medical people would have detailed knowledge of the costs of the operations. Indeed, it would be surprising if many of the medical sample knew the exact costs either. On the other hand, it would not be surprising to find that people in both groups could make some reasonable estimate of the comparative costs of, say, a kidney operation and a tonsillectomy, which might be based on information about the relative length of the operation, the complexity of it, the complications that might arise from it and the length of the hospital stay as well as from judgements of relative importance or value.

Finally, it should be noted – as an aside to the QALY research discussed in Chapter 4 – that the value ratings were not simply related to whether the operations are intended to save lives. Note, for example, that both samples rated hip replacement as more valuable than tonsilectomy, the cataract operation as more valuable than colonoscopy.

EFFECT OF MANIPULATING THE PERCEIVED COST OF SERVICES

The fact that people generally are unable to recall or to estimate accurately what the government spends to provide services is a powerful reason for believing that people's estimates of the value of such goods do not take into much account the costs of providing them. However, it is not quite a decisive one. There is now a considerable body of psychological research on memory that shows there may be (at least) two sorts of memory. In the technical language of cognitive psychology, there is an explicit and an implicit memory (Squire, 1986). Explicit memory is encountered when people can consciously remember and recount events. However, people's behaviour may also be influenced by events that they can not consciously remember. In this case, they are said to have an implicit memory for them. The implication of this distinction here is that it is possible that people's valuation of government services could be influenced, for example, by their previous reading about their costs – and we have seen that the information is there to be read – even though they are not later able to recount accurately the information they saw.

One way to examine the effect of people's implicit knowledge of costs is to manipulate the cost information itself. Accordingly the three experiments in Kemp (in press) asked respondents to value government services or proposals for government services after giving them cost information that was sometimes accurate, sometimes a factor of three too high, and sometimes a factor of three too low. In the first experiment, respondents were presented with this accurate or falsified information about current spending on 15 government-supplied services. (See Kemp, in press, Experiment 1 for details of the design and analysis.) The chief result was that neither ratings of the total value of the services nor ratings of the value of spending an extra $1 million on each of the services were affected by the 'information' people were given about their costs.

The other two experiments featured attempts to manipulate information about the marginal costs of the services rather than information about their total costs. Experiment 2 presented information like: 'Each hospital bed and operations associated with it costs on average $246 000 per year' (service = hospitals); 'Each new soldier costs around $100 000 per year' (service = defence); 'A single superannuation beneficiary receives around $10 500 per year after tax' (service = old age pensions). As in the previous experiment, respondents were given accurate costs for some services and costs that were a factor of three too high or too low for others. They were asked to assume that 'these figures tell you what extra spending in each area would bring'. For none of the 11 services valued, did the cost manipulation affect the rated value of spending an extra $1 million on the service.

As was remarked earlier in this chapter, the New Zealand government often floats proposals for augmenting services through the media. In the third experiment in this series, 15 such actual proposals were obtained from the local newspaper, *The Press*, over a period of three months. These proposals were presented to the respondents, and they were asked to rate the value of each proposal. In each case, the actual proposal cost was falsified and an amount either three times more or three times less than the actual cost substituted. As in the previous studies, there was no effect of the cost manipulation. Overall, then, these studies suggest that respondents largely ignore costs – total or marginal – when they rate the value of government services, a result that is quite consistent with the failure to recall them accurately which we have already noted.

Curiously and importantly, although the respondents' value ratings were little affected by manipulating cost information, their preferred spending on the services was markedly influenced by it. Apart from valuing the services in Experiment 1, respondents wrote down the annual per capita amount they thought should be spent on each of the services. These figures were strongly related to the cost information (or misinformation) with which they had been supplied. Indeed, when the services were accompanied by false information, the ratio of 3 : 1 : 0.33 in the costs given the respondents was approximately reflected in the average respondent's spending preferences. For services that received higher rated values, these preferred amounts were somewhat greater than those they were presented with; for services with the lower rated values, the preferred amounts were close to or below the costs they were given. Table 8.6 shows the results from one condition of this experiment. (Other conditions of the experiment counterbalanced the false information presented.)

Table 8.6. Median preferred per capita expenditure (in NZ $) and actual expenditure on government services when respondents were given misleading (one-third or three times actual) or accurate cost information

Service	Preferred expenditure	Actual expenditure
One-third actual costs presented		
Schools	400	768
Unemployment benefits	138	359
Universities	100	178
Subsidized work	15	36
Women's Affairs Dept	0.50	1.35
Actual costs presented		
Superannuation	1500	1375
Defence	300	375
Police	258	208
National Library	18	14
Hillary Commission	1.75	1.22
Three times actual costs presented		
Health	5500	1471
Domestic Purposes Benefits	1246	414
Dept of Conservation	163	49
Immigration	45	15
NZ Symphony Orchestra	8.10	2.70

Thus, while the rated values were largely unaffected by the false cost information, people's preferred spending on the different services was very strongly affected. This result has implications for our understanding of differences between the different valuation methods that were discussed in Chapter 5. Clearly, asking people how much they would like to allocate to different services is similar to the method of contingent valuation. We remarked earlier that contingent values appear relatively easy to bias. Indeed, some of the specific findings from previous research into that method might lead us to expect the kinds of results that are shown in Table 8.6. For example, Thaler (1985) found that willingness to pay for a beer that would be drunk on a beach depended on the type of outlet. People were willing to pay higher sums if the beer was to be bought from a luxury hotel, which of course would generally charge higher prices. Baron and Maxwell (1996) found respondents willing to pay more for a public good that they believed to be expensive. Thus people's willingness to pay for goods and services in these studies was influenced by what they perceived to be the 'going rate', just as the respondents in our survey seem to have based their preferences for how much the government should spend on particular services on the information they were given about current spending.

A tentative inference one might draw from the disparity between the relative volatility of the preferred spending results and the relative stability of the value rating results is that the latter are in some sense more psychologically fundamental. Such a conclusion is also supported by at least two other studies. Kemp and Willetts (1995a, Study 3) asked respondents to perform both a form of contingent valuation and category rating of the value incurring to New Zealand people from each of 16 government services. In the contingent valuation, respondents were presented with two payment cards (cf. Boyle and Bishop, 1988), each showing dollar amounts in four linear scales $0–9, $10–100, $101–1000, and $1001–10 000. The first such card showed current expenditure on the 16 services, and then respondents were asked to indicate their own choice of expenditure on the second card.

We then conducted separate multiple regression analyses on each respondent's results. We found that their contingent values (that is, the amounts they wrote down on the second cards) were very well predicted by the actual costs of the services (shown on the first cards) and the rated values. In contrast, the rated values were considerably less well predicted from the costs and the contingent values. The result suggests that their contingent valuations might have been formed from an amalgam of the cost information they were given and their underlying values of the services as measured by the rating procedure.

A similar conclusion was reached by Kahneman *et al.* (1993). In this study, respondents were confronted with 16 headlines featuring either naturally or humanly caused environmental disasters (for example, salmon extinction or forest fires) and different respondents were asked to respond using different measures. The measures were willingness to pay, simple ratings of support for intervention, satisfaction with giving to the cause, upsetness, and the importance of the issue. The different measures proved to be highly intercorrelated, with the highest inter-rater reliability for the importance measure. The authors concluded that the results suggest 'willingness to make a personal contribution of money, support for political action, and a simple rating of the importance of the problem are almost interchangeable measures of the same attitude. The core of this attitude, as identified by the simplest question that elicits it, is the importance of the issue' (Kahneman *et al.*, 1993, p. 314).

CONCLUSIONS

Obviously people are not well informed about what government costs. The work done on fiscal illusions reveals that people are not very good at perceiving what they pay in tax and what government costs as a whole. The work reviewed in this chapter demonstrates that people have very little idea of how much money the government allocates to the different services it provides.

Quite why people are so badly informed is not completely clear, but there are some good indications. In the first place, it is worth repeating that, at least in New Zealand and the UK, information is publicly available, not only through official government statistics, but also through the media. The New Zealand government at least does appear to make an honest, if not ultimately very successful, attempt to inform the public about how government money is spent (for example, Campos and Pradhan, 1997), and it is not easy to sustain the hypothesis that it is trying to restrict access to such information.

On the whole the evidence supports the contention that it is prices people remember and use rather than overall cost information. Harris and Seldon may be right in their claim that people's understanding of the costs of supplying government services would be enhanced if such prices were available. On the other hand, there is no evidence that actually having to pay for the items is particularly important. We note in this respect that even though people pay for goods like fruit and clothing they did not prove much more accurate at estimating average per capita spending on these goods than they did at estimating per capita spending on government services.

The results reported in this chapter also reinforce the notion that the rated values of different government services are in some sense a rather fundamental construct. The relative impermeability to cost information that we noted in this chapter is a counterpart to the failure to distinguish ratings of marginal and total value that we noted in Chapter 6. Contingent valuation, on the other hand, is affected by such information.

Finally, there is a pessimistic conclusion. The way people value government services in New Zealand, and probably in many other parts of the world, and their desire to spend more or less on a particular service are unlikely to be based on very in-depth cost–benefit analysis. We consider this issue in a little more detail.

In microeconomic theory, people may often not need to know anything about total utilities and total costs to make rational decisions. So, for example, my 'rational' decision to drink another glass of red wine does not require me to have an idea of the total utility I derive from red wine or any knowledge of my total spending on it. A rational decision can be made quite straightforwardly by knowing what utility I am likely to derive from the next glass and what I am going to pay for it. Presumably, although the theory does not usually dwell on this point, some sort of comparison with the marginal utility I might obtain from other products or services with a similar cost is made. The important point, however, is that rational decisions of this kind only require knowledge of marginal utility and costs, not total utility and costs.

Exactly the same logic applies to the goods and services supplied by the government. In theory there is no reason why people should need to know the total costs and total utility of government services to make rational decisions about their expansion or contraction. The problem is that with these services it is much more difficult to estimate the marginal utility and marginal costs.

As was remarked earlier, item prices and estimates of the utility to be obtained from the item (comparable to the cost of an extra glass of wine and the benefit derived from drinking it) are simply not often available for many government services. Where they are – the valuation of medical operations is a reasonable example – we find that the rated utility of these items and their costs seem to have a quite similar relationship to that found between the utility of consumer items and their costs. But what do we do if we want to find out the benefits of investing in a new fighter plane, reducing the average classroom size from 24 to 23 pupils, or increasing the subsidy to kindergartens? A marginal analysis is still possible for such decisions – obviously we are talking about small changes to an existing service – but the marginal analysis is of a somewhat different kind and here it is often useful to know what the total costs and benefits are.

So, for example, how is James to estimate how much extra benefit might be derived from increasing spending on a government service by, say, $10 million? The obvious way for him to do this would be to say something like: 'Well, we spend $X million dollars on this service now, and we get a pretty good deal from it but there is room for improvement. On the other hand, $10 million dollars is a very small proportion of $X million, so it isn't going to make very much difference'. Alternatively, James might think: '$10 million is quite a big proportion of $X million, so I guess we could expect to get some real benefit from spending it'. Note that here he is basing his estimate of the marginal utility to be derived from increasing the supply of the service on his estimate of the total utility currently derived. This is in accordance with our finding that total and marginal utility are not much distinguished for government services. This may or may not be a reasonable way to estimate marginal utility, but there is a more glaring problem with James's approach.

If James does not know what X actually is – and the evidence indicates that he does not know enough even to make a reasonable guess – he cannot use this kind of reasoning effectively.

Overall, then, it appears unlikely that people can make an informed marginal cost–benefit analysis of government services. One might go on to ask more generally how they do go about making decisions about how worthwhile government services are and what sorts of things they want the government to do. These issues are considered in the next chapter.

9. What Do People Want the Government to Undertake?

A number of researchers have suggested, on different grounds, that people's thinking about the provision of government services consists of an adherence to a few rather simple, poorly thought-out propositions. Commenting on the results of a budget game survey, De Groot and Pommer (1989, p. 131) remarked that the responses appeared to be 'generated to a large extent by very general notions on the (un)desirability of public goods: "defence is bad, education and health care are good"'. Baron (1997) concluded that many contingent valuation results showing insensitivity to quantity are consistent with the hypothesis that people's values for public goods are heavily dominated by the perceived importance of the good. As we saw in the previous chapter, Kahneman *et al.* (1993) suggested that people's willingness to pay for environmental goods was mostly driven by their perception of the importance of the issue.

The research that was outlined in the previous chapters generally supports these conclusions. In particular it is consistent with the finding that marginal and total utility appear to be poorly distinguished for government-supplied goods; with the finding that people do not appear to know much about what it costs to provide government services or to have much of a basis for making cost–benefit judgements; and with the finding that similar category rating or magnitude estimates of value are obtained with rather different instructions.

In the remainder of this chapter we look at research that seems to bear on the questions of what people want the government to do and how they perceive the way the government provides services. We look first at the area of lay economic beliefs and theories, and then at the mental picture people have of the government's role in the economy. Then we briefly consider a little research on what people think the government should do as opposed to what should be left to the market system. The final section is mainly devoted to two studies, one which looked primarily at why people thought the government should spend more or less on a service, and one which attempted to assess how involved people feel in the way the government allocates spending among different services.

LAY ECONOMIC BELIEFS AND THEORIES

In recent years there has been a good deal of interest in the beliefs that lay people have about all kinds of disciplines. So, for example, there has been a reasonable amount of interest in 'folk psychology', where researchers have studied the ideas and beliefs about psychology that ordinary folk have. These ideas and beliefs turn out to be especially interesting because they can be influential on people's behaviour, unlike, say, the ideas of naïve physicists, which have little impact on the way that non-human bodies operate in the physical world (see, for example, Fletcher, 1995; Furnham, 1988). As Heider (1958, p. 2) put it, the ordinary person 'has a great and profound understanding of himself and other people which, although unformulated or only vaguely conceived, enables him to interact with others in more or less adaptive ways'.

In a similar vein there has been some attention paid to what lay people believe about economics, and again this research is important because what people believe about economics has behavioural consequences. This point is, of course, a very obvious one. As we saw in Chapter 3, people's perceptions of the economy are a strong influence on how they vote. One might also remark that a major theme of the history of the twentieth century was the ideological conflicts produced between capitalist and communist economic theory.

Some of the research into lay economics has considered how children and adolescents learn about the way the economy operates (for example, Stacey, 1985; Roland-Lévy, 1999). There has also been a little investigation of the understanding that lay people have of economic theory and the consequences this might have. For example, Baron and Kemp (2001) found that people often had an imperfect understanding of Ricardo's theory of comparative advantage and that those with poorer understanding of it were less likely to be well disposed towards free trade.

There have been a few studies that have attempted to elucidate what people think about the government's role in the economy. One of the more interesting of these was reported by Williamson and Wearing (1996). In this study, the researchers presented a variety of Australian respondents with questionnaires that covered the present and expected state of the economy, and asked for the expression of opinions about macroeconomic policies, government spending, taxation, and a variety of other variables. Each respondent also participated in a clinical interview in which they were asked 'When you consider how the economy affects the well-being of people in Australia, what do you think about?'. Various cues (for example, role of the public sector, wages and debt) were used if respondents were unable to reply to this question.

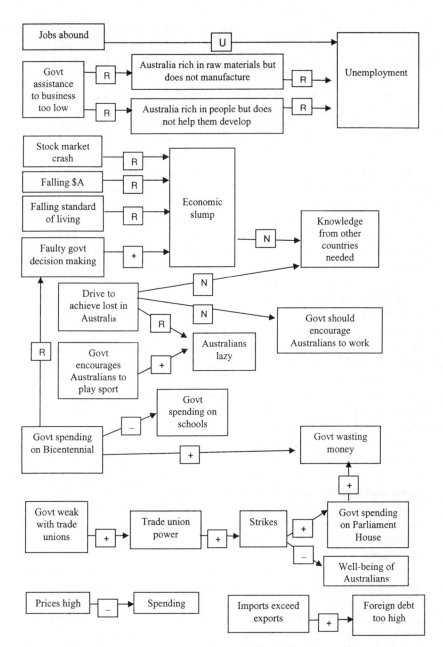

Figure 9.1. One woman's cognitive model of the Australian economy (adapted from Williamson and Wearing, 1996, Fig. 2). Key to linkage symbols: + increases; – decreases; R related; U unrelated; N a need

An interesting and important finding of this research was that the interviews and the questionnaire data produced rather different kinds of information. From the questionnaires, for example, it was evident that the sample as a whole had a fairly positive view of the government's role in the economy. On the other hand, in the authors' view, often 'questionnaire responses masked respondents' thoughts' (Williamson and Wearing, 1996, p. 27). In particular the interviews seem to have been more suitable for uncovering the beliefs about causal linkages that the respondents had: 'The cause and effect linkages derived from participants' dialogue indicated many dual (or multiple) beliefs which were masked in simple questionnaire responses.' For example, respondents were likely to select a neutral response to current tax levels if they believed simultaneously that low income earners paid too much, and high income earners too little tax.

The interviews revealed that respondents often had complex interrelationships of beliefs about the economy. Figure 9.1 illustrates the cognitive model derived by the authors from the interview of a young woman. The number of linkages produced by this respondent (24) was close to the average derived from the sample.

Some of the results of Williamson and Wearing's study had to do with government spending preferences. Overall, questionnaire responses tended to suggest that the government should spend more, particularly on welfare and education, while at the same time holding taxation constant or reducing it. However, analysis of the interviews and follow-up questions revealed that this was not necessarily a case of fiscal ignorance since often the respondents wanted to reduce spending on some areas in order to increase it in others. Moreover, they were often concerned to eliminate waste and prioritize spending within a particular area.

Williamson and Wearing's research clearly shows that laypeople's thinking about the role of the government in the economy, although undoubtedly an oversimplification of the actual processes at work, can be quite complex and sophisticated. It is also a clear indication that the way people value the services supplied by the government is influenced by a number of different sorts of consideration, and that these considerations are interrelated.

Overall, there has not been a great deal of research into lay economic beliefs (Furnham, 1988) and much of what there has been is of little relevance to the way that the government allocates funding. However, one area that is clearly relevant concerns people's beliefs regarding the fair distribution of resources of various kinds: for example, wealth, job opportunities and health funding (Furnham, 1988).

As an influential example of this research, Kluegel and Smith (1986) identified a dominant ideology in the beliefs of Americans about the sources and possible remedies of inequality. In their view, this ideology mixes conservative and liberal views in ways that are not always consistent, even within the same individual. So, for example, they suggest that

> Our liberal sympathies urge us to support children in poverty because they are not responsible for the circumstances in which they were born. The dominant ideology, on the other hand, leads to such distrust of the personal character of the parents receiving welfare that the restrictions and stigma attached to its allocation may act ... to perpetuate a life in poverty for the children we intend to help. (Kluegel and Smith, 1986, p. 7)

One important aspect of the way people perceive the causes of inequalities is the finding that people's attributions are often very much affected by their own position. So, for example, it has often been found that people who are unemployed tend to attribute their state to social or economic causes. Those who are employed often attribute the unemployment of others to their personal failings, citing such factors as laziness or lack of ability (Feather and O'Brian, 1986; Furnham, 1982).

Overall, it is likely that how people think about the government's role in the economy and how it should go about allocating resources depends on the application of a number of what might be termed ethical heuristics. These ethical heuristics might be thought of as similar to the heuristics and biases which have been found to appear when people make judgements under conditions of uncertainty (for example, Kahneman and Tversky, 1996; Shafir and Kahneman, 1999; Tversky and Kahneman, 1981).

Some important examples of ethical heuristics include the principle of needs, by which one person's needs should take precedence over another's wants, the principle of equity, by which people should receive according to their inputs, and the principle of equality, by which all people should receive the same. Each of these principles is intuitively reasonable, but applying them gives rise to considerable difficulty. We consider in a little more detail the principle of needs.

Berry (1994) in his book *The Idea of Luxury* points out that societies often operate under a principle of precedence such that 'when Adam needs something that Brenda wants but does not need, then meeting Adam's need is prima facie morally preferable to satisfying Brenda's desire' (Berry, 1994, p. 63). This is, of course, close to Rawls' (1971) prescription, and we saw in Chapter 4 that the principle appears to be important in people's health decisions.

Berry goes on to chart attitudes towards luxury in European history, showing that some but not all societies have sought to regulate it in the interests of the principle of precedence. This preference appears to persist today. Kemp (1998a) found that whether a good was perceived as a luxury or a necessity was very influential in how people wished to proceed when the good is in short supply. People preferred that scarce goods having the nature of a necessity should be distributed by some form of regulation rather than through the market system.

The application of this principle is not straightforward, since in practice it is not easy to define what is a necessity and what is a luxury. So, for example, Adshead (1992) in his book *Salt and Civilization* argues that salt was an early example of a human luxury. Kemp's (1998a) respondents gave the highest necessity rating to electricity, a commodity which was hardly in use at all a century ago. Moreover, people do not share the same views as to which goods are luxuries and which necessities, and, indeed, the same good can be more or less of a luxury depending on the circumstances of the individual who wants (or needs) it (Kemp, 1998a).

In *King Lear*, an important source of conflict between the aged king and his ungrateful daughters, Goneril and Regan, is Lear's desire to have his personal retinue of knights accommodated by them. In Act 2, Scene 4, the daughters question his need for these companions. Lear replies:

O, reason not the need: our basest beggars
Are in the poorest things superfluous:
Allow not nature more than nature needs,
Man's life is cheap as beast's: thou art a lady;
If only to go warm were gorgeous,
Why, nature needs not what thou gorgeous wear'st,
Which scarcely keeps thee warm.

Not only do the different heuristic principles become difficult to define when one attempts to go beyond common sense, but they also frequently come into conflict. For example, should a particular education opportunity – a place on a sought-after university course for instance – go to those who appear to merit it most (equity), or to those who are in most need, for example to those who are relatively uneducated because of past discrimination? Or, if everyone can not be treated equally, because it may not make sense for everyone to have a fraction of the course, should they be given an equal opportunity to take the course by distributing the places randomly? Obviously in this case only one of the principles can be followed and the others must be set aside.

Each of the principles is sometimes employed, although as a rule in somewhat different situations (Adams, 1963; Mellers and Baron, 1993; Messick, 1993). None of them seems to be universally favoured in all situations, but although some of the general outlines are apparent it is not yet clear which principles people will favour in which situations. Nor, of course, will everyone choose the same ethical heuristics to deal with each issue. For example, we would expect someone who identifies more with the political left to favour the equity principle less often than someone on the political right. We might also expect that just as different decision-making heuristics are invoked by different decision frames (for example, Tversky and Kahneman, 1981), so too might different ethical heuristics be invoked by different ethical frames. For example, drawing attention to the past discrimination that a particular minority group has suffered might encourage people to reserve some places on a university course for members of that group.

RESEARCH ON THE DESIRABILITY OF GOVERNMENT INTERVENTION IN THE ECONOMY

Even from the brief overview I have just given, it should be clear that it is not easy to derive clear, unambiguous predictions from the research into lay economic beliefs. Indeed, the general theme is of a number of different principles which will frequently conflict with one another. This suggests not only that different people will hold rather different views in similar situations but also that quite small changes in circumstances might produce rather large changes in people's preferred allocations.

On the whole economists have tended to adopt a theoretical approach when considering what the government should or should not do in the economy. Their arguments have usually focused on issues of efficiency or on maximizing social utility. Another approach is to ask people what sorts of things the government should do. We consider first research in which ordinary people have been presented with hypothetical shortages or scarcities of different goods and then asked how they think the situation should be dealt with.

One line of research has investigated people's responses to experimental simulations of social dilemmas of the 'tragedy of the commons' kind and found that people often chose some kind of regulation to prevent scarce resources being depleted. So, for example, Messick *et al.* (1983) had groups of six people undertake the 'harvest' of a slowly replenishing resource. In a (manipulated) condition in which the resource was overused, the respondents tended to vote for a regulatory leader. A subsequent study (Samuelson *et al.*, 1984) suggested that different factors influenced individual harvest decisions and the decisions about what kind of leadership to vote for to attempt to remedy the situation.

Kemp (1996, Study 1) presented lay respondents with hypothetical scenarios featuring shortages of different kinds and asked people to choose between dealing with the shortage through the market or by regulation. In the market alternative there was no intervention but, they were told, the price of the commodity would rise until the number of people willing or able to pay for it matched how much of the commodity was available. They were told that under regulation an honest committee would be set up to allocate the commodity to those people it thought might most benefit from it. None of the shortages were presented as being the producer's fault. For example, one scenario read: 'A shortage of French champagne develops in New Zealand. The shortage is caused by the hijacking of a container ship and is expected to last only for a month. Several companies import champagne regularly.' Elements of the scenarios, for example, the expected duration of the shortage and the number of importers, were varied.

The chief result was that the nature of the response was strongly affected by the type of the commodity. For example, there was overwhelming preference for the regulatory option when the good was a scarce drug needed for treating a fatal illness, and overwhelming preference for the market system when the good was a luxury such as champagne.

Subsequent studies aimed to identify important variables affecting the preferred response. This research showed that preference for regulation was increased if the good was necessary for people's health (Kemp, 1996, Studies 2 and 3; Kemp and Bolle, 1999, Studies 3 and 4); if there was only one producer or if someone stood to profit from the scarcity (Kemp, 1996, Studies 2 and 3); if a large number of people were likely to be affected by the scarcity (Kemp, 1996, Studies 2 and 3); if the good was a necessity rather than a luxury (Kemp, 1998a, Study 3); and if the scarcity was expected to last for years rather than a few months (Kemp, 1996, Studies 1, 2 and 3). Two unpublished studies by Kemp and Bolle found that changing the income distribution in a hypothetical society, curiously enough, did not produce any change in preference between regulation and the market. Thus, it did not seem to be the case that the case for regulation was related to a desire to obtain more even income or utility distributions.

Of course, in reality the choice is not simply whether to regulate or not. A variety of different non-market measures are currently used to ration out scarce goods (for example, Hardin, 1968; Frey and Pommerehne, 1993) and we should not expect people to be indifferent between them. Three such measures are waiting time, individual merit, and random choice. For example, scarce theatre tickets and some kinds of hospital operation in state-run health systems are often allocated according to the length of time people have waited for them. (In some cases, the length of time that people are willing to wait is a reasonable measure of how keen they are to obtain the scarce commodity. One might think of it as a price of time.) Organizations often attempt to determine individual merit. This is common, for example, when determining who should be the recipient of an organ transplant, merit in this case often being determined by a QALY calculation of some kind. Merit is also often used to allocate places in prestigious graduate schools. Random allocation is more rarely employed by publicly funded institutions but it is not unknown. The principle is occasionally a component of immigration policy. A polytechnic institute in Christchurch used it to allocate scarce places on a nursing course for a number of years (although there was something of an outcry when their method was discovered by the media).

Unsurprisingly, Kemp and Bolle (1999) found that preferences for different distribution methods varied with the nature of the scarce good. For example, the merit principle was preferred for scarce medical drugs, the length of wait for scarce theatre tickets. Curiously, the market system was relatively little favoured overall. Preferences to some extent mirror what actually happens in the respondent's society, but not completely. Kemp and Bolle (1999, Study 3) compared the preferences of people brought up in communist eastern Europe and more market-oriented western Germany, but did not find strong correlations between people's preferences and their upbringing. A comparison between two market-oriented societies with different current practices with respect to some goods (Germany and New Zealand) also did not show the expected difference in preferences (Kemp and Bolle, 1999, Study 4). For example, at the time the provision of housing was more strictly regulated in Germany than in New Zealand, but there was no difference in people's preferences for how to deal with a housing shortage between the two societies. In conclusion, although practice and preference are correlated, it is not true that people always prefer what they are used to.

The issues identified by the respondents in deciding between market and regulatory distribution are partly in agreement and partly in disagreement with the reasons for government intervention that economists have put forward and that were reviewed in Chapter 2. On the agreement side, obviously both economists and lay-people are concerned with the effects of unregulated monopoly. The issue of how many people are affected by a shortage bears some (though by no means a perfect) relation to whether a good is a public or a private good in the economic sense. So, people's preference for regulation when large numbers of people are affected is similar to the economist's notion that goods might be provided by the government if they are the kind of good that once provided becomes available to all. On the other hand, the obvious linked concerns with whether the good is a luxury or a necessity and whether it is a health-related issue are not really related to the economists' account. Probably the biggest contradiction comes from the respondents' concern to regulate goods that are likely to be in short supply for long periods of time. In general, long periods of regulation should have a counter-productive effect. Regulating scarce products in this way should act to remove the incentive for firms to search for substitutes or new technologies so they can take advantage of profitable opportunities.

The last twenty years have seen a trend towards privatization, and worldwide governments have turned over many of the services they formerly provided to privately owned companies or in some cases to the non-profit sectors of the economy. The driving force, of course, has been the economic belief that private companies are generally more efficient than government-owned ones. There has been curiously little research into people's preferences regarding these changes. One exception is a survey carried out by Thompson and Elling (2000) on a random sample of residents of the state of Michigan.

This survey asked whether respondents would prefer each of 14 services to be provided by profit-making firms, non-profit organizations or government agencies. A majority of the respondents favoured private supply of two services, garbage collection and janitorial services. There was no majority in favour of having non-profit organizations run any of the services. When preferences for the two non-government suppliers (profit-making firms and non-profit organizations) were combined, there were then majorities in favour of non-governmental supply for just four of the 14 services: garbage collection, clerical services, street cleaning and emergency medical services. Thus, a clear result of the study is that most people wanted most of the services (10 out of 14) to be supplied by the government. This was also true of all the services, for example, prisons, enforcement of building regulations, police and fire protection, that had an element of coercion.

A number of attitudinal questions established that, overall, private firms were regarded positively, even though people did not necessarily prefer them to be used. Regression analyses were used to predict support for privatization by individuals from a range of demographic variables. Overall, privatization was more likely to be preferred by those with higher incomes, whites, and Republican supporters, but the overall predictive power of the regression equation (accounting for 5.9 per cent of the variance in the preferences) was low.

Kemp (1998b, Study 3) asked New Zealanders to rate the values of eight government services and eight classes of market goods. An average government preference score was created by subtracting the average of the eight market goods ratings from the average of the eight government services ratings. Positive values on this score should reflect an overall preference for government services relative to market services and negative values an overall preference for market goods.

Respondents also completed an Economic Beliefs Scale devised by Furnham (1985), on which high values correspond to more left-wing or socialist beliefs. The expectation was that these two measures should be positively correlated but in fact no significant correlation was found. Nor were respondents with lower incomes more likely to have more positive scores. Thus, this study too suggests that preferences for government versus private supply of goods are not easy to predict.

Mahoney (2001) used methods similar to those of Kemp (1996) to investigate the factors affecting people's preferences for government versus private supply of services. In Study 1, New Zealanders were asked which of 18 possible factors were important in determining their supply preferences. In their approximate order of importance, the key factors turned out to be whether the service was necessary for people's health; whether everyone (rather than a few) wanted or needed the service; whether it was necessary for people's safety; whether it was a necessity rather than a luxury; whether the service contributed to education; whether there was only one supplier; whether there were negative externalities associated with it; and whether the service was a public good in the economist's sense.

Mahoney's (2001) Study 2 presented respondents with scenarios in which four of these factors were systematically varied. The study confirmed that health, the number of people needing or wanting the service, the number of suppliers, and the presence of negative externalities were important influences on their preferences. Her third study presented respondents with a list of 25 services, some currently government-supplied (for example, defence), some privately supplied (for example, dentists, bars and pubs), and some supplied by a mixture (for example, rubbish collection, buses). The respondents rated their preference (government versus private supply) for each service, their present satisfaction with the service, and the extent to which the service had six of the factors found important for determining preferences from Study 1. (For example, each service was rated for whether it was necessary for people's health.) The regression analysis of Study 3 showed important factors influencing preferences to be the number of suppliers, whether the service was necessary for people's health, and their current satisfaction with the service.

Overall, Mahoney's research suggests that people's preferences for government versus private supply are quite similar to their preferences for distributing goods in short supply via a regulating authority or the market system. For example, there is a clear preference that health goods and services be government run and distributed by regulation if scarce. The presence of monopolies also inclined people to government supply and regulation.

GOVERNMENT ALLOCATION OF RESOURCES

A fairly simple way to try to get insight into the way people think about the government's allocation of money is to ask them for their views. Kemp and Crawford (1999, Study 3) carried out a simple series of interviews with a small group of 24 respondents, 11 of them students and 13 non-students.

The interviewer asked each respondent to identify an 'area where you think the government should increase its spending', then asked why they had chosen the area, and finally asked on what information and knowledge they had based their decision. In the second part of the interview they were asked to identify 'an area where you think the government currently spends too much money'. They were again asked why they had chosen this area, and on what information and knowledge they had based the decision.

All the respondents were able to identify both an area in which they thought the government should increase its spending and an area where they thought the government spent too much. For the preferred increase, 12 respondents nominated education (or some aspect of it), 8 respondents nominated health (or some aspect of it), and there was 1 nomination for each of (state-funded) superannuation, industrial development, justice and community activities. For the preferred decrease, 8 respondents nominated some aspect of social welfare (especially the unemployment benefit), 7 defence, 4 spending on members of parliament, and 2 spending on Maori (New Zealand indigenous people) issues. Education, prisons, and the employment of consultants to provide advice for government decision-making were each nominated by one respondent. Incidentally, it is noteworthy that even for this small sample the choice of areas was in quite close agreement with the results of asking larger samples to rate the value of different government services.

The reasons advanced for the nominations were coded into four categories:

Fairness. The respondent believed that the present level of spending was unfair or advantaged or disadvantaged some group unfairly. For example, one respondent who wanted more spent on superannuation stated: 'I think it's unfair that people who work their whole life paying taxes but are unable to get retirement insurance and then when they retire they are made to get a pittance from the government for superannuation.'

Spinoff. The respondent believed either that an increase would be a good investment for society (for example, education was often seen as an investment in the society's future) or that the present level of spending was producing a negative long-term effect (for example, one respondent believed that social welfare reduced work motivation).

Service Issues or Waste. Respondents stated that increased spending would lead to a better service or commented that the present system was unworkable. Decreased spending was justified by stating that a service was unworkable, or that the money was wasted or that better uses were available. For example, one respondent wanted to decrease defence spending 'because New Zealand cannot afford nor justify buying three frigates or even one today at a price of 250 million each. This money could be better used to reduce public waiting lists for elective surgery and the suffering that goes on.'

Need. The respondent pointed to a need for the service or that people were currently missing out. For example, one respondent wanted to see increased spending on health because of '[t]he huge waiting lists for life threatening problems'.

Table 9.1. Percentages of respondents nominating different categories of reasons for advocating an increase or decrease in government spending on some area, and the first and second source of information used for the decision

	Increase	Decrease
Category		
Fairness	4	25
Spinoff	42	13
Service/Waste	0	62
Need	54	0
Information source: first source named		
Media	29	63
Personal	58	29
Theory driven	12	8
Information source: second source named		
Media	25	13
Personal	17	21
Theory driven	4	0

Table 9.1 shows the numbers of respondents nominating each of the four types of reason for the increased and decreased spending. Interestingly, the categories were differently used to justify increases and decreases. The category of need, which relates quite closely to the idea that people evaluate

government areas of spending according to their importance, appears to be significant for justifying increases but not decreases in spending. Decreases were most often justified by referring to waste or service delivery issues. The importance of spinoffs, especially where increases in expenditure were recommended, recalls the importance of interlinkages in the way Williamson and Wearing's respondents thought about the government's role in the economy.

The sources of information people claimed to have used in making their decisions divided easily into three groups: media sources, personal experiences or those of friends, and 'theory driven', a category that includes learning through formal education or consistency with one's personal beliefs. Many respondents nominated more than one source of information. As Table 9.1 shows, the predominant sources were the media and personal experience. It is noteworthy that respondents were more likely to nominate the media as the first source for justifying decreases in expenditure, while they were more likely to think of personal experience as the first source for preferred increases of spending. This suggests that one important way in which people might decide that a service needs more money spent on it is simply by hearing about individual people who appear deserving of some government provided service and are missing out or in need.

A more elaborate study was carried out by Ølander *et al.* (1999). Sixty-two respondents participated in brief interviews and completed short questionnaires about the allocation of government expenditure. In the short structured interview, they were asked six questions (shown in Table 9.2). Following the interview, they completed a brief questionnaire. They were asked to record their preferences for increased government spending versus tax cuts. They were also asked how important to them was the way the government allocated money among different services and how much attention they paid to the way the government allocated money. Responding was on a ten-point scale ranging from 0 (No importance/attention) to 10 (Great importance/attention).

Responses to the open-ended questions are shown in Table 9.2. Where respondents gave more than one answer, only the first is shown, but, overall, few respondents gave lengthy answers to any of the questions. It is possible that the brevity of the responses arose from the nature of the interview, but it is also consistent with respondents not possessing a well-developed schema that allows them to evaluate the nature and effects of government spending.

A number of features of the table are worth noting. In the first place, nearly three-quarters of the respondents felt that they had very little input into how the government allocates resources, although about the same proportion would have liked to have had more input. Secondly, many respondents placed considerable emphasis on the importance of people's wants and needs and the effectiveness of different government policies in allocation decisions. In this respect, their responses were similar to those obtained from the earlier study. Thirdly, the responses to the last two questions seem to indicate an unmet demand for more information, although there was no evident consensus about what that information should be.

Other findings from the study were that the respondents had a slight tendency to favour increased spending rather than tax cuts if the government had surplus money. Also noteworthy was that ratings of the importance of government allocation (Average = 7.9/10) were considerably higher than respondents' ratings of how much attention they paid to allocation decisions (Average = 5.0/10).

If we take the two studies together we can come up with a few tentative conclusions about the way people think about government services.

In the first place, our respondents did not seem to have very elaborate ideas about government services. Particularly noteworthy is the large gap between the rated importance of allocation decisions and the low level of attention actually given to them. Note also that most people did not think they knew much about the process of allocation, although they would have liked to.

Secondly, some of the results from Ølander *et al.*'s study suggest that many people feel alienated from the process of government decision-making. Most of the sample felt they had little influence on the way the government allocated money, although they would have liked more. Many also pointed to a need for more information, and sometimes for new types of information.

One might note in this context a worldwide trend, investigated by a number of political scientists, for people in democracies to have lost confidence in the process of government, and in particular for them to have lost confidence in governments' abilities to deliver on public expectations (for example, Birch, 1984). In New Zealand this loss of confidence has actually led to constitutional change. In November 1993, the electorate voted to change the way members of parliament were elected from a 'first past the post' basis, where each electorate separately chooses an MP (as happens in the UK or in the US House of Representative elections). As from 1996, members of the New Zealand parliament have been elected on the same system of proportional representation that is used in Germany (and in many other European countries). Under this system, the number of seats held by a party in the parliament is proportional to the number of votes received by the party, with the exception that the party has to obtain 5 per cent of the vote to have any representatives at all. Thus, perceived alienation from the process by which the government allocates spending in New Zealand might be seen as an instance of a more general process.

Table 9.2. Percentage of responses to open-ended questions on government allocation of resources (n = 62 for all questions)

---

1. Allocation Determinants: 'What do you think determines how the government allocates the money it has available to the different services it provides, for example, so much to education, so much to defence, to social welfare benefits etc?'

Public opinion/voters	26
Government/politicians	23
Needs	16
Lobbying	6
Past allocations	6
Other (including expediency)	11
Don't know	11

2. Influence: 'Do you feel that you yourself have some influence on the way the government allocates money among the different services?... [For responses other than no]: 'In what way?'

No; very little		74
Yes	- through voting	15
	- through referenda	2
	- through active commitment (e.g. lobbying)	6
	- other	3

3. Desire influence: 'Would you like to have more influence?... [If anything but no]: 'How could that come about?'

No		26
Yes	- but don't know how	11
	- voting	3
	- voting on allocation/referenda/surveys	18
	- lobbying etc.	27
	- other	15

4. Considerations: 'If you were asked how government spending should be distributed among different services, what would you take into consideration?'

Wants and needs	47
Effectiveness (effects, relative benefits, etc.)	19
Other	33

5. Information need: 'Is there some sort of information that you think you need in order to figure out whether spending should be increased in some cases or perhaps decreased in others?' [If yes]: 'What sort of information?'

Yes, wants and needs data	18
Yes, effectiveness data	29
Yes, current allocation	23
Other answers	31

6. Information sources: 'Where could you get this information?'

New types of information	
- formal undertakings, e.g. audits, analysis	10
- informally from the services themselves	6
- informally from users, market research	8
Official and other sources	
- existing 'official' sources (incl. media)	52
- other sources	3
- no idea or no answer	21

Thirdly, in both studies the wants and needs of people were perceived to be of particular importance, especially when new expenditure or the expansion of existing services is under consideration. These results also recall the distinction between luxuries and necessities that was discussed earlier in the chapter: people appear to believe that government should be responsible for ensuring people have access to necessities, whatever they are perceived to be. A twist to this finding can be seen in the acknowledgement by some that more information on wants and needs would be useful.

Fourthly, some of the results shown in Table 9.2 suggest both an awareness that the respondent does not know what is currently spent on different services (as we would expect from the previous chapter) and an awareness that he or she does not know what returns are obtained from current levels of spending. Particularly important in this regard is that over half the sample asked either for data on the effectiveness of existing services or for information about their current allocations. Thus, some people, at least, would like to see a form of cost–benefit analysis done on government services.

Fifthly, there is some suggestion from the results that different cognitive and ethical processes might be at work in different types of decision. Perhaps the clearest indication comes from the finding from Kemp and Crawford's study that different types of reason were used to advocate increases of expenditure than decreases. In particular, need was more important for preferring increases in expenditure, and service issues or waste for preferring decreases.

Sixthly, however alienated people may feel from allocation decisions, this does not stop them from wanting to see the government provide services, and, indeed, increase the level of such services. Not one respondent in either study, for example, remarked that it would be better to have the state get out of providing services such as health or education, and leave them to the market to supply.

It would be unwise to place too heavy a weight on the results from either or both of these studies, as clearly a number of important questions have been left unanswered. Moreover, Williamson and Wearing's research suggests that respondents may have a somewhat more elaborate representation of government allocations than is revealed by questionnaire studies of this type. It would also be interesting to see if the way the issues are framed influences people's allocation decisions. For example, would it be possible to manipulate people into preferring reductions or increases in social welfare benefits by using different frames (cf. Tversky and Kahneman, 1981)? One type of frame, say, might emphasize the impoverishment of the beneficiaries, another the sacrifices that must be made by taxpayers. Certainly, Lewis's (1982) work on the psychology of taxation suggests that people's willingness to pay tax can be rather easily manipulated in this way. Most important of all, it is still not clear what underlying personal values might correlate with the different preferred spending allocation patterns.

10. Conclusions

This final chapter has three related themes. Firstly, we consider how the utility provided by government services should be assessed. Secondly, some of the findings from the psychological approach to government spending are reviewed. Thirdly, there is a brief discussion of the political implications of these findings. I have entitled the chapter 'conclusions', but the word implies a degree of certainty which for the most part is not justified, as the reader will discover.

VALUING GOVERNMENT SERVICES

As was remarked in earlier chapters, it is of special importance to assess the utility of goods and services supplied by governments because inference from people's behaviour is rarely possible or meaningful. We have also seen that broadly there is a choice between objective, indirect measures of utility and subjective, direct ones. Neither kind of measure is completely satisfactory, but where different government services are to be valued and the valuations compared, for example the value of education and defence and support of the arts, the subjective, direct measures seem to be preferred, if only because there is often no objective measure which will serve equally for such different kinds of good.

Of course, as an exception to this, inference from people's voting behaviour is in theory extendable to all the different kinds of government services. The major difficulty here is that the connection between what people value and what governments provide or what political parties say they will provide seems to be very frail, as we saw in Chapter 3. It does not therefore seem very reasonable to derive people's valuations of public goods from what is known about the way people vote in representative democracies.

Ideally we should like a measure of utility to be reliable, valid and measured on a ratio scale. This would enable us to measure the construct of utility that economists would like to define. We would like the scale to have the properties of additivity, so that if the value to me of the social welfare system were 5 and the value of defence 3 then the total value would be 8. We should also like to have a scale that enables us to make interpersonal comparisons, so that we could decide, for example, that service A should be provided to Fred because he would receive 10 units of utility from it while providing service B to James would only give James 8 units of utility.

None of the subjective measures we have investigated completely fulfils these criteria. If an observer knew nothing about the research that has been conducted on the different measurement methods, she would probably opt for contingent valuation. The dependent variable used, money, is measured on a ratio scale. Sums of money can be added. Moreover, the use of the money scale does make at least some kinds of interpersonal comparison possible: If Fred is willing to pay more for A than James is for B, then, other things being equal, it does seem reasonable to conclude that Fred might value A more than James does B.

However, the research evidence reviewed in Chapter 5 indicated serious problems with contingent valuation. The adding-up and embedding effects and the relative insensitivity of the measure to the quantity of the good in question argue against contingent valuation fulfilling our ideal criteria. The research reported in Chapter 8 indicates, moreover, that when people are asked to indicate the amounts they would prefer to see spent on different government services, these amounts are extremely sensitive to what they currently believe or are told about the current amounts. Indeed, the research indicates that contingent valuations are mainly formed from a combination of a simple value rating and information about existing prices.

Of the other measures only the quality of life measures used in medical decision-making have any real claim to the scaling properties we would like our measure of utility to have, but this measure is not easily applicable to valuing the whole range of government-supplied services. Moreover, as we saw in Chapter 4, quality of life measures, too, have their problems. For example, their use in the all-important comparison between individuals is extremely questionable.

The other subjective measures reviewed may be a little less problematic because they do not give the illusion of offering more. Of the two psychophysical methods, category rating seems marginally preferable to magnitude estimation. Category rating, whether of value or happiness, is a rougher more intuitive kind of measure than the money scale of contingent valuation, and the best justification for its use is not so much that it provides an ideal measure of utility but rather that it provides a useful tool for exploring people's mental representations of the construct. In the past it has been found useful in psychology for measuring other subjective dimensions, and an important focus of the research described in Chapters 6 and 8 was the attempt to uncover the kinds of mental representation that people employ when they value government or indeed any other kind of good or service.

Asking people whether they wish to spend more, the same or less on a government service is a simpler measure still. This measure is perhaps not so well adapted for exploring the way people think about government as category rating, nor does it give much information as to strength of people's values or preferences. On the other hand, it is very simple for respondents to use, and the results obtained from it seem to be generally consistent with those obtained from the more complex methods. As none of the other methods really seems to supply a valid answer to the question of how much more or less should be spent on a given service if people wish to change the spending, this measure may at present provide nearly as much useful information to a government as methods that in theory do appear to answer the question.

Connected with the question of how we should measure the utility that people assign to government services is the question of what kind of mental representation people have of this utility. The economic theory of utility seems to assume that individuals do have in their heads a representation of a relationship (ideally a mathematical function) which relates the utility of a good to its cost. It is also assumed that people can determine the slope of this function, at least for some points, so that they can make marginal utility judgements. On the other hand, there is no reason in the theory why everyone should have the same relationship.

The research evidence we have reviewed indicates that when people value government services using the method of category rating they make little distinction between marginal and total utility and they do not seem to know much about costs. This does not seem to be the fault of the method of category rating, because, as we saw in Chapter 6, when people are asked to use category rating to value market-supplied goods, the results agree rather well with the economic theory. Moreover, the basic idea that people value government goods in a simple way is supported by others who have used other measurement techniques (for example, De Groot and Pommer, 1989). Thus, the general implication is that we do not obtain better measures of the utility of government services mainly because people's mental representation of these utilities does not support better measures. The research also leads us to doubt whether most people do have a mental representation of the utility–cost relationship for such services.

In his recent review of means of determining value, Jon Baron points up a number of problems with trying to measure values, some of which have already been reviewed. He remarks that 'it is too early for researchers to give up trying to measure values reliably and validly. I discuss these problems to encourage other researchers to try to solve them, not to promote despair' (Baron, 1997, p. 74).

Baron makes a number of suggestions as to how measurement might be improved. One, making the task easier by asking for rating judgements, has been a theme of this book, but, as we have seen, category rating does not produce the ideal measure of utility. Another solution is, in effect, to educate the survey respondents and perhaps the public at large to adopt the conceptual tools of the economist to think about government spending. This is surely not an impossible task, because they already seem to use them in valuing market goods, but better information and perhaps motivation may be required.

It seems likely that the search for more sophisticated means to value government services will attract increased effort, not because the research is likely to produce speedy rewards but because there is so much at stake. Governments do spend a colossal amount of money and there is obviously scope for improvement in the way they do it. In recent years means of valuing human life have made an increasing contribution to medical decision-making, and it is a natural extension to attempt to value the full range of publicly funded services. Whether the eventual outcome of this search will be the discovery and validation of a measure of utility that has all the properties we would like, or whether we shall eventually end up with a measure which does less and forces us to revise our theories of the way people value government services is at present still unclear.

HOW DO PEOPLE THINK ABOUT GOVERNMENT SERVICES?

This section summarizes some of the results that have been discussed in more detail in previous chapters.

We begin by echoing a conclusion from the previous section. People do not think of government services in quite the same way that they think of market-supplied goods and services. In particular, they appear to think of them in a way that is simpler, at least in terms of economic theory. One of the ways in which people think of government services in a simpler way is that the distinction between marginal and total utility of such services is less well-drawn than for market-supplied goods and services. It is likely that at least part of the failure to distinguish marginal and total utility for government-supplied services arises from the lack of item prices and marginal cost information for many government services.

Second, the distinction in economics that is made between private and public goods appears to find little echo in either the thinking or the valuations made by the lay person. There is no apparent trend for more or less pure public goods (in the economist's sense of the term) to be either over- or undervalued relative to private goods supplied by the government. Some public goods, especially defence, are rarely highly valued; others, for example police in New Zealand or transport services in other countries receive quite high valuations.

Third, there is often a mismatch between the resources that governments allocate to particular services and the allocation that the electorate would like to see made. Results obtained using the different subjective methods agree in demonstrating that the wishes of the median voter are not generally carried out. A fairly consistent result obtained using different methods in different countries is that people would like to see more allocated to health and education and less to defence. On the other hand there are also distinct differences between countries in the preferred allocation patterns.

Fourth, one might expect that not getting the mix of services they wish would discourage people from wanting the government to supply services at all. There is little evidence for this. On the contrary, people appear to want governments to provide a considerable range of goods and services, and this desire is by no means limited only to public goods as defined by economists. For example, there is considerable enthusiasm for governments to provide health services. People often place a high value on the services that governments provide, and are keen to see them provided by the government rather than by the market.

Fifth, when people value the services that the government provides they do not generally base their values only on their own self-interest. Instead, their valuations have at least some altruistic component, and reflect people's beliefs and values for society as a whole. It is, however, likely that the valuation of goods and services provided by the market also has some altruistic component.

Sixth, people are not very well informed about what it costs to provide government services. At least in New Zealand this lack of knowledge does not seem to be a consequence of government policy. Indeed, much of the information is quite readily available. The lack of knowledge has implications for people's ability to perform cost–benefit analyses and poses problems for the valid measurement of the utility of government services, especially when contingent valuation is used.

Seventh, the lack of item prices for government services seems to be an important factor in the rather poor relationships obtained between the valuations of government services and their costs.

Eighth, the valuation of a government service appears to be heavily influenced by the perceived need for the service. There is some indication that a large part of the people's desire to see more spent on particular services comes from the observation of particular individuals, either known personally or through the media, who seem in some sense to be deserving but missing out.

Finally, an odd feature of the research done to date deserves remark. Many of the surveys of people's valuations of government goods or attitudes towards them have featured attempts to try to link the values or attitudes to demographic variables (education, income, age, gender) or to their political orientation using a multiple regression or some similar analysis. The consistent finding, remarked in the preceding chapters from time to time, is that the values and attitudes have been poorly predicted by these demographic and political variables, which in combination usually explain 10 per cent or less of the variance in the measures. This result is found even though the different studies have often used quite different measures of value as the dependent variable. For example, Kemp and Willetts (1995b) found poor prediction of category ratings of value; Thompson and Elling (2000) reported little ability to predict who will favour government rather than private provision of the services they investigated.

Quite why this predictability should be so poor seems a little mysterious, at least to me. A possible partial explanation is that people do not consider their own narrow self-interest very much when they do these valuations, so that, for example, in fact elderly people are not largely driven by a desire to increase spending on old-age pensions, university students value other services besides universities, and so on. It is also likely that large political parties and their supporters do not differ much in the way they value different government services (as, incidentally, the median voter model predicts).

Whatever the explanation of the result, it has important implications. One is that there are probably some other kinds of variable that we have not yet measured, perhaps personality variables, which relate more closely to these values. There is also the practical implication that the politician who tries to woo a demographically defined portion of the electorate by increasing spending on what she thinks are likely to be its central concerns is probably often wasting her time.

Another more subtle implication is the suggestion that the important theoretical issue of how values can be compared and summed across individuals may not, in fact, be of great practical significance. The reader will recall that in, say, the category rating method we cannot generally say that a value rating of 6 from Patricia has the same meaning as a value rating of 6 given by Quentin. Now in many practical applications (medical decision-making is an exception here) differences between individuals are not of much consequence because, as pointed out in Chapter 5, they can simply be averaged out so long as the variation in rating use is not connected with some variable of interest.

It clearly would be a concern, however, if different groups within society gave quite different values, because it would then be hard to interpret the significance of the differences between the groups. For example, suppose we found that women generally gave average value ratings of 7 to education and 8 to health, while men gave average value ratings of 9 to education and 7 to health. How would we balance the relative valuations of the two sexes? The consistent finding that this kind of result does not arise thus enables us to downgrade (although not to eliminate) the practical significance of the interpersonal comparison problem.

POLITICAL IMPLICATIONS

Obviously the research that has been reported in this book has implications for the general question of how many and what sorts of government services are to be supplied. As an important determinant of the way these services are allocated at present is political ideology, we consider how the different ideologies line up against the research findings.

We begin by caricaturing the economic left and right of the present western ideological spectrum. In these caricatures we could represent the right as being concerned to have the government restrict itself mainly to supplying public goods as defined by economists, such as the police, justice and defence, with perhaps the addition of a low, cheap, rather harshly administered safety net to deal with the problems of the 'deserving poor'. One reason for this restriction is the belief that governments tend to be inefficient providers of services such as education, health and old-age pensions.

The left, on the other hand, is viewed as advocating that governments provide a rather extensive range of government services, certainly including health and education, and often extending to housing and an elaborate transport network. An important reason for this broader provision is the belief that otherwise poor but deserving members of the community miss out on such services.

Various other attributions are made by those favouring one position or the other. For example, the right may complain that the left is not concerned about personal freedom, the left that the right is fundamentally uncaring for deserving but unfortunate members of society, but these attributions, although important, are not really our concern here.

The research we have reviewed in this book does not completely endorse either of these caricatured positions. If we consider specific services in New Zealand for example, the lesser valued services are defence (usually thought to be a favourite of the right) and certain classes of welfare benefits (usually thought to be favourites of the left). Other anomalies come up when the values of other societies are considered. A further indication that the left–right divide might not be of overwhelming significance in valuing government services is given by the consistent finding from the surveys discussed above that people's valuations are not very well predicted by which political party they support.

Problems also surface for both of these caricatured orientations on a more general level. Problematic for the right is, firstly, the consistent finding that people want to see certain classes of service provided by the government. This is particularly true of health services. Virtually all the valuation studies suggest that people want to see the government provide such services, greatly value what is currently provided, and would like to see the level of spending on them increased. In addition, people are not happy to see health services provided by the free market and would prefer to see scarcities of health goods dealt with by regulation rather than by the free market.

Secondly, the distinction made in economics between private and public goods seems to have little reflection in the valuations. Although defence is typically valued rather poorly, the police and other public goods are often valued quite highly. Similarly, the partly private services of health and education are valued highly, while cultural goods (for example, the New Zealand Symphony Orchestra) tend to receive lower valuations.

The major general difficulty raised for the left stems from the lack of a sensitive mechanism by which the values of the public might influence the way government spending is allocated to different services. In fact the present valuations of people who live in representative democracies are not closely related to actual levels of spending, and the wishes of the median voter are not well met.

It is not clear how much governments are at fault in failing to match their spending more closely to the valuations of the public. Ordinary people often know little about the costs of supplying different government services, and have a less sophisticated idea of the value of such services than they do of the value of goods they purchase in the marketplace. It is difficult to see in these circumstances how they might make informed judgements about the relative value for money of supplying different services. Perhaps governments are behaving intelligently. Tying government spending too closely to the apparent values of the public might produce policies that simply reflect 'a bundle of unrelated prejudices' (Williams, 1966, p. 11).

If people really want the government to supply goods and services but under representative democracy the mix of services that people would like is not supplied and they do not have the knowledge necessary to make very informed judgements about them, what might be done? On a political level, at least three kinds of choice suggest themselves.

One possibility is that decisions about allocating government funds could be taken out of the hands of elected politicians and entrusted to, say, a group of officials who would be charged to take account of public opinion in their allocation decisions. The officials could proceed by conducting frequent surveys to measure people's values along the lines we have reviewed above. This solution has a number of fairly obvious drawbacks. First, it is hard to see why the officials should be more responsive to public demand than the elected politicians are. Second, it is hard to see why the general public should inform itself better about the actual costs and benefits of government services under such a regime. Third, it is not clear how the officials should be instructed to react if they suspect that public opinion might be based on misperception of the costs and benefits of some of the services.

A second possibility is to adopt a solution of the economic right and simply to turn most government services over to the market system. This has the obvious advantage of allowing individuals to choose for themselves which services they will consume. It also has the advantage of allowing components of the services to be priced, and the research reviewed in Chapter 8 suggests that the provision of prices is likely to lead to better informed individual decisions about what should be spent on what. It is also noticeable from Chapter 9 that some people at least are aware of this lack, since they believed their decisions would be improved by better access to data on the cost effectiveness of different government services.

On the other hand, it is not obvious that, for example, the privatization of the health system would lead to more equitable or even more efficient provision of health services. Perhaps more important, the evidence indicates that people would not willingly embrace such a system. A consistent theme of all the research reviewed is that there is a general consensus that services such as health or education should be provided by governments.

Of course, advocates of the economic right might reasonably claim, on the basis of the research done to date, that because people are badly informed they are not now in a position to make reasonable judgements about such matters. If services like health and education were privatized there might be an initial period of resistance but in the long run, the citizenry would change its mind.

It seems to me that this argument cannot be decisively refuted on the basis of the research done to date, but there are some indications that it might not be correct. The research we have discussed in this book does not suggest large international differences on this kind of issue. Moreover, where comparisons have been made between societies (for example, Kemp and Bolle, 1999), these suggest that people do not simply prefer the kind of service delivery that they currently have. A number of indicators suggest that people generally want governments to provide or at least heavily support health services. For example, people prefer to allocate scarce health resources by rationing than through the market system. In fact, as Ubel (2000) points out, even in the rather market-oriented US health system, many health decisions are made using rationing criteria rather than market-driven ones.

A third possibility for change is to have allocation decisions made by direct democratic vote. In this case, the citizenry would vote on the funds to be allocated to each service, perhaps in a complex series of individual votes, perhaps in a single annual decision to approve or reject a proposed budget of total government spending. The evidence to date suggests that this process is likely to bring allocations more into line with public demand, although this might depend on the precise voting processes adopted. Moreover, there are some indications from the previous chapter that some New Zealanders at least would like more input of this kind.

Again one has to question how effective such a change would be. The indications from the research reviewed in Chapter 3, especially that comparing different Swiss local jurisdictions, is that the supply of public services would become better aligned with demand, that there might be a small increase in personal happiness and that perhaps people would be more willing to pay taxes to provide the services. However, it should be remembered that there is a difference between the kinds of service typically provided by local jurisdictions and those supplied by central governments, and, more important, that the effect of any individual vote in a national referendum is normally likely to be less than in a local one. It may also be that the success of direct democracy on a national scale would depend on precisely what kind of institutional procedures were adopted.

There is also a question as to how much better informed individuals might be about the costs and benefits of the services than they are at present. It is easy to see that members of the public might have a rather greater motive to do so, but the research we reviewed in Chapter 8 suggests that a major reason for the public's present lack of knowledge is the lack of prices. This lack would not necessarily be remedied by adapting direct democratic procedures, although perhaps the adoption of such a process would lead to a greater demand for such information and greater attention to it when it is provided. Certainly there are indications from the Swiss research that this might happen.

This line of thinking suggests that changes to the political process might produce change in the way people think about government services. Such thinking in turn opens up the possibility of a rather complex interplay between the search for an appropriate method to value public goods, the mental representations of the value of such goods that people have, and the political process which allocates them.

At first it appears that the proper decision procedure in this issue should be to follow the sequence of this chapter. We would decide first on a suitable measurement method. Then we would use this to investigate how people value government services. Finally, we would make use of the results to make policy recommendations. But a number of the results we have looked at suggest grave problems with this plan of attack.

In this book we have reviewed a good deal of evidence that measurement methods are not performing as well as we should like them to and that part of the reason for this may be that people do not value government services using a procedure as complex as that suggested by economic analysis. In part this simplicity might be attributed to a lack of item prices for such services and perhaps to a lack of involvement with the process of allocating funds to such services.

It may be, as Baron (1997) suggests, that both the complexity of people's processes and the viability of some of the measurement methods would be increased if people were better educated in the process of valuation. But the reason they do not have the more complex concepts available to them now may be in part a consequence of the current political process. Why should people have a complex understanding of this (or any other) issue if there can be little payoff from it?

Perhaps a different, more involving political process would lead to a more complex understanding of the issue. The more complex representations of the value of government services that resulted would then provide support for more complex measures of value. This second proposition, at least, should not surprise academic readers. In any discipline, attempting to match the results obtained from a particular research method with the predictions of a theory may serve as a test of the theory. Alternatively, the attempt may serve as a validation (or invalidation) of the method. Occasionally the matching attempt might serve both these services. Certainly, researchers in any discipline are taught that when the results obtained from a method do not agree with the theoretical predictions one should look carefully at both the method and the theory to see which is at fault.

Finally, having considered three major changes to the way that governments go about allocating resources and suggesting that changes might affect both the way people think about government services and, in the end, the outcome of the search for better means to value them, we come to a less far-reaching and controversial consideration for change.

Why do governments not put more effort into finding out what the wishes of the public are in regard to the services they supply? It is doubtful whether most elected politicians at present do have a good idea of the mix of government services the electorate desires. While one can debate whether politicians should necessarily be attempting to follow all the public's wishes, information about the wishes should be useful to these policymakers even if it were not always acted on.

Part of the resistance to obtaining measures of the public's valuations of government services may arise because many politicians hold the quite reasonable belief that elections are not normally determined by the level of provision of these services. Another source of resistance may come from advisors trained in the discipline of economics. Such advisors are likely to have acquired a mistrust of subjective valuation methods, which, at least at present, is partly justified. As we have seen, none of the methods is ideal.

However, decisions about government services must still be made, even if ideal methods for determining the value of the services are not available. Moreover, many decisions that are currently made do breach the principle of Pareto optimality and leave some people worse off in some sense. Would it not be better to make these decisions with the benefit of information, even imperfect information, about the value people place on the services?

Although the simpler methods we have discussed in this book, particularly the psychophysical methods and the 'more, the same, less' method, are not ideal measures of the value of government services, they do produce results that are often in reasonable agreement. Not all the results obtained from using them are intuitively obvious, and it is likely that at least some information from surveys based on them will not have been previously known to decision-makers. The methods are not particularly difficult for respondents to use, and the results are not difficult for policy analysts to interpret. Representative surveys that incorporate them are not very expensive, and certainly not expensive in comparison to what governments spend. Why not use them?

References

Adams, J.S. (1963), 'Towards an understanding of inequity', *Journal of Abnormal and Social Psychology*, **67**, 422–36.

Adshead, S.A.M. (1992), *Salt and Civilization*, Christchurch, NZ: Canterbury University Press.

Ainslie, G. (1992), *Picoeconomics: The Strategic Interaction of Successive Motivational States within the Person*, Cambridge: Cambridge University Press.

Ajzen, I. and M. Fishbein (1977), 'Attitude–behavior relations: A theoretical analysis and review of empirical research', *Psychological Bulletin*, **84**, 888–918.

Algom, D. and L.E. Marks (1990), 'Range and regression, loudness scales, and loudness processing. Towards a context-bound psychophysics', *Journal of Experimental Psychology: Human Perception and Performance*, **16**, 706–27.

Allingham, M.G. and A. Sandmo (1972), 'Income tax evasion: A theoretical analysis', *Journal of Public Economics*, **1**, 323–38.

Alvarez, R.M., J. Nagler and J.R. Willette (2000), 'Measuring the relative impact of issues and the economy in democratic elections', *Electoral Studies*, **19**, 237–54.

Anderson, N.H. (1990), 'Integration psychophysics', in H.-G. Geissler (ed.), *Psychophysical Explanations of Mental Structure*, Toronto: Hogefe and Huber, pp. 71–93.

Aristotle (2000), *Nicomachean Ethics*, trans. R. Crisp, Cambridge: Cambridge University Press.

Arrow, K.J. (1963), *Social Choices and Individual Values*, 2nd edition, New York: John Wiley.

Ashton, T., J. Cumming and N. Devlin (2000), *Priority Setting in New Zealand: Translating Principles into Practice*, Unpublished manuscript.

Bagnoli, M. and B.L. Lipman (1989), 'Provision of public goods: Fully implementing the core through private contributions', *Review of Economic Studies*, **56**, 583–601.

Barnes, J. (1992), *The Porcupine*, London: Jonathan Cape.

Baron, J. (1997), 'Biases in the quantitative measurement of values for public decisions', *Psychological Bulletin*, **122**, 72–88.

Baron, J. and J. Greene (1996), 'Determinants of insensitivity to quantity in valuation of public goods: Contribution, warm glow, budget constraints, availability, and prominence', *Journal of Experimental Psychology: Applied*, **2**, 107–25.

Baron, J. and S. Kemp (2001), *Attitudes toward Free Trade and Understanding of Comparative Advantage*, Unpublished manuscript.

Baron, J. and N.P. Maxwell (1996), 'Cost of public goods affects willingness to pay for them', *Journal of Behavioral Decision Making*, **9**, 173–83.

Becker, G. and K.M. Murphy (1988), 'A theory of rational addiction', *Journal of Political Economy*, **96**, 675–700.

Belk, R.W. and G.S. Coon (1993), 'Gift giving as agapic love: An alternative to the dating paradigm based on dating experiences', *Journal of Consumer Research*, **20**, 393–417.

Belk, R.W. and M. Wallendorf (1990), 'The sacred meanings of money', *Journal of Economic Psychology*, **11**, 35–67.

Bergstrom, T.C. and R.P. Goodman (1973), 'Private demands for public goods', *American Economic Review*, **63**, 280–96.

Berry, C.J. (1994), *The Idea of Luxury: A Conceptual and Historical Investigation*, Cambridge: Cambridge University Press.

Binswanger, H.P. (1991), 'Brazilian policies that encourage deforestation in the Amazon', *World Development*, **19**, 821–9.

Birch, A.H. (1984), 'Overload, ungovernability and delegitimation: The theories and the British case', *British Journal of Political Science*, **14**, 135–60.

Black, D. (1987), *The Theory of Committees and Elections*, Boston: Kluwer. (Originally published in 1958.)

Black, J. (1997), *Oxford Dictionary of Economics*, Oxford: Oxford University Press.

Blais, A. and R. Young (1999), 'Why do people vote? An experiment in rationality', *Public Choice*, **99**, 39–55.

Blomquist, S. and V. Christiansen (1999), 'The political economy of publicly provided private goods', *Journal of Public Economics*, **73**, 31–54.

Boadway, R. (1997), 'The role of second-best theory in public economics', in E.B. Curtis and R.G. Harris (eds), *Trade, Technology and Economics: Essays in Honour of Richard G. Lipsey*, Cheltenham, UK and Lyme, US: Edward Elgar, pp. 26–43.

Bondonio, P. and C. Marchese (1994), 'Equilibrium in fiscal choices: Evidence from a budget game', *Public Choice*, **78**, 205–18.

Bonetti, S. (1998), 'Experimental economics and deception', *Journal of Economic Psychology*, **19**, 377–95.

Bowen, H.R. (1943), 'The interpretation of voting in the allocation of economic resources', *Quarterly Journal of Economics*, **58**, 27–48.

Boyle, K.J. and R.C. Bishop (1988), 'Welfare measurements using contingent valuation: A comparison of techniques', *American Journal of Agricultural Economics*, **70**, 20–28.

Boyne, G.A. (1987), 'Median voters, political systems and public policies: An empirical test', *Public Choice*, **53**, 201–19.

Breetvelt, I.S. and F.S.A.M. van Dam (1991), 'Underreporting by cancer patients: The case of response-shift', *Social Science and Medicine*, **32**, 981–87.

Brodsky, S.L. (1988), *The Psychology of Adjustment and Well-being*, New York: Holt, Rinehart, and Winston.

Brookshire, D.S. and T.D. Crocker (1981), 'The advantages of contingent valuation methods for benefit–cost analysis', *Public Choice*, **36**, 235–52.

Brookshire, D.S., R.C. d'Arge, W.D. Schulze and M.A. Thayer (1981), 'Experiments in valuing public goods', *Advances in Applied Microeconomics*, **1**, 123–72.

Buchanan, J.M. (1968), *The Demand and Supply of Public Goods*, Chicago: Rand McNally.

Buchanan, J.M. and G. Tullock (1962), *The Calculus of Consent*, Ann Arbor: University of Michigan Press.

Burgoyne, C.B. and D.A. Routh (1991), 'Constraints on the use of money as a gift at Christmas: The role of status and intimacy', *Journal of Economic Psychology*, **12**, 47–69.

Burrows, C. and K. Brown (1993), 'QALYs for resource allocation: probably not and certainly not now', *Australian Journal of Public Health*, **17**, 278–86.

Campos, J.E. and S. Pradhan (1997), 'Evaluating public expenditure management systems: An experimental methodology with an application to the Australian and New Zealand reforms', *Journal of Policy Analysis and Management*, **16**, 423–45.

Caplow, T. (1984), 'Rule enforcement without visible means: Christmas gift giving in Middletown', *American Journal of Sociology*, **89**, 1306–23.

Carroll, J. and P. Green (1995), 'Psychometric methods in marketing research: Part 1, Conjoint analysis', *Journal of Marketing Research*, **32**, 385–91.

Citrin, J. (1979), 'Do people want something for nothing: Public opinion on taxes and government spending', *National Tax Journal*, **32**, 113–29.

Clarke, P.M. (1998), 'Cost–benefit analysis and mammographic screening: A travel cost approach', *Journal of Health Economics*, **17**, 767–87.

Clotfelter, C.T. (1976), 'Public spending for higher education: An empirical test of two hypotheses', *Public Finance*, **31**, 177–95.

Coase, R.H. (1960), 'The problem of social cost', *Journal of Law and Economics*, **3**, 1–44.

176 *Public Goods and Private Wants*

Coase, R.H. (1974), 'The lighthouse in economics', *Journal of Law and Economics*, **17**, 357–76.

Cook, T.D. and D.T. Campbell (1979), *Quasi-experimentation: Design and Analysis Issues for Field Settings*, Chicago: Rand McNally.

Costa, P.T., R.R. McCrae and A.B. Zonderman (1987), 'Environmental and dispositional influences on well-being: Longitudinal follow-up of an American national sample', *British Journal of Psychology*, **78**, 299–306.

Craig, P. (1991), 'Costs and benefits: A review of research on take-up of income-related benefits', *Journal of Social Policy*, **20**, 537–65.

Cullis, J.G. and A. Lewis (1985), 'Some hypotheses and evidence on the tax knowledge and preferences', *Journal of Economic Psychology*, **6**, 271–87.

Cullis, J.G. and A. Lewis (1997), 'Why people pay taxes: From a conventional economic model to a model of social convention', *Journal of Economic Psychology*, **18**, 305–21.

Daum, J.F. (1993), 'Some legal and regulatory aspects of contingent valuation', in J.A. Hausman (ed.), *Contingent Valuation: A Critical Assessment*, Amsterdam: North-Holland, Elsevier, pp. 389–414.

Davis, R. (1963), 'Recreation planning as an economic problem', *Natural Resources Journal*, **3**, 239–49.

Dawkins, R. (1989), *The Selfish Gene*, 2nd edition, Oxford: Oxford University Press.

De Groot, H. and E. Pommer (1987), 'Budget-games and the private and social demand for mixed public goods', *Public Choice*, **52**, 257–72.

De Groot, H. and E. Pommer (1989), 'The stability of stated preferences for public goods: Evidence from recent budget games', *Public Choice*, **60**, 123–32.

Diamond, P.A., J.A. Hausman, G.K. Leonard and M.A. Denning (1993), 'Does contingent valuation measure preferences? Some experimental evidence', in J.A. Hausman (ed.), *Contingent Valuation: A Critical Assessment*, Amsterdam: North Holland Press.

Diener, E. and E. Suh (1997), 'Measuring quality of life: Economic, social and subjective indicators', *Social Indicators Research*, **40**, 189–216.

Diener, E., M. Diener and C. Diener (1995), 'Factors predicting the subjective well-being of nations', *Journal of Personality and Social Psychology*, **69**, 851–64.

Diener, E., B. Wolsic and F. Fujita (1995), 'Physical attractiveness and subjective well-being', *Journal of Personality and Social Psychology*, **69**, 120–29.

Diener, E., E. Sandvik, L. Seidlitz and M. Diener (1993), 'The relationship between income and subjective well-being: Relative or absolute?' *Social Indicators Research*, **40**, 189–216.

Diener, E., E.M. Suh, R.E. Lucas and H.L. Smith (1999). 'Subjective well-being: Three decades of progress', *Psychological Bulletin*, **125**, 276–302.

Downs, A. (1957), *An Economic Theory of Democracy*, New York: Harper and Row.

Drummond, M.F., B.J. O'Brien, G.L. Stoddart and G.W. Torrance (1997), *Methods for the Economic Evaluation of Health Care Programmes*, 2nd edition, Oxford: Oxford University Press.

Eatwell, J., M. Milgate and P. Newman (1987), *The New Palgrave: A Dictionary of Economics*, London: Macmillan.

Edwards, W. (1977), 'How to use multiattribute utility measurement for social decision-making', *IEEE Transactions on Systems, Man and Cybernetics*, **SMC–7**, 326–40.

Edwards, W. (1992), 'Discussion: Of human skills', *Organizational Behavior and Human Decision Processes*, **53**, 267–77.

Elffers, H. (1991), *Income Tax Evasion: Theory and Measurement*, Deventer: Kluwer.

Elffers, H. (1999), 'Tax evasion', in P.E. Earl and S. Kemp (eds), *The Elgar Companion to Consumer Research and Economic Psychology*, Cheltenham, UK and Northampton, MA, US: Edward Elgar, pp. 556–60.

Elffers, H., R.H. Weigel and D.J. Hessing (1987), 'The consequences of different strategies of measuring tax evasion behaviour', *Journal of Economic Psychology*, **8**, 311–37.

Endres, A.M. (1999), 'Utility theory', in P.E. Earl and S. Kemp (eds), *The Elgar Companion to Consumer Research and Economic Psychology*, Cheltenham, UK and Northampton, MA, US: Edward Elgar, pp. 599–604.

Falkinger, J. (1995), 'Tax evasion, consumption of public goods and fairness', *Journal of Economic Psychology*, **16**, 63–72.

Fandel, G. and J. Spronk (eds) (1985), *Multiple Criteria Decision Methods and Applications*, Berlin: Springer.

Fanshel, S. and J.W. Bush (1970), 'A health-status index and its applications to health-services outcomes', *Operations Research*, **18**, 1021–66.

Feather, N.T. and G.E. O'Brian (1986), 'A longitudinal study of the effects of employment and unemployment on school-leavers', *Journal of Occupational Psychology*, **59**, 121–44.

Fechner, G.T. (1860), *Elemente der Psychophysik*, Leipzig: Breitkopf and Harterl.

Feld, L.P. and G. Kirchgässner (2000), 'Direct democracy, political culture, and the outcome of economic policy: A report on the Swiss experience', *European Journal of Political Economy*, **16**, 287–306.

Ferris, J.M. (1983), 'Demands for public spending: An attitudinal approach', *Public Choice*, **40**, 135–54.

Ferris, J.M. (1985), 'Interrelationships among public spending preferences: A micro analysis', *Public Choice*, **45**, 139–53.

Finke, R.A. (1989), *Principles of Mental Imagery*, Cambridge, MA: MIT Press.

Fletcher, G.J.O. (1995), *The Scientific Credibility of Folk Psychology*, Mahwah, NJ: Lawrence Erlbaum.

Font, A.R. (2000), 'Mass tourism and the demand for protected natural areas: A travel cost approach', *Journal of Environmental Economics and Management*, **39**, 97–116.

Forte, F. (1967), 'Should "public goods" be public?', *Public Choice*, **3**, 39–46.

Frank, R.H. (1997), 'The frame of reference as a public good', *The Economic Journal*, **107**, 1832–47.

Freud, S. (1960), 'The psychopathology of everyday life', in J. Strachy (ed.), *The Standard Edition of the Complete Psychological Works of Sigmund Freud. Vol. VI*, London: Hogarth Press. Original work published in 1901.

Frey, B.S. (1994), 'Direct democracy: Politico-economic lessons from Swiss experience', *American Economic Review (Papers and Proceedings)*, **84**, 338–42.

Frey, B.S. (1997), 'A constitution for knaves crowds out civic virtues', *The Economic Journal*, **107**, 1043–53.

Frey, B.S. and W.W. Pommerehne (1993), 'On the fairness of pricing – an empirical survey among the general population', *Journal of Economic Behavior and Organization*, **20**, 295–307.

Frey, B.S. and A. Stutzer (2000), 'Happiness, economy and institutions', *The Economic Journal*, **110**, 918–38.

Friedland, N., S. Maital and A. Rutenberg (1978), 'A simulation study of income tax evasion', *Journal of Public Economics*, **10**, 107–16.

Funk, C.L. and P.A. Garcia-Monet (1997), 'The relationship between personal and rational concerns in public perceptions about the economy', *Political Research Quarterly*, **50**, 317–42.

Furnham, A. (1982), 'Explanations for unemployment in Britain', *European Journal of Social Psychology*, **12**, 335–52.

Furnham, A. (1985), 'A short measure of economic beliefs', *Personality and Individual Differences*, **6**, 123–6.

Furnham, A. (1988), *Lay Theories: Everyday Understanding of Problems in the Social Sciences*, Oxford: Pergamon.

Furnham, A. and A. Lewis (1986), *The Economic Mind*, Brighton: Harvester.

Galanter, E. (1962a), *New Directions in Psychology*, New York: Holt.

Galanter, E. (1962b), 'The direct measurement of utility and subjective probability', *American Journal of Psychology*, **75**, 208–20.

Galanter, E. (1974), 'Psychological decision mechanisms and perception', in E.D. Carterette and M.P. Friedman (eds), *Handbook of Perception: Vol. 2*.

Psychophysical Judgment and Measurement, San Diego, CA: Academic Press, pp. 85–125.

Galanter, E. (1990), 'Utility functions for nonmonetary events', *American Journal of Psychology*, **103**, 448–70.

Galbraith, J.K. (1969), *The Affluent Society*, 2nd edition, London: Hamish Hamilton.

Garber, A.M. (2000), 'Advances in cost-effectiveness analysis of health interventions', in A.J. Culyer and J.P. Newhouse (eds), *Handbook of Health Economics. Vol. 1A*, Amsterdam: Elsevier, pp. 181–221.

Garber, A.M., M.C. Weinsten, G.W. Torrance and M.S. Kamlet (1996), 'Theoretical foundations of cost-effectiveness analysis', in M.E. Gold, J.E. Siegel, L.B. Russell and M.C. Weinstein (eds), *Cost-effectiveness in Health and Medicine*, Oxford: Oxford University Press, pp. 25–53.

George, R.N. and S. Kemp (1991), 'A survey of New Zealanders with tinnitus', *British Journal of Audiology*, **25**, 331–36.

Gerdtham, U.-G. and B. Jönsson (2000), 'International comparisons of health expenditure: Theory, data and econometric analysis', in A.J. Culyer and J.P. Newhouse (eds), *Handbook of Health Economics. Vol. 1A*, Amsterdam: Elsevier, pp. 11–53.

Gescheider, G.A. (1988), 'Psychophysical scaling', *Annual Review of Psychology*, **39**, 169–200.

Gold, M.R., D.L. Patrick, G.W. Torrance, D.G. Fryback, D.C. Hadorn, M.S. Kamlet, N. Daniels and M.C. Weinstein (1996a), 'Identifying and valuing outcomes', in M.E. Gold, J.E. Siegel, L.B. Russell and M.C. Weinstein (eds), *Cost-effectiveness in Health and Medicine*, Oxford: Oxford University Press, pp. 82–134.

Gold, M.E., J.E. Siegel, L.B. Russell and M.C. Weinstein (eds) (1996b), *Cost-effectiveness in Health and Medicine*, Oxford: Oxford University Press.

Gouveia, M. (1997), 'Majority rule and the public provision of a private good', *Public Choice*, **93**, 221–44.

Groenland, E.A.G. and G.M. van Veldhoven (1983), 'Tax evasion behaviour: A psychological framework', *Journal of Economic Psychology*, **3**, 129–44.

Haig, B.D. (1992), 'From nuisance variables to explanatory theories: A reformulation of the third variable problem', *Educational Philosophy and Theory*, **24**, 78–97.

Hallgren, M.M. and A.K. McAdams (1997), 'The economic efficiency of internet public goods', in L.W. McKnight and J.P. Bailey (eds), *Internet Economics*, Cambridge, MA: MIT Press, pp. 455–78.

Hanley, N. and C.L. Spash (1993), *Cost–Benefit Analysis and the Environment*, Aldershot, UK and Brookfield, US: Edward Elgar.

Hardin, G. (1968), 'The tragedy of the commons', *Science*, **162**, 1243–8.

Harris, R. and A. Seldon (1979), *Over-ruled on Welfare*, London: Institute of Economic Affairs.

Harris, R.J. (1985), *A Primer of Multivariate Statistics*, 2nd edition, Orlando, FA: Academic Press.

Hausman, J.A. (ed.) (1993), *Contingent Valuation: A Critical Assessment*, Amsterdam: North-Holland, Elsevier.

Hayek, F.A. (1945), 'The use of knowledge in society', *American Economic Review*, **35**, 519–30.

Heider, F. (1958), *The Psychology of Interpersonal Relations*, New York: Wiley.

Helson, H. (1947), 'Adaptation-level as frame of reference for prediction of psychophysical data', *American Journal of Psychology*, **60**, 1–29.

Hessing, D.J., H. Elffers and R.H. Weigel (1988), 'Exploring the limits of self-reports and reasoned action: An investigation of the psychology of tax evasion behavior', *Journal of Personality and Social Psychology*, **54**, 405–13.

Hey, J.D. (1998), 'Experimental economics and deception: A comment', *Journal of Economic Psychology*, **19**, 397–401.

Heyndels, B. and C. Smolders (1995), 'Tax complexity and fiscal illusion', *Public Choice*, **85**, 127–41.

Hockley, G.C. and G. Harbour (1983), 'Revealed preferences between public expenditures and taxation cuts: Public sector choice', *Journal of Public Economics*, **22**, 387–99.

Holcombe, R.G. (1989), 'The median voter model in public choice theory', *Public Choice*, **61**, 115–25.

Hudson, J. and P.R. Jones (1994), 'The importance of the "ethical voter": An estimate of "altruism"', *European Journal of Political Economy*, **10**, 499–509.

Humphreys, P. (1977), 'Application of multi-attribute utility theory', in H. Jungermann and G. de Zeeuw (eds), *Decision Making and Change in Human Affairs*, Dordrecht: Reidel.

Hurley, G. (2000), 'An overview of the normative economics of the health sector', in A.J. Culyer and J.P. Newhouse (eds), *Handbook of Health Economics. Vol. 1A*, Amsterdam: Elsevier, pp. 55–118.

Ingberman, D.E. (1985), 'Running against the status quo: Institutions for direct democracy referenda and allocations over time', *Public Choice*, **46**, 19–43.

Jahoda, M., P. Lazarsfeld and H. Zeisel (1933), *The Sociography of an Unemployed Community*, London: Tavistock.

Jungermann, H. and G. de Zeeuw (eds) (1977), *Decision Making and Change in Human Affairs*, Dordrecht: Reidel.

Kahneman, D. and J.L. Knetsch (1992), 'Valuing public goods: The purchase of moral satisfaction', *Journal of Environmental Economics and Management*, **22**, 57–70.

Kahneman, D. and A. Tversky (1984), 'Choices, values and frames', *American Psychologist*, **39**, 341–50.

Kahneman, D. and A. Tversky (1996), 'On the reality of cognitive illusions', *Psychological Review*, **103**, 582–91.

Kahneman, D., I. Ritov, K.E. Jacowitz and P. Grant (1993), 'Stated willingness to pay for public goods: A psychological perspective', *Psychological Science*, **4**, 310–15.

Kawachi, I., P. Bethwaite and J. Bethwaite (1990), 'The use of quality-adjusted life years (QALYs) in the economic appraisal of health care', *New Zealand Medical Journal*, **103**(883), 46–8.

Keeney, R.L. (1977), 'The art of assessing multiattribute utility functions', *Organizational Behavior and Human Decision Processes*, **19**, 267–310.

Kemp, M.C. and C. Maxwell (1993), in J.A. Hausman (ed.), *Contingent Valuation: A Critical Assessment*, Amsterdam: North-Holland, Elsevier, pp. 217–65.

Kemp, S. (1988), 'Magnitude estimation of the utility of nonmonetary items', *Bulletin of the Psychonomic Society*, **26**, 544–7.

Kemp, S. (1991), 'Magnitude estimation of the utility of public goods', *Journal of Applied Psychology*, **76**, 533–40.

Kemp, S. (1996), 'Preferences for distributing goods in times of shortage', *Journal of Economic Psychology*, **17**, 615–27.

Kemp, S. (1998a), 'Perceiving luxury and necessity', *Journal of Economic Psychology*, **19**, 591–606.

Kemp, S. (1998b), 'Rating the values of government and market supplied goods', *Journal of Economic Psychology*, **19**, 447–61.

Kemp, S. (in press), 'The effect of providing misleading cost information on the perceived value of government services', *Journal of Economic Psychology*.

Kemp, S. and F. Bolle (1999), 'Preferences in distributing scarce goods', *Journal of Economic Psychology*, **20**, 105–20.

Kemp, S. and C.D.B. Burt (1999), 'Why are we reluctant to sell friendship?' *Journal of Applied Social Psychology*, **29**, 2272–91.

Kemp, S. and C.D.B. Burt (2001), 'Estimation of the value and cost of government and market supplied goods', *Public Choice*, **107**, 235–52.

Kemp, S. and J. Crawford (1999), *Could Valuations of Government Goods be Estimates of their Marginal Utility?* Unpublished manuscript.

Kemp, S. and Willetts, K. (1995a), 'Rating the value of government-funded services: Comparison of methods', *Journal of Economic Psychology*, **16**, 1–21.

Kemp, S. and Willetts, K. (1995b), 'The value of services supplied by the New Zealand government', *Journal of Economic Psychology*, **16**, 23–37.

Kemp, S., S.E.G. Lea and S. Fussell (1995), 'Experiments on rating the utility of consumer goods: Evidence supporting microeconomic theory', *Journal of Economic Psychology*, **16**, 543–61.

Kershaw, D. and J. Fair (1976), *The New Jersey Income-maintenance Experiment. Vol. 1. Operations, Surveys and Administration*, New York: Academic Press.

Kinder, D.R. (1981), 'Presidents, prosperity and public opinion', *Public Opinion Quarterly*, **45**, 1–21.

Kinsey, K.A. (1988), *Measurement Bias or Honest Disagreement? Problems of Validating Measures of Tax Evasion*, ABF Working Paper 8811, Chicago: American Bar Foundation.

Kirchsteiger, G. and C. Puppe (1997), 'On the possibility of efficient private provision of public goods through government subsidies', *Journal of Public Economics*, **66**, 489–504.

Kluegel, J.R. and E.R. Smith (1986), *Beliefs about Inequality: Americans' Views of What is and What Ought to Be*, New York: Aldine de Gruyter.

Knopf, K.A. (1991), *A Lexicon of Economics*, San Diego, CA: Academic Press.

Kristensen, O.P. (1982), 'Voter attitudes and public spending: Is there a relationship?' *European Journal of Political Research*, **10**, 35–52.

Krueger, L.E. (1989), 'Reconciling Fechner and Stevens: Towards a unified psychophysical law', *Behavioral and Brain Sciences*, **12**, 251–320.

Kryter, K.D. (1985). *The Effects of Noise on Man*, 2nd edition, Orlando FA: Academic Press.

Lane, R.E. (1991), *The Market Experience*, Cambridge: Cambridge University Press.

Lazarus, R.S. and C.A. Smith (1988), 'Knowledge and appraisal in the cognition–emotion relationship', *Cognition and Emotion*, **2**, 281–300.

Ledyard, J.O. (1995), 'Public goods: A survey of experimental research', in J.H. Kagel and A.E. Roth (eds), *The Handbook of Experimental Economics*, Princeton: Princeton University Press, pp. 111–94.

Lewis, A. (1982), *The Psychology of Taxation*, Oxford: Martin Robertson.

Lewis, A. and D. Jackson (1985), 'Voting preferences and attitudes to public expenditure', *Political Studies*, **33**, 457–66.

Lipscomb, J., W.C. Weinstein and G.W. Torrance (1996), 'Time preferences', in M.E. Gold, J.E. Siegel, L.B. Russell and M.C. Weinstein (eds), *Cost-effectiveness in Health and Medicine*, Oxford: Oxford University Press, pp. 214–46.

Lipsey, R.G. (1989), *An Introduction to Positive Economics*, 7th edition, London: Weidenfeld and Nicolson.

Lipsey, R.G. and K.J. Lancaster (1956), 'The general theory of second best', *Review of Economic Studies*, **24**, 11–32.

MacFadyen, A.J. (1999), 'Well-being', in P.E. Earl and S. Kemp (eds), *The Elgar Companion to Consumer Research and Economic Psychology*, Cheltenham, UK and Northampton, MA, US: Edward Elgar, pp. 615–9.

Mackenzie, A. (1998), *Tax and the Small Business Owner: Is it a Fair Relationship?*, unpublished M.Sc. Thesis, Christchurch: University of Canterbury.

Mahoney, M. (2001), *Important Factors in Preferences for Supply of Services: Government versus Private Supply*, unpublished M.Sc. Project, Exeter: University of Exeter.

Maital, S. (1979), 'Measurement of net benefits from public goods: A new approach using survey data', *Public Finance*, **34**, 85–99.

Marshall, A. (1961), *Principles of Economics*, 9th edition, London: Macmillan.

Marwell, G. and R. Ames (1979), 'Experiments on the provision of public goods I: Resources, interest, group size, and the free-rider problem', *American Journal of Sociology*, **84**, 1335–60.

Mason, R. and L.D. Calvin (1978), 'A study of admitted tax evasion', *Law and Society Review*, **13**, 73–89.

Maxwell, S.E. and H.D. Delaney (1985), 'Measurement and statistics: An examination of construct validity', *Psychological Bulletin*, **97**, 85–93.

Mayer, R.N. (1999), 'Consumer protection', in P.E. Earl and S. Kemp (eds), *The Elgar Companion to Consumer Research and Economic Psychology*, Cheltenham, UK and Northampton, MA, US: Edward Elgar, pp. 121–8.

McDaniel, T. and C. Starmer (1998), 'Experimental economics and deception: A comment', *Journal of Economic Psychology*, **19**, 403–9.

McDaniels, T.L. (1996), 'The structured value referendum: Eliciting preferences for environmental policy alternatives', *Journal of Policy Analysis and Management*, **15**, 227–51.

McKean, J.R., R.G. Walsh and D.M. Johnson (1996), 'Closely related good prices in the travel cost model', *American Journal of Agricultural Economics*, **78**, 640–46.

Mead, W.J. (1993), 'Review and analysis of state-of-the-art contingent valuation studies', in J.A. Hausman (ed.), *Contingent Valuation: A Critical Assessment*, Amsterdam: North-Holland, Elsevier, pp. 305–32.

Meehl, P.E. (1970), 'Nuisance variables and the ex post facto design', *Minnesota Studies in the Philosophy of Science*, **4**, 373–402.

Mellers, B.A. and J. Baron (eds) (1993), *Psychological Perspectives on Justice: Theory and Applications*, Cambridge: Cambridge University Press.

Messick, D.M. (1993), 'Equality as a decision heuristic', in B.A. Mellers and J. Baron (eds), *Psychological Perspectives on Justice: Theory and*

Applications, Cambridge: Cambridge University Press, pp. 11–31.

Messick, D.M., H. Wilke, M.B. Brewer, R.M. Kramer, P.E. Zemke and L. Lui (1983), 'Individual adaptations and structural change as solutions to social dilemmas', *Journal of Personality and Social Psychology*, **44**, 294– 309.

Mill, J.S. (1909), *Principles of Political Economy*, ed. W.J. Ashley, London: Longmans, Green and Co. Originally published in 1848.

Milne, A.A. (1978), *Winnie-the-Pooh*, London: Methuen.

Misiolek, W.S. and H.W. Elder (1988), 'Tax structure and the size of government: An empirical analysis of the fiscal illusion and the fiscal stress arguments', *Public Choice*, **57**, 233–45.

Mitchell, R. and R. Carson (1989), *Using Surveys to Value Public Goods: The Contingent Valuation Method*, Washington, DC: Resources for the Future.

Mouritzen, P.E. (1987), 'The demanding citizen: driven by policy, self-interest or ideology?' *European Journal of Political Research*, **15**, 417–35.

Murray, D.J. (1993), 'A perspective for viewing the history of psychophysics', *Behavioral and Brain Sciences*, **16**, 115–86.

Musgrave, R.A. (1986), *Public Finance in a Democratic Society. Vol. 1. Social Goods, Taxation and Fiscal Policy*, Brighton: Wheatsheaf.

Musgrave, R.A. and P.B. Musgrave (1984), *Public Finance in Theory and Practice*, 4th edition, New York: McGraw-Hill.

Nannestad, P. and N. Paldam (1995), 'It's the government's fault. A cross-section of economic voting in Denmark, 1990/3', *European Journal of Political Research*, **28**, 33–62.

Nelson, P. (1999), 'Multiattribute utility models', in P.E. Earl and S. Kemp (eds), *The Elgar Companion to Consumer Research and Economic Psychology*, Cheltenham, UK and Northampton, MA, US: Edward Elgar, pp. 393–400.

Nisbett, R.E. and T.D. Wilson (1977), 'Telling more than we can know: Verbal reports on mental processes', *Psychological Review*, **84**, 231–59.

Noam, E.M. (1982), 'Demand functions and the valuations of public goods', *Public Choice*, **38**, 271–80.

Ølander, F., S. Kemp and J. Crawford (1999), *How Should the Government Allocate Resources?* Unpublished manuscript.

Olson, M. (1982), *The Rise and Decline of Nations: Economic Growth, Stagflation, and Social Rigidities*, New Haven: Yale University Press.

Organization for Economic Cooperation and Development (2000), *Main Economic Indicators*, Paris: OECD, September, pp. 256–9.

Parducci, A. (1982), 'Category ratings: Still more contextual effects', in B. Wegener (ed.), *Social Attitudes and Psychophysical Measurement*, Hillsdale, NJ: Erlbaum.

Pitz, G.F., J. Heerboth and N.J. Sachs (1980), 'Assessing the utility of multiattribute utility assessments', *Organizational Behavior and Human Decision Processes*, **26**, 65–80.

Pocket Strategy (1998), London: The Economist Books.

Pommerehne, W.W. (1978), 'Institutional approaches to public expenditure: Empirical evidence from Swiss municipalities', *Journal of Public Economics*, **9**, 255–80.

Pommerehne, W.W. (1990), 'The empirical relevance of comparative institutional analysis', *European Economic Review*, **34**, 458–69.

Pommerehne, W.W. and F. Schneider (1978), 'Fiscal illusion, political institutions, and local public spending', *Kyklos*, **31**, 381–404.

Poulton, E.C. (1989), *Bias in Quantifying Judgements*, Hove: Erlbaum.

Price, S. and D. Sanders (1995), 'Economic expectations and voting intentions in the UK, 1979–1989. A pooled cross-section approach', *Political Studies*, **43**, 451–71.

Quiggin, J. (1999), 'Utility', in P.E. Earl and S. Kemp (eds), *The Elgar Companion to Consumer Research and Economic Psychology*, Cheltenham, UK and Northampton, MA, US: Edward Elgar, pp. 590–94.

Rao, A.R. and K.B. Monroe (1989), 'The effect of price, brand name, and store name on buyer's perceptions of product quality: An integrative review', *Journal of Consumer Research*, **15**, 253–64.

Rawls, J. (1971), *A Theory of Justice*, Boston: Harvard University Press.

Ridley, M. (1997), *The Origins of Virtue: Human Instincts and the Evolution of Cooperation*, New York: Viking.

Riker, W.H. and P.C. Ordeshook (1968), 'A theory of the calculus of voting', *American Political Science Review*, **62**, 25–43.

Robbins, L. (1938), 'Interpersonal comparisons of utility: a comment', *Economic Journal*, **48**, 635–41.

Roland-Lévy, C. (1999), 'Economic socialization', in P.E. Earl and S. Kemp (eds), *The Elgar Companion to Consumer Research and Economic Psychology*, Cheltenham, UK and Northampton, MA, US: Edward Elgar, pp. 171–81.

Rosenhan, D.L. and M.E.P. Seligman (1989), *Abnormal Psychology*, 2nd edition, New York: Norton.

Russell, L.B., J.B. Siegel, N. Daniels, M.R. Gold, B.R. Luce and J.S. Mandelblatt (1996), 'Cost-effectiveness analysis as a guide to resource allocation in health: Roles and limitations', in M.E. Gold, J.E. Siegel, L.B. Russell and M.C. Weinstein (eds), *Cost-effectiveness in Health and Medicine*, Oxford: Oxford University Press, pp. 3–24.

Rutherford, D. (1992), *Dictionary of Economics*, London: Routledge.

Samuelson, C.D., D.M. Messick, C.G. Rutte and H. Wilke (1984), 'Individual and structural solutions to resource dilemmas in two cultures',

Journal of Personality and Social Psychology, **47**, 94–104.

Samuelson, P.A. (1954), 'The pure theory of public expenditure', *The Review of Economics and Statistics*, **36**, 387–9.

Samuelson, P.A. (1955), 'Diagrammatic exposition of a theory of public expenditure', *The Review of Economics and Statistics*, **37**, 350–56.

Samuelson, P.A., K. Hancock and R. Wallace (1975), *Economics: Second Australian edition*, Sydney: McGraw-Hill.

Schkade, D.A. and J.W. Payne (1993), 'Where do the numbers come from? How people respond to contingent valuation questions', in J.A. Hausman (ed.), *Contingent Valuation: A Critical Assessment*, Amsterdam: North-Holland, Elsevier.

Schram, A.J.H.C. (1990), 'A dynamic model of voter behavior and the demand for public goods among social groups in Great Britain', *Journal of Public Economics*, **41**, 147–82.

Schram, A.J.H.C. (1991), *Voter Behavior in Economic Perspective*, Berlin: Springer.

Schram, A.J.H.C. and F. van Winden (1989), 'Revealed preferences for public goods: Applying a model of voter behavior', *Public Choice*, **60**, 259–82.

Schram, A.J.H.C. and F. van Winden (1991), 'Why people vote: Free riding and the production and consumption of social pressure', *Journal of Economic Psychology*, **12**, 575-620.

Schwartz, C.E. and E.A. Laitin (1998), 'Using decision theory in clinical research: Applications of quality-adjusted life-years', in M.J. Staquet, R.D. Hays and P.M. Fayers (eds), *Quality of Life Assessment in Clinical Trials: Methods and Practice*, Oxford: Oxford University Press, pp. 119–41.

Schwartz, S., J. Richardson and P.P. Glasziou (1993), 'Quality-adjusted life years: origins, measurements, applications, objections', *Australian Journal of Public Health*, **17**, 272–8.

Shabman, L. and K. Stephenson (1994), 'A critique of the self-interested voter model: The case of a local single issue referendum', *Journal of Economic Issues*, **28**, 1173–86.

Shafir, E. and D. Kahneman (1999), 'Heuristics and biases', in P.E. Earl and S. Kemp (eds), *The Elgar Companion to Consumer Research and Economic Psychology*, Cheltenham, UK and Northampton, MA, US: Edward Elgar, pp. 284–9.

Singer, M.S. (1999), 'Fairness', in P.E. Earl and S. Kemp (eds), *The Elgar Companion to Consumer Research and Economic Psychology*, Cheltenham, UK and Northampton, MA, US: Edward Elgar, pp. 230–33.

Skinner, B.F. (1971), *Beyond Freedom and Dignity*, New York: Knopf.

Sloan, F.A. (ed.) (1995), *Valuing Health Care: Costs, Benefits, and Effectiveness of Pharmaceuticals and Other Medical Technologies*,

Cambridge: Cambridge University Press.

Smith, A. (n.d.), *An Enquiry into the Nature and Causes of the Wealth of Nations*, London: Routledge. (Originally published in 1776.)

Smith, E.R. and F.D. Miller (1978), 'Limits on perception of cognitive processes: A reply to Nisbett and Wilson', *Psychological Review*, **85**, 355–62.

Smith, R. and M. Wearing (1987), 'Do Australians want the welfare state?' *Politics*, **22**(2), 55–65.

Smith, V.L. (1980), 'Experiments with a decentralized mechanism for public good decisions', *American Economic Review*, **70**, 584–99.

Sorensen, R. (1992), 'Fiscal illusions: nothing but illusions', *European Journal of Political Research*, **22**, 279–305.

Spash, C. (1999), 'Contingent valuation', in P.E. Earl and S. Kemp (eds), *The Elgar Companion to Consumer Research and Economic Psychology*, Cheltenham, UK and Northampton, MA, US: Edward Elgar, pp. 128–34.

Squire, L.R. (1986), 'Mechanisms of memory', *Science*, **232**, 1612–19.

Stacey, B. (1985), 'Economic socialization', *Annual Review of Political Science*, **2**, 114–28.

Staquet, M.J., R.D. Hays and P.M. Fayers (eds) (1998), *Quality of Life Assessment in Clinical Trials: Methods and Practice*, Oxford: Oxford University Press.

Stevens, S.S. (1946), 'On the theory of scales of measurement', *Science*, **103**, 677–80.

Stevens, S.S. (1957), 'On the psychophysical law', *Psychological Review*, **64**, 153–81.

Stevens, S.S. (1975), *Psychophysics: Introduction to its Perceptual, Neural, and Social Prospects*, New York: Wiley.

Stigler, G.J. (1972), 'Economic competition and political competition', *Public Choice*, **12**, 91–106.

Stiglitz, J.E. (1988), *Economics of the Public Sector*, 2nd edition, New York: Norton.

Storer, P. and M.A. van Audenrode (1995), 'Unemployment insurance take-up rates in Canada: Facts, determinants and implications', *Canadian Journal of Economics*, **28**, 821–35.

Strauss, R.P. and G.D. Hughes (1976), 'A new approach to the demand for public goods', *Journal of Public Economics*, **6**, 191–204.

Suetonius, *Lives of the Caesars*, trans J.C. Rolfe, London: Heinemann, 1951.

Tan, G. and S. Murrell (1984), 'Respondent characteristics in citizen evaluation of municipal services', *Social Indicators Research*, **14**, 29–52.

Thaler, R. (1985), 'Mental accounting and consumer choice', *Marketing Science*, **4**, 199–214.

Thibaut, J., N. Friedman and L. Walker (1974), 'Compliance with rules:

Some social determinants', *Journal of Personality and Social Psychology*, **30**, 792–801.

Thompson, L. and R.C. Elling (2000), 'Mapping patterns of support for privatization in the mass public: The case of Michigan', *Public Administration Review*, **60**, 338–47.

Tullock, G. (1967), *Towards a Mathematics of Politics*, Ann Arbor: University of Michigan.

Tullock, G. (1976), *The Vote Motive*, London: Institute of Economic Affairs.

Tversky, A. and D. Kahneman (1981), 'Framing decisions and the psychology of choice', *Science*, **211**, 453–8.

Ubel, P. (2000), *Pricing Life: Why it's Time for Health Care Rationing*, Cambridge, MA: Bradford.

von Neumann, J. and O. Morgenstern (1944), *Theory of Games and Economic Behavior*, Princeton: Princeton University Press.

von Winterfeldt, D. and W. Edwards (1986), *Decision Analysis and Behavioral Research*, Cambridge: Cambridge University Press.

Wagner, R.E. (1976), 'Revenue structure, fiscal illusion, and budgetary choice', *Public Choice*, **25**, 45–61.

Wärneryd, K.-E. and B. Walerud (1982), 'Taxes and economic behaviour: Some interview data on tax evasion in Sweden', *Journal of Economic Psychology*, **2**, 187–211.

Watson, J.B. (1930), *Behaviorism*, New York: Norton.

Webley, P., S.E.G. Lea and R. Portalska (1983), 'The unacceptability of money as a gift', *Journal of Economic Psychology*, **4**, 223–38.

Webley, P., H.S.J. Robben, H. Elffers and D.J. Hessing (1991), *Tax Evasion: An Experimental Approach*, Cambridge: Cambridge University Press.

Wegener, B. (ed.) (1982), *Social Attitudes and Psychophysical Measurement*, Hillsdale, NJ: Erlbaum.

Weigel, R.H., D.J. Hessing and H. Elffers (1987), 'Tax evasion research: A critical appraisal and theoretical model', *Journal of Economic Psychology*, **8**, 215–35.

West, E.G. and Winer, S.L. (1980), 'Optimal fiscal illusion and the size of government', *Public Choice*, **35**, 607–22.

White, P. (1980), 'Limitations on verbal reports of internal events: A refutation of Nisbett and Wilson and of Bem', *Psychological Review*, **87**, 105–12.

Williams, A. (1966), 'Tax policy – can surveys help?' *Political and Economic Planning*, **32** (494), 4–40.

Williamson, M.R. and A.J. Wearing (1996), 'Lay people's cognitive models of the economy', *Journal of Economic Psychology*, **17**, 3–38.

Winkelmann, L. and R. Winkelmann (1998), 'Why are the unemployed so unhappy? Evidence from panel data', *Economica*, **65**, 1–15.

Winter, S. and P.E. Mouritzen (1998), *Why People Want Something for Nothing: The Role of Asymmetrical Illusions*, Unpublished manuscript, Aarhus University.

Woodworth, R.S. and H. Schlosberg (1955), *Experimental Psychology,* 3rd edition, London: Methuen.

Zanardi, A. (1996), 'The distribution of benefits of public expenditure programmes: Evidence from Italy from a budget game experiment', *Public Finance*, **51**, 393–414.

Index